Acclaim, Applause, and Appreciation for
The Ultimate Game of Thrones and Philosophy!

"Game of Thrones *isn't just beautiful and exhilarating. It's deep, and this collection of essays shows it. From investigations of the ethics of violence and sexuality to reflections on matters of faith, knowledge, and political power, this volume, like* Game of Thrones *itself, collects a vast world of thought and feeling. It does so, too, in a way that's both fascinating and accessible. The North may remember, but the authors of these chapters know how to think! Winter's coming, so sharpen not only your swords but also your ideas."*

> —PETER S. FOSL, Professor and Chair of Philosophy, Transylvania University

"*Just as the three-eyed raven appears to Bran Stark in his vision-dreams, inspiring his quest beyond the wall to the cave where his body resides, this book shall stimulate, counsel, and enlighten the reader about the multifarious philosophical themes at work in the people who battle for the Iron Throne of the Seven Kingdoms. It's fire for the passionate soul and food for thought. After all, don't forget, winter is coming!*"

> —KIMBERLY BALTZER-JARAY, author of *Doorway to the World of Essences* (2011) and contributor to *Clear and Present Thinking: A Handbook in Logic and Rationality* (2013)

"*A highly addictive show deserves a highly addictive analysis.* The Ultimate Game of Thrones and Philosophy *is the definitive source for all of us who didn't want the experience to end with viewing but aren't satisfied with the ordinary water-cooler banter. Although this volume doesn't include nearly as much gratuitous nudity or violence (or any for that matter) it is the essential* Game of Thrones *companion.*"

> —DANIEL MIORI, author and medical practitioner

"*In a world where you never really know whom you can trust, and losing is never an option, it pays to have a reliable guide on hand at all times.*

If you can't call on Tyrion Lannister, then this book is your guide. It's filled with clear-cut answers to the exhausting range of philosophical questions raised in Game of Thrones. *You'll soon be sitting on your very own Iron Throne—with one sword for each question!"*

> —JOHN V. KARAVITIS, CPA, MBA, popular writer on pop culture and philosophy

---

"The Ultimate Game of Thrones and Philosophy *traverses the vast lands of Westeros and the territory north of the Wall and across the Narrow Sea to examine, among other things, who may be truly worthy to sit on the Iron Throne. Like any mega-popular television franchise,* Game of Thrones *tells us just as much about ourselves as about the fictional kings, queens, bastards, and broken things who populate this world.*

The maesters of this book help us understand why we love this show— and the books on which it is based—so much, even when it frustrates or disturbs us. You don't have to travel to the Citadel or pray to 'the old gods and the new' to gain insight into the human condition so aptly depicted by Game of Thrones *and the thirty-one chapters in this scholarly tome."*

> —JASON T. EBERL, Semler Endowed Chair for Medical Ethics, Professor of Philosophy, College of Osteopathic Medicine, Marian University

---

"The best of fantasy is rooted in reality, and in Westeros we find ourselves, our demons (aka the Lannisters), and our better angels, even if the latter are quite rare, and named Jon Snow. The authors in this book use Game of Thrones *to explore our shared human condition. From Jon Snow as moral exemplar to the redemption of the Hound, readers will learn about themselves by engaging their favorite, and most hated, residents of the Seven Kingdoms. Westeros should look familiar, it's our world—a world of injustice and cruelty. But it's also a world of redemption, sacrifice, honor, and integrity. All this is captured in* The Ultimate Game of Thrones and Philosophy."

> —JACOB M. HELD, Director of the UCA Core, Associate Professor of Philosophy, Department of Philosophy and Religion, University of Central Arkansas

---

"The Ultimate Game of Thrones and Philosophy *takes the reader on a fascinating journey through the Seven Kingdoms with critical essays including those on the humor of Tyrion, why we love to hate Joffrey, questioning the meaning of prophecy for Daenerys and Stannis, the "misshapen" Christ analogs in Jon Snow's resurrection, Brienne of Tarth and feminine recognition, the ambiguity of Jaime Lannister as sinner and savior, and whether Samwell Tarly will save them all by delving into the Citadel library in Oldtown. Readers will enjoy exploring deeper thinking on their favorite characters and the major themes of the series up to and including Season Six."*

—PATRICIA L. BRACE, Professor of Art, Southwest Minnesota State University

---

"A must read for any fan of Game of Thrones *who has the slightest interest in philosophy. From morality, politics, sex, and the family in Westeros to the philosophy of art as it relates to the* Game of Thrones *saga, this book covers a wide variety of philosophically interesting subjects in thirty-one provocative and entertaining essays."*

—GREG LITTMANN, Associate Professor of Philosophy, Southern Illinois University at Edwardsville

---

"In unfolding the philosophical issues raised by Game of Thrones, *this book is crucial for anyone prowling the seven kingdoms. Find out with Freud about the true meaning of our hate for vile Joffrey and what Karl Marx has to say on who's really pulling the strings in Westeros. Apart from solving Varys's riddle, the authors also shed light on the moral significance of characters like Bran and Aemon. And with their guidelines on when (and whom!) to trust in times of treachery, the Iron Throne will soon be yours!"*

—JANELLE PÖTZSCH, Ruhr-University Bochum, co-editor of *Dracula and Philosophy: Dying to Know* (2015)

---

*"*Game of Thrones *is an intense fantasy thriller that is, at its heart, an intellectual show, and its hardcore fans appreciate its cerebral core. That's why any dedicated fan of the show will become engrossed in the thought-provoking chapters of* The Ultimate Game of Thrones and Philosophy, *written by top scholars who are also loyal* Game of Thrones *fans, skewering many of the philosophical ideas in* Game of Thrones—*ideas that you have long been thinking about yourself!"*

—JAMES ROCHA, Assistant Professor of Philosophy, California State University at Fresno

"Do you ever feel like the whole world is out to get you, that your life is filled with horrifying violence and gratuitous sex, and that you just want to spend your days guarding your homeland from weird ice walkers, solving esoteric riddles from creepy advisors, or giving birth to shadow spawn? Well, prepare yourself for the real game of thrones—philosophy! The Ultimate Game of Thrones and Philosophy *will twist and turn you through adventures of truth, reality, disabilities, deception, faith, your hatred of Joffrey, a little incest, and of course, your favorite imp, Tyrion."*

> —COURTLAND LEWIS, editor of *The Philosophy of Forgiveness* (2016), and co-editor of *Red Rising and Philosophy: Break the Chains!* (2016)

"Bertrand Russell once observed: 'Most people would sooner die than think; in fact, they do so'. The Ultimate Game of Thrones and Philosophy *helps us improve our chances of staying alive by reflecting on real-life issues—freedom, power, sex, evil, and honor—while holding our own lives up to the same sort of examination. This book exposes the real richness of* Game of Thrones *while also bringing that same richness to our own existence."*

> —JACK BOWEN, author of *If You Can Read This: The Philosophy of Bumper Stickers* (2010) and *The Dream Weaver: One Boy's Journey through the Landscape of Reality* (2006)

"Like the army of White Walkers, a rich and expansive Game of Thrones *and philosophy book has been a long time coming. This exciting volume covers an incredible diversity of topics from ethics to epistemology to sex. Any thoughtful fan of the* Game of Thrones *universe will find this book of insightful essays more welcome than the end of Joffrey's wedding feast."*

> —BENJAMIN MCCRAW, philosophy instructor at the University of South Carolina Upstate, and co-editor of *The Problem of Evil: New Philosophical Directions* (2015) and *The Concep of Hell* (2015).

The Ultimate
Game of Thrones
and Philosophy

Popular Culture and Philosophy® Series Editor: George A. Reisch

For full details of all Popular Culture and Philosophy® books, visit www.opencourtbooks.com.

Popular Culture and Philosophy®

The Ultimate Game of Thrones and Philosophy

You Think or Die

Edited by

ERIC J. SILVERMAN AND ROBERT ARP

OPEN COURT
Chicago

Volume 105 in the series, Popular Culture and Philosophy ®, edited by George A. Reisch

To find out more about Open Court books, call toll-free 1-800-815-2280, or visit our website at www.opencourtbooks.com.

Open Court Publishing Company is a division of Carus Publishing Company, dba Cricket Media.

Printed and bound in the United States of America.

A portion of Dr. Silverman's time on this project was supported by a generous grant from Christopher Newport University, Newport News, Virginia.

The Ultimate Game of Thrones and Philosophy: You Think or Die

ISBN: 978-0-8126-9950-0

Library of Congress Control Number: 2016951387

This book is also available as an e-book.

Contents

Invitation to Initiation

MARIANNE CHAILLAN

As wise as Maester Aemon, as cunning as Tyrion Lannister, and as strategic as Lord Varys . . .

In the fifth-season episode of HBO's *Game of Thrones* titled "Hardhome," Stannis Baratheon speaks with Sam Tarly in the library of Castle Black and learns that Sam has indeed killed a White Walker with a dagger made from Dragon Glass. Stannis asked how Sam knew that this dagger could kill the Walker, and Sam confesses that an old manuscript revealed this precious knowledge to him. So as danger grows beyond the Wall, the advice that Stannis gives to Sam for the people of Westeros is, "Keep reading, Sam Tarly."

Isn't it surprising that Stannis—a man of action—acknowledges that true power has its roots in a contemplative man? Not really, once we understand that knowledge is a weapon. When he was young, Sam wanted to become a sorcerer. Hasn't he, in a way, accomplished his dream? As indeed it is in books that we can discover highly precious powers.

This book will make you a sorcerer too! It will give you the power to understand the secrets of the fascinating universe of *Game of Thrones*. Not only will you discover the incredible philosophical depth of a series that its detractors wrongly portray as merely an unleashing of violence and sex, but you might also find, between the lines, an intuition about the one who will manage to sit on the Iron Throne . . .

The book that you are holding in your hands has summoned experts as wise as Maester Aemon, as cunning as Tyrion Lannister, and as strategic as Lord Varys—the philosophers! Here you will meet Maester Kant on the King's Road, or Lord Machiavelli in the corridors of King's Landing's Castle. Here Maester Seneca will help you discover all the wisdom included in the expression *Valar Morghulis*, while Lord Kierkegaard provides unexpected analysis on Stannis's sacrifice. In the following pages, Tyrion will initiate you to existentialism, while Daenerys will lead you along the path of the notion of freedom.

In this book, you will find all the answers to the questions you asked while watching the TV series. You will even discover the questions that maybe you didn't ask yourself. Like perhaps, to know if it is immoral to watch *Game of Thrones*. Or why there is so much violence in each episode, or even if it's possible to morally justify the Red Wedding!

Come, join the precious and skillful Night's Watch that, in its own way, represents the philosophers. If you wish, it is time to say your vows. Repeat the words that could have been those of Maester Kant, the Age of Enlightenment philosopher: *"I am the fire that burns against the cold, the light that brings the dawn, the horn that wakes the sleepers, the shield that guards the realms of men."*

If you said those words, welcome, Brother, your initiation begins on page 3.

_____

Marianne Chaillan is the author of *Game of Thrones: Une Métaphysique des Meurtres (Game of Thrones: A Metaphysics of Murder)* (Paris: Le Passeur Éditeur, 2016).

And now it begins.

—SER ARTHUR DAYNE

I

Life Is Not
a Song

1
Arya Stark as a Rough Hero

E.M. DADLEZ

I killed a boy when I was eight, Arya almost said, but she thought she'd better not.

—GEORGE R.R. MARTIN, *A Storm of Swords*

Imagine a headline that actions like Arya's could inspire in the present day:

Pre-teen Defendant to Be Tried as Adult in Harrenhal Slaying (*Lannister Herald*)

A Westerosi prosecutor says that evidence of premeditation warrants charging the young person (referred to only as 'A. Girl' in court documents) implicated in the grisly murder of a guardsman at Harrenhal's postern gate, to the full extent of the law. The deadly assault was committed in the course of an armed robbery during which three horses were stolen. Pieter Snow, the unfortunate guardsman slain by the youthful miscreant, is survived only by his heartbroken maternal parent, a senior serving-wench at the well-known Bolton Dreadfort facility. Rumored to be a multiple-felony offender, 'A. Girl' is nevertheless held by the public defender not to be irretrievably depraved. 'A. Girl's' lack of maturity and wartime experiences all contributed to a character prone to impulsiveness and heedless risk-taking, the defense avers. It is argued that the young are more vulnerable to negative influences and lack the ability to extricate themselves from crime-producing settings. The defense will maintain on this basis that sociopathic tendencies can develop as a result of immersion in horrific environments. Roose Bolton's representatives have strongly repudiated these aspersions on the climate at Harrenhal, amid the furor to which such an unusual defense strategy was bound to give rise. At last report, 'A. Girl's' Public Defender has taken up residence in a local Sept under armed guard, until repudiations diminish.

This is how a contemporary news piece on an eleven-year-old multiple murderer might look (except that until trial the accused could be referred to only as a 'suspect'). Some would want to see the juvenile tried as an adult.

It would matter that the murder was linked to other crimes, that the young killer was armed and looking for trouble. It would matter to most that the youthful offender had killed more than once. Others might regard the perpetrator's youth as partly exonerating on the ground of an underdeveloped capacity for moral judgment and diminished impulse control. Personal trauma and insalubrious environments would also be held to diminish responsibility, as would the limited options for survival open to a person in her particular circumstances.

What not even the most sympathetic pundit would claim, however, is that the Girl of the news report is admirable and courageous, an embattled and heroic figure whose success we crave, whose endeavors we applaud, and whose triumphs we celebrate. But that, in a nutshell, is the most frequent audience response to Arya Stark. The question here is whether there's anything morally deficient about a work that elicits such positive responses to a character whose deeds are (as even the text concedes) morally troubling.

Hume's Rough Heroes

In his essay "Of the Standard of Taste," the great eighteenth-century philosopher David Hume argues that the "rough heroes" celebrated by the ancient poets cannot properly engage our imagination, since "we cannot prevail on ourselves to enter into their sentiments, or bear an affection to characters, which we plainly discover to be blameable."

More recently, Anne Eaton has written an essay on "Robust Immoralism" in which she takes a more severe line than David

Hume. Hume's strictures apply to works in which a hero performs morally objectionable actions which the narrator nonetheless endorses. Since we cannot imagine what we cannot conceive, such a textual feature leads to imaginative disengagement. If, for instance, a text endorses as morally correct something that we believe is always wrong (the torture of innocents, say) we will not be able to imagine its rightness without making amendments to the story.

So Hume is concerned with works that explicitly *endorse* the morally problematic act, whereas Anne Eaton looks at works which do not do that, but merely exert a "halo effect" on immoral actions. Such works invite us to imagine attractive, compelling people who perform bad actions. Admirable traits like courage or intelligence are combined with troubling moral ones. So the question isn't about whether a work is immoral for inviting us to approve of immoral things by imagining they're acceptable. It is, rather, about whether a work is immoral for exerting a halo effect on morally problematic traits.

Eaton's Rough Heroes, differ from Hume's in that their negative traits are acknowledged by the text to *be* negative. Martin's books never endorse Arya's problematic actions. The narrator acknowledges them as problematic, shows us the psychological harm that doing them inflicts on her, and never portrays them as commendable. Yet, for all that, Arya's positive traits have so won us over (via, Eaton would contend, the halo effect) that we root for Arya in a way that would give us serious pause in real life. Does this demonstrate that there's something morally questionable about the story itself? Eaton would say yes, but my answer is, ultimately, no.

Eaton does seem to be correct in claiming that this kind of morally disruptive figure can have a profound impact on readers or viewers and can contribute enormously to fictional works. Works that permit us to explore morally alien perspectives, that allow us to see what the world looks like through the eyes of someone who does what we wouldn't do ourselves, are often more engaging than others. This is true not just because there's a kind of fascination with breaking conventional rules, but because such works are truer to life than those in which every heroine is as good as she is beautiful.

Because these works are so likely to fascinate, there is some concern that the sheer sympathetic interest which the characters arouse will overwhelm any repugnance felt toward their actions. However, I don't think that works which do not endorse an immoral perspective outright, but only show us how an otherwise appealing character might act upon it, are on that account ethically flawed.

A Sympathetic Killer

Consider the almost uniformly positive reaction to Arya. Thrust into the maelstrom of war in the Seven Kingdoms, she's forced to endure her father's execution, her mother's murder, and her brother's assassination. Only her wits and fortitude enable her to survive. Her self-control and intelligence are shocking and admirable, her self-reliance and growing ability to fight even more so. Unlike her sister Sansa, who develops a spine only well into the series, Arya does the best she can with the hand that she's been dealt.

If she allows herself to become an instrument of vengeance, well, the reader is allowed to see how that could happen, how much it costs her, how hard such a course would be for anyone to resist. The text never endorses Arya's killings, but it lets us see them through Arya's eyes. She will kill in self-defense, where the alternative is her death or that of her friends. She will kill for the sake of vengeance, but all Arya's revenge killings, without exception, are of despicable people the world is better off without.

Her gruesome murder of Ser Meryn in a brothel is the execution of a sadistic pedophile. Her elimination of Walder Frey and his sons rids the world of treacherous murderers. There is at least a strong utilitarian justification for the elimination of most of her victims. The *explanation* for these choices of Arya's is forcefully presented without yet becoming a justification.

Indeed, Arya is shown to rebel against the orders of the Faceless Men at the end of Season Six. She prevents the actress Lady Crane from drinking poison, thereby incurring the wrath of those who ordered her to kill Lady Crane. Moreover, her ultimate triumph over the Waif, sent to kill her for violating assassin protocol, earns her full acceptance in the House of Black and White—but it is an acceptance she repudiates:

> Finally, a girl is no one.

> A girl is Arya Stark of Winterfell.

Arya, who has been longing for assimilation and the loss of identity, is brought back to a sense of self by her refusal to kill for no reason. Of course that reclamation of identity leads her to organize a House of Atreus scenario for the benefit of the man who engineered the infamous Red Wedding at which her mother and brother were betrayed and murdered. Walder Frey is presented with a pie made from the bodies of his sons. Arya thereafter reveals her identity and cuts his throat, having informed him that the last thing he'll see will be "a Stark smiling down at you as you die."

The television series in particular arouses a revulsion intended to conflict with our positive response to Arya's youth and courage. Arya's obsession with revenge is dwelt on as, night after night, she relentlessly repeats the names of those for whose death she prays. This is not presented as a healthy state in which to be, but it is made understandable. We're intended to empathize with Arya and share her hatreds.

The clearest case of a morally deplorable action of Arya's which is never endorsed by the text involves her first assassination—the killing of a stranger at the behest of the House of Black and White. Once she's assigned her target—an old insurance seller in a soup shop—she spends some time observing him and attempting to invent rationalizations for his elimination. But she's told that it's not her business to judge him, only to kill him. And she does.

She puzzles over the most effective tactics, given the old man's bodyguards, and implements an ingenious and effective strategy. The text characterizes the action as wrong, even making it clear that Arya is suppressing concerns about its morality. Yet our investment in Arya is not diminished. We don't want her to be caught. We worry about what doing such a thing will do to her. We fear for her stability, we are concerned for her, but we nonetheless want her to emerge unscathed well before she redeems herself at the end of Season Six.

Does the Story Make Us Approve Bad Actions?

Is that kind of imaginative engagement a harmful thing? Does it lead us to take Arya's actions lightly? Or even to consider them permissible just because she has done them? The case has to be more complicated than that.

The combining of positive with negative traits in a single individual reflects what is true of the world. Witty, entertaining people can be cowards, honest rule-following types can carp and criticize intolerably, gifted artists can be despicable. Often, we will put up with bad traits (even if we still disapprove) because we value the good ones so highly. If a beloved sibling or parent or family pet did something unacceptable, such as injuring another, we wouldn't sanction that action, but we would seek to explain it in such a way as to encourage compassion. Our love for the miscreant would probably not be altered in the least.

Anne Eaton may well believe that such inclinations are reinforced by characters like Arya and our responses to them, very much to our moral detriment. I disagree. To seek explanations for behavior—as I might in the case of a badly behaved pet or relative and as most readers of Martin's series do in the case of Arya—isn't to exonerate the agent and can be a commendable impulse in itself.

We may also forgive wrongs without on that account considering them less wrong. Indeed, our investment in an actual person or a beloved fictional character may involve a genuine fear for their future well-being simply on account of the morally problematic nature of their actions. Such interests and concerns will not consume us in response to a newspaper story (such as that ventured at the outset of this chapter). They only become compelling when the case involves someone with whose story and with whose feelings we are well acquainted, whether in life or art.

How the Halo Effect Works

The halo effect is a well-documented phenomenon, but it need not be the case that some positive trait will lead us to develop pro-attitudes toward negative moral traits. If we love Arya, that doesn't mean we will always be inclined to justify everything she does. It means that we will view her morally suspect actions with particular concern—sometimes with an eye to mitigating explanations, but often with a concern for the ultimate consequences for the agent in whose well-being we are invested.

Another point about the halo effect. Tests purporting to show our tendency to endow attractive people about whom we are otherwise ignorant with traits toward which we have pro-attitudes often rely on situations in which the test subject must guess the other traits of the person under observation. In the absence of evidence, association rules. Traits that we value (intelligence, fairness, generosity) are ascribed to a character whose appearance is valued. However, this is less often true when the test subject has evidence to go on and is not simply guessing. So there's reason to believe that the power of association is mitigated by evidence of the sort provided by an intricately conceived fiction.

Moreover, negative traits cohabiting with positive ones in a single individual ought, according to the preceding principle, to be just as likely to exert a cooling effect on our estimation of the positive traits. In other words, a character's negative moral traits might make that character's attractiveness less compelling. Seeing an actor portray a repulsive evildoer can form such strong negative associations that it becomes difficult to find that actor attractive in even the most do-gooding roles. Biases of this kind can work in both directions.

Empathy with the Guilty

Consider characters like Shakespeare's Macbeth, whose actions appall us and yet with whom we can't help but sympathize, whose eloquence and perspicacity we cannot but admire. Those who sympathize with Macbeth at the last will not be inclined to justify the murder of MacDuff's wife and children. One of the things we sympathize *with* is the horror of having done certain things and the way that can empty the world of meaning.

Even in the case of less literary works, a well-drawn character can elicit similar reactions. So it appears inappropriate to condemn *Game of Thrones* for its depiction of Arya. It is possible, of course, that some readers may misinterpret the text, and take Arya's acts of vengeance to be heroic exercises of justice in which all right-thinking persons should engage. But this is a simple-minded misinterpretation of the text for which neither the author nor the story should be held accountable.

Killings in Martin's stories are ugly when Arya does them. We are made to see how they can appear desirable from Arya's perspective, but they are never endorsed—indeed, the reverse is often true, especially in the case of the assassination of the individual whose culpability is never established. If a text simply endorsed vengeful bloodshed, we might bring David Hume's strictures to bear. But that is not the case with Arya, who, if she is a Rough Hero, is not a hero whose transgressions we will come to embrace as good deeds.

Arya's transgressions compel interest and concern rather than approval, because of their ultimate effects on Arya and her development. So there is a pro-attitude of a sort toward Arya's moral failings (interest and concern, emotional investment) but it is not an attitude that corrupts or desensitizes.

2

Ned Stark: One Man in Ten Thousand

CHRISTOPHER C. KIRBY

> And the gods, who set mortals on that brutal voyage toward under-
> standing, have decreed that we must suffer into learning . . . Harsh is
> the grace of gods ruling from their terrible thrones.
>
> —AESCHYLUS. *Agamemnon,* lines 176–180

> It's always the innocents who suffer.
>
> —VARYS, "The Pointy End"

Winter is coming, but life in Westeros was *already* tragic. Where else could taking a new job cause you to lose your head . . . literally? Fans of *Game of Thrones* might be tempted to call the series tragic because of its dark themes of desolation and desperation . . . or simply because it continues to kill off all of the best characters!

But, it's neither an untimely death, nor utter despair that makes a story truly tragic. To understand what tragedy *really* is, in the classical sense, we have to go back to its inventors, the ancient Greeks.

Game of Thrones draws its inspiration from a wide array of myths, legends, and folklore. And, it was just the same for the first Greek tragedians, who used Greek mythology as material for their own stories.

Like *Game of Thrones*, the action in those ancient tragedies centered on the stories of four ruling dynasties: House Atreus in Mycenae, House Cadmus in Thebes, House Erichthonius in Athens, and House Minos in Crete. And, like the main houses

11

in *Game of Thrones*, these tragic dynasties suffered terrible fates of their own making. Yet, the most tragic of all was House Cadmus, which became famous for the magnitude of its *unmerited* suffering and the determination its members showed in overcoming such undeserved hardship.

This is probably why most people now associate tragedy with *any* tale that depicts terrible suffering. However, the *most* tragic stories almost always include the self-inflicted suffering of *innocents*. The saga of Ned Stark is a prime example of this sort of tragedy.

What Makes Tragedy

The man who passes the sentence should swing the sword.

—EDDARD STARK, "Winter Is Coming"

Aristotle (384–322 B.C.E.), the first philosopher to take a close look at tragedy, thought the main ingredient in any tragic tale is the demise of a *mostly* good person with a fatal character flaw.

Such a tragic flaw—which the Greeks called *hamartia*— might even consist in having too much of a good trait. Aristotle thought human beings were at their best when they aimed for everything in moderation. It's obvious that Ned's overblown sense of honor is what Aristotle would call excessive, and it's what continues to land him in hot water.

Another major component in tragedy for Aristotle is an error (or errors) caused by the character flaw that ends up reversing someone's fortune. He called such reversals *peripeteia*, which means "to fall down around," like when we say "things have come crashing down" around someone.

Finally, Aristotle believed a tragic hero or heroine must wind up in the sort of misery that could elicit fear and pity in an audience, so they could feel sympathy for the character's plight and identify with it. In this way, tragedy can fulfill its main social function, *catharsis,* which is the purging of negative emotions in its audience. For Aristotle, the story of Oedipus as told by Sophocles was the shining example of tragedy, precisely because it: 1. moved its audience to tears by 2. showing a decent man trying his best to do the right thing, but 3. mucking it up in a perfect storm of circumstance, character flaws, and dumb luck.

Fortunately, *Game of Thrones* delivers in droves on Aristotle's three criteria, especially in how Ned's story plays out. From the first episode, Ned is depicted as an honorable man who performs his duty with dignity. "The man who passes the sentence should swing the sword," he tells Bran. And this is meant to give us insight into the quality of his character; Ned is nothing if not decent. He's the sort of man who follows the old ways. Yet, as the first episode unfolds, we get glimpses into Ned's *hamartia* after he learns King Robert is coming to name him Hand:

Too Much of a Good Thing

NED: He's coming this far North, there's only one thing he's after.

CATELYN: You can always say no, Ned.

But, Ned *can't* say no, his tragic obsession with honor and duty won't allow it. As if he needed prodding, Luwin reminds Ned of this after Catelyn points out the mortal danger involved, "The king rode for a month to ask Lord Stark's help . . . You swore the king an oath, my lord." Sure enough, by the end of the first episode Ned has agreed and rides south with the king.

That was Ned's reversal of fortune. Since his decision stemmed strictly from duty and honor, his role as Hand will remain dominated by those values. He's been set on a path that ensures his tragic flaw will continue to come into play. In the next episode he kills Sansa's direwolf by order of the king, even though he could have refused, or simply let the animal escape. It would be reasonable to expect his longtime friend to forgive such a transgression. But, Ned's reluctance to defy the king stems directly from his commitments to honor and duty.

You think my life is some precious thing to me?

—EDDARD STARK, "Baelor"

In "The Wolf and the Lion," we finally see Ned defy the king when he steps down as Hand after hearing King Robert's plan to assassinate Daenerys and her unborn child. In venting his anger, Robert recognizes why Ned is now refusing to obey:

> ROBERT: You're the King's Hand, Lord Stark. You'll do as I command or I'll find me a Hand who will.
>
> NED: And good luck to him. I thought you were a better man.
>
> ROBERT: Out! Out, damn you! I'm done with you. Go! Run back to Winterfell! . . . You think you're too good for this? Too proud and honorable? This is a war!

Doomed by Honor

Once again, Ned's decisions, even the ostensibly defiant ones, are dominated by his sense of honor. Although it appears it might work out for Ned, he gets pulled back into the king's service while dutifully searching for the secret Jon Arryn died chasing. From there, Ned's fortune really begins to spiral downward, as his honor obliges him to make a series of errors: like confronting Cersei, refusing Renly's help, and ignoring Littlefinger's advice to take advantage of the power Robert bequeathed to him as Lord Protector of the Realm.

It turns out Ned's not just decent . . . he's virtuous and damn likeable! Most fantasy stories would kill to have a hero like him as the protagonist; but *Game of Thrones* simply *kills him off*. In "Baelor," Varys visits Ned in the dungeons one last time in an effort to convince him to forsake his honor in favor of survival:

> VARYS: Cersei knows you as a man of honor. If you give her the peace she needs and promise to carry her secret to your grave, I believe she will allow you to take the Black and live out your days on the Wall with your brother and your bastard son.
>
> NED: You think my life is some precious thing to me? That I would trade my honor for a few more years of . . . Of what? . . . I learned how to die a long time ago.

By now, *Game of Thrones* is known for its refusal to deliver the hackneyed, hero-wins-in-the-end trope of more conventional fantasy tales. The classical tragedians would, no doubt, smile at such a move, since they did the same thing by challenging the heroic epics of Homer (the *Iliad* and the *Odyssey*) that came before them. This is where that third Aristotelean element, *catharsis*, comes into focus.

Those two episodes which depict Ned's imprisonment and execution set viewership records for the first season, but the online reaction was pretty hostile after his beheading. Many had a hard time accepting how a noble figure could meet such an ignoble end. Then something interesting developed. Fans began to commiserate online about those feelings and a sense of community grew from their interactions, as fans purged their own emotions to like-minded folks.

Weeping Together

This same sort of *catharsis* took place whenever the ancient Greeks attended classical tragedies. We can only imagine how much more *intense* this would have been sitting side by side on the walls of those ancient amphitheaters, watching the suffering on stage and witnessing the outpouring of emotions among our fellow watchers on the walls. The ancient Greeks realized that weeping alongside others, even strangers, created a bond almost as strong as kinship. And this was the social function of tragedies, to bring together the citizens of a city-state and bind them to one another through the common feelings of fear and pity.

> As we sin, so do we suffer.
>
> —PYCELLE, "Baelor"

More recently Martha Nussbaum has revived the moral and social relevance of classical tragedy in contemporary life. For her, the most important concept in Greek tragedy is the idea that people are, simultaneously, victims *and* agents in their own stories. Like Oedipus and Ned, they find themselves constrained by circumstances and chance, but they also tend to put themselves in those situations because of their character habits.

Classical tragedy reminds us of that through the exercise of what Nussbaum calls fearful compassion. She identifies three components of such compassion. First, we recognize another's suffering is substantial. Second, we realize the suffering person didn't deserve so much misery. Third, we understand how such tragedy could easily happen to us.

Nussbaum concludes that when it comes to passing moral judgment on the actions of others, we should remember they may have landed in those circumstances because of some catastrophe, but the actor still has some responsibility for their actions.

Nussbaum also believes our moral lives are filled with moments of "tragic conflict"—cases where luck constrains a person in such a way that they *must* choose between two competing and equally valid moral claims. This is where *Game of Thrones* is at its *most* tragic. Nearly *every* lead character lands in tragic conflict which leads to their demise.

The paradigmatic example of tragic conflict for Nussbaum is the decision laid before Agamemnon of House Atreus. Agamemnon was the commander of the Greek fleet that was ready to set sail for Troy. Unfortunately, the weather made things too treacherous for his army to leave the Greek shores safely. He was given a choice: sacrifice your daughter to placate the angry gods, or risk your army's destruction. This mirrors the choice which Melisandre places in front of Stannis when his army is frozen in its tracks on the way to Winterfell.

Like Stannis, Agamemnon chose to kill his daughter—even though killing your own family was deemed a heinous act by the ancient Greeks. But, Agamemnon doesn't make the decision lightly. He recognizes that both choices are not "without their evils," and he struggles to prioritize those evils in his mind and reconcile them to his choice of action.

We often find ourselves in similar scenarios involving a practical conflict between two competing values. Because our lives are full of all manner of commitments—to our families, our careers, our own hopes and dreams—we frequently find ourselves in a place where we're damned if we do and damned if don't. But, this brute fact about our moral lives isn't something from which we should try to hide; it's something we should embrace.

Embracing this fact helps us realize we too are victims, as well as agents, in our own moral stories. It's not that we should wish for suffering, but we should accept that, like these tragic heroes, we must suffer into learning and moral maturity.

Tragic Conflicts

When word reaches Castle Black that Ned has been captured, his "son" Jon Snow finds himself in his own tragic conflict. The wise Maester Aemon advises him about his situation:

> AEMON: Tell me, did you ever wonder why the men of the Night's Watch take no wives and father no children?
>
> JON: No.
>
> AEMON: So they will not love. Love is the death of duty. If the day should ever come when your lord father was forced to choose between honor on the one hand and those he loves on the other, what would he do?
>
> JON: He . . . He would do whatever was right. No matter what.
>
> AEMON: Then Lord Stark is one man in ten thousand. Most of us are not so strong.

Jon has faith in Ned to do what's right when it comes to practical conflicts in value, but as we've just seen, the problem with such scenarios is that there's no *truly* right choice, because neither option is "without its evils."

This raises another point about tragedy highlighted by Nussbaum. Most people believe that the wisest way to deal with tragic conflict is to prioritize the competing values and act according to that hierarchy. This is just what Stannis and Agamemnon did when they chose to sacrifice their daughters. Most moral philosophers would see prioritization as the best strategy because they *assume* any adequate moral theory should not allow for the possibility of genuine practical conflict. But, there are some real problems to thinking in this way.

First, we must admit that even if it *were* possible to arrange moral values hierarchically, sometimes situations arise where the *same* value gives rise to conflicting obligations. For instance, wanting to be a good father, by itself, might cause a practical conflict wherever competing commitments to multiple children pop up. Moreover, if reason *really* could provide a clear resolution through prioritization, then in such scenarios there should be no "moral residue" (that unpleasant feeling which comes from second-guessing our choices). Yet, we do often feel guilt and remorse for choosing the lesser of two evils and we look at figures like Stannis and Agamemnon with some contempt because of the decisions they've made.

A good tragedy doesn't attempt naive solutions to the problems of practical conflict—the way most moral philosophies try to do—through prioritization. Instead, it shows us the fullness and complexity of the problem itself. It teaches us that the best a tragic hero can do is to acknowledge his or her own suffering and recognize it as an expression of a commitment to moral goodness. So, the key is to learn from suffering *without* succumbing to the misguided optimism of philosophical safety. The best that we, the watchers on our own walls, can do for the tragic heroes we encounter in life is to honor the significance of those troubles by seeing them as real possibilities for ourselves. Aemon recognizes that Jon *must* face his own conflict in order to grow morally:

> Aemon: We're all human. Oh, we all do our duty when there's no cost to it. Honor comes easy then. Yet sooner or later in every man's life there comes a day when it's not easy. A day when he must choose.

The aim of tragedy isn't some romantic notion of happiness, but rather the greater range of emotion and nuance in action that comes with moral maturity. Ned was unable to open himself up to such possibilities, to the extreme of not even telling Jon who his real parents were, and it led to his eventual demise. As a member of the Night's Watch, Jon followed Ned in choosing honor and duty, and it got him killed.

Perhaps there's still an opportunity for Jon, as King in the North, to grow beyond Ned's single-minded prioritizations and learn that, in the *Game of Thrones*, like life, there is no escape from moral suffering. Every choice involves a tragic loss.

3
There's Only One God and His Name Is Death

MATTHEW MCKEEVER

Ned, Catelyn, and Robb Stark die. Joffrey and Tywin Lannister die. Viserys Targaryen dies. Khal Drogo dies. Jon Snow dies. Well, for a while. A lot of people die in *Game of Thrones*.

That a lot of people die in some work of fictional art is not in and of itself interesting: in a typical action movie, there's plenty of death. What's interesting about *Game of Thrones* is that, as the above list indicates, a lot of *central* characters die *unexpectedly* in *Game of Thrones*. Indeed, it's from this fact that a lot of the dramatic power of the series emerges. And this, in turn, may be because it's quite rare, in art, for central characters to die unexpectedly.

But we should be puzzled by this. For a tradition going all the way back to Plato and Aristotle has it that the function of art is representation (*mimesis*). Plato and Aristotle disagreed as to the worth of art. Plato didn't look too kindly on art. For him, art was a copy of a copy, because he divided the world into concrete particular objects and the abstract forms. A particular concrete drinking goblet—say, Tyrion Lannister's—with its scratches and chipped paint, is a copy of the abstract form of the goblet, the perfect example of gobletness. And it's the abstract forms which really exist, for Plato. But a representation of Tyrion's goblet, in a film or on a page, is itself a copy of the goblet, and so it's a copy of a copy, even further removed from reality than the goblet itself.

Aristotle agreed with Plato that art is a copy of the physical world, but didn't think it's any the worse for that. In his *Poetics*, he notes that art (such as tragic plays) works by virtue of representing people's misfortune, and this enables it to perform its central role: of letting us vent or purge emotions like pity and fear by presenting stories which arouse these emotions.

These differences notwithstanding, they both agreed that art is about representing the world. And certain modern and post-modern art excepted, this seems reasonable and has remained a popular view. But bearing this in mind, it becomes unclear why it is quite rare, in art, for central characters to die unexpectedly. For it's an important and tragic fact of life that the central characters *in our lives* sometimes die unexpectedly: the unexpected death of someone close to us is invariably deeply shocking, emotionally and existentially, as we pine for someone taken from us and are made viscerally aware of the fragility of life.

Given this, it seems there must be an explanation for *why* most art doesn't represent sudden unexpected death. And there *is* such an explanation: it's that the representational capacity of art in general excludes the portrayal of sudden, unexpected death of central characters. But this raises another question: how does Martin nevertheless manage to portray it?

The Unexpected Death of Central Characters Is Rare

The unexpected death of central characters in narrative art is rare. It's quite hard to argue directly for such a claim, because there are so many stories available. I hope the reader can consult works with which she is familiar and will find it true.

But we can consider how odd it would be had central characters in major works of art died early. A *King Lear* in which Lear dies at the end of the first act would be an odd thing. Similarly an Anna Karenina catching a bad cold leading to fatal pneumonia halfway through the novel would be somewhat lacking. And a lot of the fun would be taken from *Breaking Bad* if Walt succumbed to his cancer in Season Two. For such plays, novels, and TV shows—which can be multiplied at will—death often marks the dramatic and emotional culmination of the work. It's not something that pops up halfway through, as Joffrey's death does in the second episode of Season Four.

Tolstoy is a useful foil here. Like Martin, he was concerned with telling stories on an epic scale, but his approach to death is notably different: it is something marked off or saved for conclusions. His most masterful treatment of death, the novella *The Death of Ivan Ilyich*, forms a work of its own which, as the title suggests, is centered on death. The sole chapter of *Anna Karenina* to bear a title has the title "Death." For Tolstoy, death is something artistically sequestered away and signposted, or reserved for big conclusions, whereas for Martin it's always ready to pop up when least expected.

I have said it's rare for main characters to suddenly die—not that it never happens. That's too strong a claim. An interesting contemporary example is Omar in *The Wire*. In Season Five, he is fighting with Marlow, gradually taking down some of his men. The expected plot arc is that either he will kill or be killed by Marlow. But no: out of nowhere, when he's in the store buying cigarettes, a prepubescent kid shoots him in the back of the head.

This is an unexpected death of a central character as shocking and powerful as those which occur in Westeros. But it still doesn't quite evince the brio Martin has for killing off his main players: it occurs very near the end of the final season. This is in marked contrast to the death of, say, Ned Stark, who died one season into a long series of at least seven seasons. So, it's rare for main characters in art to suddenly die.

We Should Expect Main Characters Often to Die Unexpectedly

We should surely expect that it would be common for main characters to die unexpectedly. The reason for this is that narrative art aims to represent the world, and it's a vital feature of life that the main characters in our own real lives can suddenly die. This is uncontroversial: both emotionally and intellectually, it's fundamental. Emotionally, there are few events more upsetting than the death of a loved one. Intellectually, it's a reminder of perhaps the defining feature of life: its finitude.

The idea that death can strike anyone at any moment is ubiquitous in art, philosophy, and religion. In art we can see it in Epicurean poems like Catullus's fifth ode, or Andrew Marvell's *To His Coy Mistress*, in which the respective authors remind their girlfriends of the transitoriness of life in a bid to get them into bed. Or think of the visual art in the *momento mori* tradition (Latin for 'remember you must die'), often of a religious nature. In philosophy, we can think of Montaigne's essay "That to Study Philosophy Is to Learn to Die," which, having mentioned some famous unexpected death, counsels us always to keep before our mind the certainty that we will some day die, so as not to stand in fear of it and so as to be able to enjoy life.

And in religion we can find it at the heart of Buddhism, with its fundamental precept that *sabba anicca*, that everything, including ourselves, is impermanent (see, for example, the final verses of *Dhammapada*, Chapter 20, which warn that death can come like a flood overwhelming a village, and that one should seek refuge in Buddhist practice). Again, examples could be easily multiplied, if we had more space.

Given the importance in our emotional and cognitive lives of the thought that we or those whom we love could die at any time, and given that art is meant to represent the cognitive and emotionally important features of our life, then we might expect that main characters would often die unexpectedly. So, why doesn't this happen? Why is it as rare as I have suggested to kill off main characters unexpectedly?

There Are Strong Arguments Against the Unexpected Death of Main Characters

Although we might expect stories to kill off main characters because this would be true to life, there are several possible reasons, in the form of strong arguments, against the portrayal of the sudden unexpected death of central characters.

The first challenges the very possibility of such portrayal: if a character dies suddenly and unexpectedly, then that character is obviously not central.

The thought here is that to be central, it's necessary to see the whole, or most of, the story through. If a character fails to do that, they are at best a peripheral character. That seems reasonable to me. Imagine a novel depicting the life of someone who dies halfway through the story, and the rest is concerned with the effects this has on the other characters. I think there's good sense to be made of the idea that this novel isn't really *about* the one who dies, but rather about those left behind and their grief or lack of it. The dead person functions merely as a plot point to bring out the theme of grief and the grieving, and thus is not a central character.

The second argument goes from a different angle. It holds, not that it's impossible, a contradiction in terms, for a central character to die unexpectedly, but rather it's just a bad artistic move. The reason it's a bad artistic move is because the author has presumably spent time introducing and telling the audience about the character. If the author then quickly and unceremoniously disposes of that character, then that time seems wasted. It would be, one might say, bad aesthetic economics to invest all that effort into a character only to waste it by having them die unceremoniously. This would explain why, oftentimes, the central characters' deaths come at the end of the story: because the work is about to end, we won't have wasted the effort put into the character, since there's no other chance to put the character to use in the work. Moreover, the audience might well get annoyed: you are bound to have heard fans of *Game of Thrones* threaten to quit the series after the death of this or that favourite character.

Limits of Representation

If either of these arguments convinces you, then we have an interesting conclusion: that there's a difficulty in representing this feature of life in art. We've come across what looks like a *representational limit of art*: a feature of the world that art can't represent.

Let's look at a couple of other such limits, as I hope that my eventual resolution of the puzzle as to how Martin overcomes the limit concerning death can shed light on these other limits.

The first limit concerns "Hollywood ugliness." This is a typical trope in romantic comedies: the man pursues the glamorous girl, ignoring the less glamorous best friend, until, in the final scene, he realizes the less glamorous girl is actually the one for him, and she removes her glasses and ponytail to reveal that she too is in fact glamorous. The important point for us is before this big final reveal: the actor playing the best friend will typically be conventionally beautiful (most actors are). That her character is meant to appear not to be beautiful is conveyed by such things as her glasses and clothes and hair.

The reason for this is that if the actor were indeed conventionally unattractive, then audiences wouldn't get that she was meant to be representing unattractiveness. Rather, they'd most likely be confused by the presence in a film of an actor who is not, relative to their standards, conventionally attractive. So in order to represent plainness, the film-maker has to use an attractive person and certain props that connote plainness, and so can't represent actual plainness.

The second limit concerns representing people from different times or places. If we want to depict an eighteenth-century character, then it's necessary to pepper their speech with the sort of archaisms that the contemporary viewer would expect such a person to say (loads of 'methinks' and verbs ending in 'eth', perhaps) even if that's not how the character would speak.

In the same vein, Bumblebee Guy from *The Simpsons* speaks a terrible Spanish which no real Mexican would ever use, but which would be just about recognizable to someone who had taken a couple of Spanish classes in high school. This is a reflection of the general fact that it's necessary, to convey something artistically, to tailor the representations to the audience's knowledge of the thing represented, rather than the thing itself, and this induces a failure of accurate representation.

The Epic Answer

First, I suggested that sudden unexpected death of central characters is rare in art. Second, I suggested that we should not expect it to be rare, because it represents a central feature of our experience, as art is meant to. Third, I gave reasons for explaining death's rarity, and suggested that its rarity is the result of a representative failure of art, an antecedently recognizable notion. But now one question looms large: how does Martin manage to get around this representational limit, and can we learn anything from it?

Here's my answer to the first question: he gets around the limit by the epic nature of *Game of Thrones*. In brief: the failure of good aesthetic economy resulting from the fact that he spends so much time portraying Ned Stark only to kill him off is offset by the fact that there are so many other characters around for us to shift our attention to. Moreover, this epicness can serve to make a character both central and, in a sense, peripheral. He simply has "world enough and time" as poor Marvell and his coy mistress don't.

This isn't an especially interesting answer. You could probably have guessed it yourself without reading this chapter. But the real interest lies in the fact that it suggests a general-purpose means for overcoming the representational limits of art: make the work bigger.

Return to our Hollywood ugliness example. Because such stories work within a dichotomous ugly-beautiful framework, we can quite easily get away with using a conventionally attractive actress and some props to convey her plainness. But say we wanted to present a story on a *larger* scale about how people look: say we were telling a story about a beauty contest, and we wanted to represent not only ugly and beautiful characters, but various gradations: quite ugly, plain, quite beautiful, and so forth. In such a case, the quick resort to props wouldn't help much. What would help, however, is if we had actors who were as attractive as their characters were meant to be. And that would overcome the representational limit: we'd have plain actors playing plain characters.

Similarly for the archaic speech example. It would no longer be sufficient, if we wanted to tell a story that spanned both the seventeenth and the eighteenth centuries, to lazily use the common stock of archaisms, because the audience then couldn't tell, if a character were to say 'methinks the wind rageth too fierce' which century the character was meant to be from. And again, it seems the way around this, at least in part, would be to have the characters from the different eras speak differently, and the obvious way to achieve this would be to have them speak roughly like the people they are portraying actually would have spoken.

What this suggests to me is that epicness is the way to overcome representational limits in art. And this makes some sense, because the goal of an epic is to present as much of life as possible. We may therefore conclude: if we want to portray certain aspects of life that resist immediate representation, go big! Make your work epic, like *Game of Thrones*, and the problem will go away.

There's one one final question though, to which I don't know the answer. The idea of the epic is not a new one. Again, return to Tolstoy: his *War and Peace* contains over five hundred characters! Why is it only now that writers are exploiting the vastness of the epic to portray the kind of deaths with which we have been concerned? Is it a good thing, as representing more of life, or is it a simple shock tactic?

I don't have answers to these questions, but I hope you'll agree they're interesting and worth asking, and show the merits of considering *Game of Thrones* not merely as a good story and a good show, but as something that can teach us about the nature of art and society.

4
Tyrion's Humor

JARNO HIETALAHTI

Tyrion Lannister is a monster, and everyone in the Seven Kingdoms knows it. He is commonly known as Half-Man, the Imp, and even his sister Cersei calls him the Beast.

True, Tyrion is a short-statured person, but he's also a Lannister, and therefore a highborn; a rare mix in Westeros. This contradictory blend of nobleness and freakiness is not easily digested by all, and least of all by his father Tywin Lannister.

Tywin has always wanted his son dead, and would rather let himself be consumed by maggots before making Tyrion heir to their family's castle, Casterly Rock. For Tywin, Tyrion is a lecherous little stump full of envy, lust, and low cunning ("Valar Dohaeris").

Tyrion is a living paradox, and this causes troubles for him and the honor of family. But then, as a real-world humanist Erich Fromm puts it, the essence of humanity is based on a contradiction. Human beings are freaks of the universe as we are the only creatures endowed with self-consciousness.

We have the option to choose our deeds, and these choices are, in the end, all that matters. To understand our choices and actions, it's necessary to understand our character. This is the proper starting point when analyzing Tyrion's humor.

The Jocular Clown

BRONN: Stay low! If you're lucky, no one will notice you.

TYRION: I was born lucky. ("Baelor")

If your father is the most powerful man in Westeros, you are not expected to, say, urinate from the Great Wall. Well, Tyrion does just that. Also, Lannisters are expected to fight for honor with swords and armors, but Tyrion prefers dusty books over knight's well-polished equipment.

Vain glory does not suit him as there are much more important things in the world. Like reading or chasing prostitutes. Obviously, Tyrion is a funny fellow, though possibly in an insolent manner. He has the capability to point out the ridiculousness of other people's thought patterns, and he's not afraid to share his observations. Thanks to his wit, Tyrion's exceptional mind is on display.

Of course, there are those—like Joffrey Baratheon—who see Tyrion as just a midget. For some, the deepest joy is to see other's suffering, and the mirth is great when they can say something like: "Hahaha, look, a dwarf!" Obviously, because of his body, Tyrion is associated with the tradition of court jesters. He's a dwarf and nothing can change it.

As Tyrion remarks in "Winter Is Coming," a person should never forget what he is, as the rest of the world will not. Hard facts have to be accepted, but this does not mean that we should submit to be slaves of external conditions. Tyrion is an oddity and a jester, or as he himself says, a practical joke of the gods, but he embraces his situation productively.

Laughter has always followed Tyrion, and already as a child he entertained his companions with silly deeds like turning cartwheels. His father tried to cut this short when he witnessed one of his son's acts. At a dinner, Tyrion surprised his family by walking the length of a table on his hands. Tywin's reaction was freezing: "The gods made you a dwarf. Must you be a fool as well? You were born a lion, not a monkey" (*A Dance with Dragons*). This did not end Tyrion's tomfoolery but made it more profound.

Tyrion makes the philosophy of humor come alive with his wits and deeds. Great minds, such as Immanuel Kant and Søren Kierkegaard, have realized that in the heart of humor lies a contradiction. Roughly put, humor stems from an incongruity between our expectations and what actually happens; for instance, if a careless stroller steps on a banana peel, slips, and hits his buttocks to the ground, others will laugh.

In this example, the incongruity lies in the actions: you should be aware of your surroundings, and not step on slippery fruits. Other philosophers, like Plato and Thomas Hobbes, have argued that in our laughter we feel superior to the object of the joke. For Hobbes, laughter is an expression of glory when we suddenly realize that we're better than the ridiculous fruit slipper. Sigmund Freud maintains that we express hidden hostility in our laughter.

The previous three theories are intertwined in the character of Tyrion Lannister, and this is underlined in "The Lion and the Rose." King's Landing is celebrating King Joffrey's wedding, and the king presents a show called "The War of the Five Kings," in which short-statured actors play roles of different kings in a mocking manner; and the winner of the war is, naturally, Joffrey himself.

Then, he encourages Tyrion to join the slapstick show. By this, Joffrey sets himself above all other kings, and represents himself as the unquestioned winner, and at the same time he mocks his uncle's physical features. These two, as everyone familiar with the show knows, share a history of confrontation. For instance, as witnessed in "The Old Gods and the New":

JOFFREY: You can't insult me!

TYRION: We've had vicious kings, and we've had idiot kings, but I don't think we've ever been cursed with a vicious idiot for a king!

JOFFREY: You can't!

TYRION: I can, I am!

JOFFREY: They attacked me!

TYRION: They threw a cow pie at you so you decide to kill them all? They're starving, you fool! All because of a war you started!

JOFFREY: YOU'RE TALKING TO A KING!

[*Tyrion slaps Joffrey across the face*]

TYRION: And now I've struck a king! Did my hand fall from my wrist?

Generally, Tyrion is the only one who has the courage to challenge the king's commands. And the king, supposedly an omnipotent ruler, hates this. Because Tyrion dares to tell

Joffrey who he really is, the king wants revenge by humiliating the Imp. So, the long-built tension reaches its highest peak in the wedding show, and Tyrion's paradoxical situation as a dwarf and a highborn gets its clearest manifestation. Equally clear is that Tyrion is screwed.

But no need to get into the details of the plot twists. The observation is that even though others may laugh at the dwarf because of his bodily features, the core of Tyrion's humor lies beyond his height. Tyrion's humor is not "only jokes," but he expresses something much more in his witty remarks, and does not let others' opinions deter him from speaking. His humor is a form of social criticism.

The Critical Outsider

That's what I do. I drink and I know things.

—TYRION, "Home"

Jesters are on the outskirts of the society. In their humor, they present an outsider's perspective. Some, like Cersei Lannister, think that everything's just a joke for Tyrion, but this view is limited. Tyrion does not mock simply for the sake of mocking, but he observes cultural paradoxes and offers critical observations on the prevailing value systems.

Erich Fromm argues that disobeying social rules just for the sake of disobedience is eventually empty. Thus, social criticism—even in a humorous form—has to be based on some values. Tyrion's critical humor is based on the affirmation of life, which refers to a deeper attitude than to the basic instinct to stay biologically alive.

We can get a grasp of Tyrion's humor by comparing his wit to another humorous fictional character, the Joker. In the movie *Dark Knight*, the Joker is a herald of Chaos, and wants nothing but to see the world burn. In short, the Joker states that nothing is serious, so there cannot be any principles nor foundations on which to base human life. For him, humans are worthless and ludicrous creatures, and any attempt to build a world is ridiculous. Life is an absurd joke.

Tyrion does not want to see the world burn, but he wants to see the rottenness of the Seven Kingdoms burned. True enough, as a Lannister he has privileges which permit him to achieve positions like Hand of the King and Master of Coin—titles out of the reach of commoners and midgets. But despite his background, Tyrion loathes empty rituals and hollow fawning.

For Tyrion, court etiquette is meaningless if the court itself is worthless. The same holds for religions and other official systems of belief. In his eyes, gods are contemptible if they want their enemies burned, or drowned, or whatever nasty termination happens to suit the whim of the Supreme Being ("The Prince of Winterfell"). And when religious system and political power are combined, the life of a commoner or a freak may easily be brushed aside. Trials are one of his favorite objects of derision, as he demonstrates in "A Golden Crown" when facing the inhumane justice of the Vale:

> TYRION: Where do I begin, my lords and ladies? I'm a vile man, I confess it. My crimes and sins are beyond counting. I have lied and cheated, gambled and whored. I'm not particularly good at violence, but I'm good at convincing others to do violence for me. You want specifics, I suppose. When I was seven, I saw a servant girl bathing in the river. I stole her robe. She was forced to return to the castle naked and in tears. If I close my eyes, I can still see her tits bouncing. When I was ten, I stuffed my uncle's boots with goatshit. When confronted with my crime, I blamed a squire. Poor boy was flogged and I escaped justice. When I was twelve I milked my eel into a pot of turtle stew. I flogged the one-eyed snake. I skinned my sausage. I made the bald man cry into the turtle stew, which I do believe my sister ate. At least I hope she did. I once brought a jackass and a honeycomb into a brothel . . .
>
> LYSA ARRYN: SILENCE! What do you think you're doing?
>
> TYRION: Confessing my crimes.

This does not mean that Tyrion wouldn't respect other families and formal relationships. Quite the contrary, he understands the meaning of social interaction in the Seven Kingdoms. Tyrion has a sharp eye for realpolitik, and he's aware how the game of thrones should be played. But his interest in the political afflictions strives from his passion to enhance life and humane growth.

Often this life-affirmative attitude is manifested in cruel remarks which are pointed against the twisted ways of living in the courts. Tyrion's humor brings out that even if the world is currently rotten, it doesn't need to be. For Tyrion, all human beings are equal. This holds for highborn and lowborn, free men and wildlings, dwarves and people of average height. He has sympathy for life, not for names. In this, he comes close to Erich Fromm who claims that we all carry the whole humanity within ourselves as we all share the paradoxical core of humanity.

The Life-Loving Outcast

PETYR BAELISH: I hear you owe that boy a significant debt.

TYRION: Only my life. Not at all that significant, I'm afraid. ("Walk of Punishment")

Living in Westeros is not easy for a dwarf even if you're a Lannister. Fate can be cruel, and Tyrion's faith in life is stretched as every fragile moment of happiness is followed by a disaster. The gods, or George R.R. Martin, test Tyrion as Job was tested in the Bible. Eventually, the dwarf has lost everything: his social prestige, family, love, power, and in the book version, half of his nose.

And still, after being stripped of all earthly possessions, Tyrion does not give up. He does not have goals or dreams, but he is alive. In *A Dance with Dragons* Tyrion is offered a sweet death in the form of delicious deadly mushrooms. While weighing his options, Tyrion ends up pondering what he has to live *for*. He realizes that he has no family legacy, no land to rule, no loved ones to take care of, all in all, nothing.

This moment of illumination would be devastating if you think that life's meaning derives from these external things. However, Tyrion declines the opportunity to end his life. This moment of reflection echoes what Fromm argues about the meaning of life: there is no meaning of life besides the act of living itself. And still, you can live viciously or virtuously, as the ideal is to fulfill your human potential.

Even though Tyrion is an outcast, he has not lost his hope for life and how this life could be more favorable for the less fortunate. Tyrion's biting humor reminds us how empty the political system in Westeros is if the only important things are family name, money, and armies. When mocking social hierarchies and the stupidity of life in such a society, Tyrion expresses affirmation of an equal life for all.

Even though Tyrion throws his jabs at certain individuals, he mocks the least flattering sides of humanity in general. Tyrion laughs at the highest rungs of the social ladder, but also at the stupidity of the masses. Still, he only laughs because of his deep compassion and fondness for life. His humor should be seen in relation to this aspect of his character, even though there are bitter tendencies in his jokes.

Tyrion often appears to be cynical, but these doubtful moments do not overcome his passion for life. For him, death is dreadfully final whereas life is full of possibilities ("The Kingsroad"). The imp might be known by his bodily features and quick wit, but his character lies beyond these aspects. Tyrion reminds us that humor is not merely jokes and silly deeds, but can be an expression of deeper emotions and a way to relate to the world.

There are a number of ways we can enjoy the humor that glows around Tyrion. First, it's possible to laugh at his physical attributes, but that is hardly satisfactory. Second, his one-liners are funny and enjoyable, but mere laughter does not capture the inner core of his humor.

In a philosophical sense, Tyrion's humor is an affirmation of life. Despite the bitter tone of his witticisms, Tyrion is an optimist even when he has lost everything. True, he states that the future is shit just like the past ("The Wars to Come") but that does not mean that this woeful outlook is the only possibility he is able to imagine. His character-rooted compassion for the tormented and oppressed conveys that we can build a kingdom where the powerful do not prey upon the weak.

Tyrion's humor stems from practical paradoxes. His jests underline the senselessness of conventional common sense, which appears to make sense only because everyone keeps repeating it. The dwarf understands that life is full of ironies, and how you relate to those ironies is pivotal. Tyrion's message is that even if the world is built by killers, there can be room for kindness.

In an absurd world, the voice of reason often sounds like a joke.

II

There Are
No Men Like Me,
Only Me

5
Guilty of Being a Dwarf

KIMBERLY S. ENGELS

Who are we? Are we defined by our physical characteristics? By how others perceive us? By our own choices? A complex combination of all of these things?

In an intensely dramatic scene, Tyrion Lannister, on trial for killing the king, declares that he is guilty of a crime—the crime of "being a dwarf." He further asserts that "I have been on trial for my entire life." With this declaration, Tyrion directly confronts a life-long struggle—that all of his choices are judged against the backdrop of his "crime" and social status as a dwarf. However, throughout his life, Tyrion is aware of his ability to challenge and transcend the social categories he is born into and attempts to be his own person.

His journey exemplifies Jean-Paul Sartre's existentialist concepts of nausea, bad faith, and authenticity. What does this mean?

Jean-Paul Sartre argues that human beings are free to create their own identities—they are, as he puts it, "radically free." In his lecture *Existentialism Is a Humanism,* he famously says that human existence precedes human essence. When he says "Existence precedes essence," Sartre doesn't mean simply that human beings are capable of making choices about what to do, but that they are free to choose who they are and to create their own values.

Many religious traditions and theories of human nature are grounded in the belief that we have an unchanging true self or soul. Sartre rejects this, and as he says, "gets rid of the blue print" of human nature. However, we only choose our own

37

essence within the constraints of characteristics that we cannot control—for example our race, biological sex, physical limitations, or cultural heritage, which he calls "facticity." These traits not only place limitations upon what we can accomplish, they affect how we are perceived and treated by others.

Sartre argues that "bad faith" arises when we either accept our facticity without recognizing our freedom to transcend it, or, alternatively, focus only on our freedom of choice without recognizing that some of our characteristics are beyond our control. If we deny certain unchangeable aspects about ourselves, we're living in bad faith. Similarly, if we deny that we are anything *but* those characteristics, we are lying to ourselves about our freedom.

Instead of living in bad faith, we should live "authentic" lives. Authenticity is usually associated with reflecting on one's "true self," but according to Sartre there is no "true self." Authenticity means acknowledging our facticity *and* recognizing that we have the freedom to choose what to make of it. In the series premier, Jon Snow shows offense when Tyrion refers to him as a bastard. Tyrion in turn gives him a piece of advice, "Never forget what you are, the rest of the world will not. Wear it like armor, and it can never be used to hurt you" ("Winter Is Coming").

Jon Snow exemplifies bad faith by hiding from his social categorization as a bastard—something he cannot change. Tyrion recognizes that people will always judge Jon for this just as they judge him for being a dwarf, and suggests that Jon own it and use it to his advantage.

Authenticity is not easy. We are often tempted to fall back on existing social categories to define us, avoiding the burden of choosing our own path. Sartre refers to the accompanying anguish as "nausea." Nausea is the feeling of sickness and dread we get when we realize that we are the ones responsible for creating ourselves through our choices, and cannot rely on an inherent nature to define us. To avoid nausea, many retreat into bad faith.

More than any other character, Tyrion exemplifies Sartre's existentialism and how people are a complex, multifaceted product of their facticity and the choices they make. In Tyrion's full acceptance of himself as a dwarf and his determination to still be his own person, he embodies Sartrean authenticity.

I Am Guilty

What does Tyrion mean when he says he is, "guilty of being a dwarf"? Tyrion is pointing out that because of his facticity as a dwarf he is judged more harshly by others. Now, this is a very real challenge that people can face due to a disability, their race, their looks, sexual orientation, or other social categories. Tyrion's presumed guilt is first evident when he is presupposed guilty by Catelyn Stark for the attempted murder of her son Bran. Upon hearing that the specific dagger wielded by Bran's attempted assassin was last seen in Tyrion's hand, Catelyn instantly jumps to the conclusion that Tyrion was guilty of conspiring to murder him ("Lord Snow").

When captured, Tyrion refuses to falsely confess that he is the one who conspired to have Bran killed. He *does* make a confession however, "I am a vile man, I confess it. My crimes and sins are beyond counting. I have lied and cheated, gambled and whored . . . You want specifics, I suppose?" before presenting a very humorous list of some of his practical jokes. Here we see Tyrion's authenticity: he refuses to confess to a crime he did not commit but takes responsibility for the things he has done ("A Golden Crown").

Tyrion is also presumed guilty by his own family. When Tyrion jokes with his sister Cersei when she is upset about a ruling decision he made, she ends the conversation with a jab that Tyrion's finest joke was killing his mother with his birth ("The Night Lands"). After Tyrion plays a key role in staving off Stannis's attack on King's Landing, his father Tywin strips him from his position as Hand of the King and refuses to believe he had any role in saving the city, calling him a drunk and "ill-made, spiteful little creature," who is lying about his accomplishments. Tywin repeats Cersei's accusation that Tyrion killed his mother during childbirth. Tywin demonstrates that he too judges Tyrion as a criminal by nature and refuses to believe that he could be a brave, wise, or effective leader ("Valar Dohaeris").

The climax of Tyrion's guilty verdict comes when Joffrey is murdered at his own wedding ceremony in "The Lion and the Rose." In a scene that gave many characters (and viewers!) pleasure, Joffrey convulses and chokes to death from poison, and Cersei is instantly convinced that Tyrion is responsible for her son's demise. This is a moment for which Cersei has been waiting a long time—when he is finally caught in the act of being the monster that she and others have always believed him to be. Tyrion is not only instantly judged guilty by Cersei but by all those around him.

Tyrion's Authenticity

Despite his presumption of guilt, Tyrion refuses to be defined by his label as a monster and builds his own essence, accepting that he cannot change the guilty verdict forced upon him. It would be easy for him simply to fall back into a state of bad faith—either by believing that he will always be nothing more than a dwarf and thus to embrace the guilt forced upon him, or by denying that his facticity as a dwarf affects his possibilities. But Tyrion is more authentic than any other character, accepting that his actions are always subject to intense scrutiny, while at the same time using his power of choice.

One striking way that Tyrion acts as his own person is by showing sympathy for others he sees having similar experiences to his own. When Tyrion encounters Bran and builds him a saddle that will allow him to ride a horse despite his accident, Tyrion states that he has a weakness for "cripples, bastards, and broken things" ("Cripples, Bastards, and Broken Things"). Tyrion's own experience of being considered broken fostered in him a sense of empathy for marginalized others.

When Tywin orders Tyrion to marry Sansa in "Kissed by Fire," he protests that Sansa is still a child and should not have to suffer being married to a dwarf. Tyrion seems genuinely more concerned with Sansa's happiness than his own, and knows Sansa has no control over her predicament. After the wedding, in the bedroom chamber, he tells Sansa that they will only sleep together if and when she actively wills to do so. With this act he shows virtue and compassion far beyond the other men in King's Landing ("Second Sons"). Tyrion shows he will use the power of his choice to be a compassionate person in spite of circumstances beyond his control, promising Sansa that even in these dire straits he will act justly.

Tyrion also strives to be a cautious and wise ruler in the time he serves as the King's Hand, approaching ruling decisions with acumen and caution, even though his efforts go unappreciated. He shows skilled strategy as Hand of the King when Stannis's army is approaching King's Landing. Due to his size and stature, Tyrion has never been able to get what he wants through brute force, so it is natural that he comes up with a unique plan for defeating Stannis. You remember the scene—he sends a single ship leaking Wildfire out into the sea into the midst of Stannis's ships, then sends fire arrows onto the surface of the water, causing an explosion that devastates Stannis's fleet!

When Joffrey cowardly retreats from the battle, Tyrion stays and rallies the troops, using his stature to shame the rest of the men into defending the city, "If I am half a man, what does that make all of you?" ("Blackwater"). While his ruling efforts go unappreciated, he accepts what he cannot change and defines his own essence in spite of it.

The Monster You Say I Am

Now, let's return to where we began: Tyrion's dramatic speech in the "Laws of Gods and Men." Tyrion's outburst is the result of frustration built over the years as he attempted to be his own person while always being met with a presumption of guilt. At his trial, witness after witness testifies against him, including his lover Shae.

With frustration and rage Tyrion directly confronts his accusers. He snarls, "I saved you. I saved this city and all your worthless lives. I should have let Stannis kill you all! Yes, I am guilty. Guilty. Is that what you wanted to hear?" Asked if he admits to killing the king, he responds, "No. Of that I am innocent. I am guilty of a far more monstrous crime. The crime of being a dwarf! I have been on trial for that my entire life."

He denies killing Joffrey, but says he wishes he had. He addresses the crowd once more, growling, "I wish I was the monster that you say I am." Tyrion expresses a desire he has never explicitly acknowledged until now. Embracing his social categorization would enable him to avoid the nausea that accompanies the acceptance that existence precedes essence, and the deep burden that comes with self-creation. A belief that being a monster is his pre-given essence would relieve him from the sickness that accompanies the responsibility to choose.

We then see a different side of Tyrion, in which he finally embraces the accusation of others. After he has lost the trial by combat, his brother Jaime sets him free, and he does not slip away quietly into the night ("The Children"). He enters the King's quarters and encounters Shae, who has slept with Tywin. In the past, Tyrion may have left the situation in order to take the moral high ground and prove that he is not a monster. But having embraced the verdict of others, he strangles Shae, takes a crossbow, and finds Tywin sitting on the toilet. When Tywin mocks him and calls Shae a whore, Tyrion shoots him.

Has Tyrion finally become the monster that others have accused him of being all these years? Tyrion's choice was made against the backdrop of a presumption of guilt that he could never fully escape, and a betrayal from both his lover and his father. Although Tyrion appears to have given in to a moment of weakness, the upside of Sartre's existentialism is that he still has the opportunity to change himself through his choices. In Seasons Five and Six, we see Tyrion do just that.

Someone to Look Up To

Immediately following the murders it appears that Tyrion is willing to resign from the burden of self-determination and, in bad faith, accept a predestined future. Drunk and hopeless, he tells Lord Varys, "The future is shit, just like the past" ("The Wars to Come"). But Lord Varys insists he still has a choice: to drink himself to death, or come to Meereen to meet Daenerys Targaryen. Tyrion chooses the latter.

As he continues his journey, he even does away with some of his old habits. Meeting a prostitute on the road to Meereen, he finds himself, to his own surprise, unable to sleep with her ("High Sparrow"). Realizing that aspects of his past behavior are not desirable moving forward, he resumes the burden of self-responsibility. Tyrion's authenticity returns; he does not hide from his physical condition and the social categorization that accompanies it. When Missandei speaks of Tyrion saving her life during the battle in Meereen, "I would be dead if it were not for the . . . little man," he corrects her: "Dwarf. I believe that's the word" ("Mother's Mercy").

As Tyrion grows to have faith in Daenerys, we see him flourish with a friend who finally appreciates his talents. Tyrion sees something unique in Daenerys—possibly because she does not judge him with the harsh presumption of guilt that has characterized his life. He also sees some of himself in her. Her life path has been shaped by the difficulty of being the daughter of the notorious Mad King, which she refuses to allow to control her life path.

Rewarding his wise ruling decisions in stabilizing Meereen, Daenerys names Tyrion Hand of the Queen. While preparing their army to sail to Westeros, Tyrion recalls how he had long ago stopped believing in things, but he cannot help believing in Daenerys ("The Winds of Winter"). Tyrion shows a remarkable change from his previous resignation that his future was destined to be just as awful as his past.

And this shows the power of Sartre's existentialism. His philosophy is often interpreted as pessimistic because it argues that our lives are inherently meaningless and that we are responsible for who we are, leading to nausea and bad faith. But Sartre insists that his philosophy is extremely *optimistic*— it provides us with an opportunity to create our own meaning and identity for those willing to take on this difficult task.

While maintaining awareness and unwavering acceptance of the things about himself that he cannot change, Tyrion chooses to foster the best that is in him: his unique empathy and sympathy for marginalized others, his acumen and creativity, and his adherence to his own moral code.

Sartre's message is always the same—Tyrion's essence is his for the making: he is the dwarf who roared and the Hand of the Queen.

6
Jaime the Savior

DANIELLE KARIM COX AND JONATHAN COX

Whether it be Jon Snow and his tryst with Ygritte, Ned Stark's seeming infidelity, or the High Sparrow's heavy handed religiosity, many of George R.R. Martin's characters strike a difficult moral balance in *A Song of Ice and Fire*. Perhaps chief among them is the infamous Kingslayer, Ser Jaime Lannister.

Jaime grew up a wunderkind, confident—perhaps overly— but indebted to the brave knights such as Ser Barristan the Bold, who brought him into the Order of the Kingsguard. Jaime was the youngest knight ever to receive an invitation into the venerable order which required him to swear an oath to serve and protect the king at all costs, including his life. As we all know, at the end of Robert's Rebellion when Ned Stark took the throne room in King's Landing, Jaime was already sitting upon the Iron Throne, wiping the blood of King Aerys II off his blade.

The question is, was this morally justifiable? Aristotle, in his *Nicomachean Ethics*, spends nearly an entire book within this work discussing the role duress or force of circumstances might play in judging whether an action is morally justifiable. If key circumstances were outside of Jaime's control, or if the Mad King Aerys were truly tyrannical, then, according to Aristotle, Jaime might be morally justified. Can we say that the pressures upon Jaime Lannister and the way his options were restricted by his circumstances takes away some of the blame for breaking his oath?

The Violated Oath

The Kingsguard is a sworn brotherhood. Our vows are taken for life. Only death relieves us of our sacred trust.

—SER BARRISTAN SELMY

The Kingsguard is an order that reaches back for hundreds of years—having been founded by Aegon the Conqueror more than 250 years before Robert's Rebellion. At any given time there are never more than seven members of the order. Jaime, at the time of the Siege of King's Landing, was guarding Aerys by himself due to the fact that most of the Kingsguard were either at the Battle of the Trident to help defend against Robert, or at the Tower of Joy in Dorne for reasons which are not entirely clear—they were apparently protecting Lyanna Stark during childbirth on Rhaegar's orders.

The gates to King's Landing and the Red Keep were closed and Aerys was killing his own people within the gates with wildfire. When Tywin and his army approached the gate, Aerys refused to open it. Only through Maester Pycell's urging did The Mad King reconsider and allow his Warden of the West to enter the city. Once the gates were opened with the King's permission, Tywin began to sack the city and take over. When Aerys became aware of his Warden's betrayal, he ordered Jaime to bring him Tywin's head.

In the face of this order—to kill his own father—Jaime unsheathed his gilded sword and assassinated the Mad King in the throne room. Ned Stark then entered the room and saw Jaime on the Iron Throne with Aerys lying on the ground—the king's lifeblood filling the grooves across the tiled floor. This regicide would be in violation of Jaime's sacred Oath—which in the culture and customs of Westeros is one of the gravest offenses that can be committed.

Several times throughout *A Song of Ice and Fire*, oath-breaking is treated as the worst of crimes. The reputations of those who commit such acts are forever tarnished, regardless of the reasons that may have otherwise justified their deeds. Ned Stark—ever the noble man—routinely decried Jaime as a Kingslayer, such as in the following discussion between Ned and King Robert from *A Game of Thrones* (1996):

"He swore a vow to protect his king's life with his own. Then he opened that king's throat with a sword."

"Seven hells, someone had to kill Aerys!" Robert said, reining his mount to a sudden halt beside an ancient barrow. 'If Jaime hadn't done it, it would have been left for you or me."

"We were not Sworn Brothers of the Kingsguard," Ned said.

Ned's response highlights the fact that the offensive act was not so much the regicide in itself, as it was the breaking of an oath. This viewpoint seems well represented by the kind of ethics, which focuses on motives and duty, and tends to disregard the specific consequences of actions.

Similar sentiments arise in discussions of Jon Snow's relationship with Ygritte, Walder Frey, and the infamous Red Wedding, and Tyrion's kinslaying. We even see another instance of supposed kingslaying in Loras Tyrell's accusation of Brienne of Tarth. The culture seems committed to an extreme view of oath-keeping, allowing no exceptions. But personal interpretations existed. For example, Jaime believed his oath also extended to the Queen. While the other members of the Kingsguard agreed, they surmised that their oath was to the king first. This would entail that the oath of the Kingsguard is primarily between the guard and the king, with the rest of the Royal Family as secondary.

Force of Circumstances

In Book III of his *Nicomachean Ethics*, Aristotle discusses the difference between voluntary and involuntary actions for the purpose of differentiating which actions are blameworthy or vicious and which ones are laudable or virtuous. He also offers a third option, which is an act comprised of voluntary and involuntary elements which he calls appropriately, a "mixed action."

While harmful acts committed strictly voluntarily are blameworthy and thus subject to praise or condemnation, involuntary actions are said to be performed either under compulsion or out of complete ignorance. An act that is forced or compelled is constrained by some outside agency. Aristotle illustrates his point with the example of someone being carried away by the wind, or—more relevant to our purposes—where a person is in possession of another or is being forced to act in accordance with their captor.

We see an instance of this belief in the episode, "No One," from Season Six. Edmure, Lord of Riverrun, demanded entry into the castle, and his uncle, the Blackfish, belayed the order. To this, the soldier responded that he was sworn to obey the commands of his lord. The Blackfish, however, thought that Edmure was not truly speaking for himself, but was under a kind of duress from the Kingslayer. When Edmure insists further the soldier says, "My Lord has given an order." To which the Blackfish responds: "With a knife to his throat. That is not a valid order." While Jaime's situation with Aerys might not fit cleanly in this later example (after all, Jaime was not a captive of The Mad King) the threat of either killing his own father and being dubbed a kingslayer, or the threat of the entire city, himself included, being immolated by wildfire seems to count as a kind of knife to his throat.

> Explain to me why it is more noble to kill ten thousand men in battle than a dozen at dinner.
>
> —TYWIN LANNISTER

Aristotle then describes situations that are similar to Jaime's where the choice is between the prevention of a greater evil or the promotion of something regarded as noble. Not only does Aristotle specifically mention a tyrant who orders someone to commit an evil act, but he describes the situation in which the crew of a ship needs to throw goods overboard to lighten the load in order to prevent sinking and thus save those on board.

Aristotle leads us through deliberation over actions that appear to be a mix of both voluntary and involuntary and he suggests that those actions are praiseworthy. The agent is presumed to have endured "something base or painful in return for great and noble objects gained." The praise is due to the voluntary aspect of the action. The crew which decided to throw the cargo overboard is said to have made the best choice available.

But there is also an involuntary aspect to their predicament, since the storm forced the crew to act at least partially involuntarily they were forced to make the choices that they otherwise would not have made. Essentially, their choices were restricted to a few unattractive options by the storm—a situation outside of their control.

Jaime, likewise, had limited choices—obey Aerys and kill his own father, kill Aerys and spare his father, run away into a city under siege, or remain and refuse to act as ordered and face the consequences of disobedience. The latter two are contrary to Jaime's character as we know of him, since he's neither so cowardly as to flee nor foolish enough to disobey the king and likely be executed after standing idly by as the city and its citizens burn.

Assuming that his only options were either to kill the King or kill his father, making the choice he did, arguably the least harmful one, is voluntary. The act could even be considered praiseworthy, in that it is the least injurious option available overall, and certainly not blameworthy, since all available options were bad through no fault of his own.

Jaime's actions weren't strictly voluntary due to his unusual circumstances. Aristotle, despite being considered a father of virtue ethics (and therefore a foe of utilitarian ethics), looks at the consequences of the mixed action, not entirely unlike the way utilitarian philosophers such as J.S. Mill or Jeremy Bentham would look at them.

Justified Killing

Like the sailors, Jaime's partially voluntary and partially involuntary action is only praiseworthy if it's the least injurious option. Therefore to see if Jaime's decision was the best option, we must decide whether committing regicide can ever be morally condoned.

John Locke, famous as one of the proponents of social contract theory states that:

> whenever the legislators endeavour to take away and destroy the property of the people, or to reduce them to slavery under arbitrary power, they put themselves into a state of war with the people, who are thereupon absolved from any farther obedience, and are left to the common refuge which God hath provided for all men against force and violence.

Thus, according to Locke, a leader who fits this profile forfeits the power and authority through which he presides and opens him or herself to a revolution, violent or otherwise. With this in mind, if Aerys perpetuates this tyranny, which Locke defines as "When the governor, however entitled, makes not the law, but his will, the rule, and his commands and actions are not directed to to the preservation of the properties of his people, but the satisfaction of his own ambition, revenge, covetousness, or any other irregular passion," then it would seem that Jaime would be justified in his Regicide.

> Burn them all!
>
> —KING AERYS II

We must therefore establish whether or not Aerys II was truly tyrannical, so that killing him represented the least harmful of Jaime's options. The King, whose love of violence was so renowned that he became known as the Mad King, would indeed qualify as a tyrant because of the campaign of democide that marked the later years of his reign.

He enjoyed watching others suffer, like when Ned Stark's father and brother, Rickard and Brandon Stark, were unjustly executed in the throne room, Rickard was set aflame, while Brandon strangled himself to death trying to save his father; all while Aerys sat on the throne and laughed. He was continuously brutal, inflicting sexual abuse upon his sister-wife, Queen Rhaella. When Jaime observed Rhaella leaving King's Landing, and the state in which the King had left her, the cuts and bruises made Jaime conclude that Aerys was nothing but a "crowned beast" (*A Feast for Crows*).

The characters in the series have led us, the readers, to believe that at the beginning of Aerys's reign, he was simply a boastful, ambitious, young king who replaced many old councilors with younger ones, including Tywin Lannister as the Hand of the King. Throughout the remainder of Aerys's reign, he gradually descended into madness, as shown through a series of unwise and unjust decisions brought about by fear. In the episode "Lord Snow," Jaime's account of the Mad King's last words that he had apparently uttered repeatedly were "Burn them all"—seeming to imply the king's command to use wildfire to burn the populace throughout the city.

Bad Consequences

It is most likely that if Jaime had left the Mad King alive then the city would have continued to burn. The damage would have been even worse if Jaime also helped to inflict the wildfire on King's Landing. It's also likely that if Jaime had obeyed his King, then Tywin Lannister would have been murdered by his own son. The repercussions of losing a player like Tywin at this time would have been too numerous to discuss in its entirety. Tywin, by virtue of being dead, would almost certainly fail to take King's Landing, resulting in a much slower takeover and a longer rebellion.

> So many vows, they make you swear and swear. Defend the King, obey the King, obey your father, protect the innocent, defend the weak . . . It's too much. No matter what you do, you are forsaking one vow or another.
>
> —Ser Jaime Lannister

Jaime was justified in killing the Mad King—despite his oath. Regicide can be morally condoned considering the king's absolute rule and thirst for unjust blood and widespread pain. Aristotle's concept of a not fully voluntary action due to extreme circumstances to avoid a greater evil is what frees Jaime from the Kingsguard's obligation.

Oaths were seen as binding for life, or until the oath has been fulfilled. The entire rebellion was comprised of oath breakers, they broke the oath of fealty. What was it that made the leaders of the rebellion rebel in the first place? Duty to family came first. Lyanna Stark's kidnapping was what brought the Starks and the Baratheons to rebel against the crown. Loyalty to family made them want to be traitors, just as loyalty to his father made Jaime want to break his oath as well.

Jaime's choice was to become either kingslayer or kinslayer. However, in addition to not becoming kinslayer, assassinating the King meant saving the entire city of thousands—which explains Jaime's confusion as to why he was "reviled by so many for my finest act" (*A Clash of Kings*). This is why Jaime Lannister, despite being constantly derided as the infamous Kingslayer, may indeed have been the savior of King's Landing.

7

Jon Snow, a Misshapen Christ Figure

Evan Rosa

I don't always watch extreme violence and brutality on TV, but when I do, I prefer *Game of Thrones*. There's nothing like capping off a sunny weekend of church picnics, playing dress-up with my daughters, and mowing the lawn with a good-ol' foray into moral atrocity and over-ripened horror. "Honey, do you have the barf-bag ready? I think Ramsay's gonna flay some more dudes in this episode."

Game of Thrones isn't the only series to fall like Lucif . . . err, I mean Joffrey . . . into moral decrepitude. But George R.R. Martin's exploration of evil has particularly dark contours. His moral imagination introduces exaggerated categories of wrongness that might be viewed as embodied experimentation and testing around the nature, acquisition, and effects of vice and evil. Or maybe it's just entertainment. *Stay bloodthirsty, my friends.*

Set against this backdrop of skull-crushing horror, moral lights emerge, but only because of the stark contrast (yes, I did that). There is such a dearth of goodness that even dim lights blind us. Jon Snow is just such a dim light. I may be in the minority against a host of thirty-something women on this one, but no: He's not perfect.

Jon redeems the *Game of Thrones* world, but not without getting dragged through the mud of moral conflict. The negative, nihilistic, morally desolate, and tragic direction of the *Game of Thrones* narrative can be understood as a severe lack of moral exemplars; it is, among other things, a thought experiment or test case for moral malformation and the need for moral reform and redemption. In this context, Jon Snow's moral example—his character and actions—exert moral influence to offer a unique, if dim, moral light for redemption in the *Game of Thrones* world.

Looking for Moral Lights

Game of Thrones is not a series without moral heroes, of course; it's just that the heroes lose. They die, and with them their moral principles and rules. So, like Ned's head and Jaime's hand, we detach. "The Red Wedding" and "The Mountain and the Viper" taught us to set our moral expectations on a totally different level.

But, that kind of detachment from and total disillusionment with moral heroes is psychological impossible. We're born looking for moral attachment to figures that provide for us a standard and guide toward the good. We're magnetized toward leaders and lights that represent a vision of the good life—what moral philosophers like Aristotle would call 'eudaimonia' (Greek for "flourishing" or "happiness"). There are certain excellences (or "virtues") to go along with whatever vision of flourishing you have. And there are moral agents who exhibit those virtues. As we watch the show—and especially for the young characters *in the show*—we can't help but identify with the most virtuous moral agents.

The moral landscape of reality is similar to the scene outside Winterfell at the "Battle of the Bastards." Even when things start orderly and lined up, it doesn't take long for them to unravel into confusion and chaos. So, it's very difficult to find exemplars of moral virtue. In just the same way that we see Jon—apparently by random luck alone—barely dodge arrows, swords, firebombs, horses, bodies, and other shrapnel as the bastards' battle begins, we moral agents ought to thank the Old Gods, the New Gods, the Lord of Light, and—why not?—go ahead and even thank the High Sparrow himself that Jon comes out alive. But in the moral fog of war that is *Game of Thrones*, like Jon, you don't escape without first getting trampled, stabbed, or dishing your own dose of damage.

Loosing Arrows, Missing the Mark

Into this moral abyss where "villains gotta vill," enter Jon Snow. Hero shot. Locks and pelt blowing in the winter wind.

But he's a bastard—dishonored and shamed from birth, and unfit even for a family name let alone any kind of claim to honor and rule.

From the very beginning of the series, Jon exhibits a moral guidance and leadership that extends beyond the rights of his last name. In "Winter Is Coming" we're introduced to a beacon—perhaps dim, but a beacon nonetheless—of moral light. He cares for his half-siblings, respects the family name he is denied, and lives out his lot the best way he knows how.

Jon's stewardship over and personal attention to Bran in "Winter Is Coming" provide a good example and metaphor for the kind of moral formation I'm thinking of. Especially salient are Jon's active leadership and example for Bran.

We meet the Starks in the middle of Bran's archery lesson—a perfect metaphor for moral life and development: You aim for the bull's-eye, or "eudaimonia"—the good. The arrows loosed—your choices, behaviors, and other moral action—belong in the middle of the target. The archer and his bow—that is, the moral agent and the tools of individual virtues, will, emotions, and reason—propel his arrows. The Greek "hamartia" or "sin" means "to miss the mark when shooting an arrow."

Though Bran keeps missing the mark, he's *expected* to do so at such a young age. As Ned says, "And which one of you was a marksman at ten? Keep practicing, Bran." The same is true for a person's moral formation and development. Young archers in the moral life will often miss the mark, but if they practice, observe better archers, study their habits, imitate their movements, heed their advice, and then practice a whole lot more, well, eventually (so this approach to moral theory goes), they'll become experts in the moral life, consistently living life in the bull's-eye.

Aristotle says that it's a *complete* life—the whole package of what I just described—that is required for eudaimonia. A truly good person necessarily exercises the virtues in doing the right thing in specific life contexts. Just like Bran, as an archer, seeks not just to hit the bull's-eye, but to hold his bow and arrow correctly, and perhaps most importantly—to know when to use it.

Watching Jon Snow, Watching in the Night

You are what you watch. That may well have some application in the context of violence on TV, but for now, I just mean "watching" in the sense of observation and experience. Your own moral development will follow the moral exemplars available to you.

When Ned insists that Bran watch his execution of the Night's Watch deserter, it's about *forming* him in a particular way. And Jon is the operative guide as he watches. "Don't look away," he instructs. "Father will know if you do." After the head rolls, he affirms to Bran: "You did well." Even if Bran looked away, or if he wasn't there at all, he still would have been formed. As we watch, observe, imitate, practice… all of these micro-moments of events—whether positive or negative, whether whispers or screams—everything is character formation. We are constantly being formed.

Jon acts as a constant guide and exemplar for the viewer. When he's not a beacon himself, he points us (and the other characters) in the direction we ought to look. That's what it is to be a moral exemplar. That's what it is to form an individual's moral character.

But, as we all know, "the night is dark and full of terrors." And it is largely barren and bereft of goodness, kindness, peace, forgiveness, freedom, patience . . . (the list of absent virtues goes on and on). And the moral fabric of the world Martin constructs just doesn't appear to have moral principles and rules in place to guide its inhabitants. So, while there can be shock, resentment, anger, horror, and other "reactive attitudes"—the characters are left with few resources to respond with substantive moral goodness *because substantive moral goodness is embodied in particular people, their dispositions, and their behaviors.*

How do characters like Cersei, Joffrey, the Mountain, Ramsay Snow/Bolton, and the hoards of other lesser devils come into being and thrive? How has such little light snuck into the moral sphere of Westeros and Essos? Again, *everything is formation* and it is the nature given to free moral agents to attach and imitate other moral agents, for better or worse. As the heroes die off, we lose our moral exemplars, representing further cracks in the moral ceiling or further tears in the moral tapestry—which results in the spreading of vice.

Jon Snow as Christ Figure

In a world as morally dark and empty as *Game of Thrones*, moral beacons appear even brighter. The moral example of Jon

Snow appears in the cracks created by the lust for gold, flesh, and power that animate the key players in the vying for the Iron Throne, as well as the less prestigious positioning for power over more local dominions. Jon's own moral beacon is Ned Stark, and so he is raised with a deep and abiding sense of justice, loyalty, and honor.

Christ figures appear in texts in many ways and their shared attributes with Jesus Christ vary from being a super-human, being of humble origin, to self-emptying and sacrificial love, to miracle work, to having the same initials! The specific attributes I'm concerned with are by now major cues:

> **Humble King.** Jon is of humble and mysterious birth, continually bearing the shame of his alleged illegitimate birth. But as we discover in "The Winds of Winter" through Bran's vision of Ned and Lyanna: Yes, he is a bastard, but he's a bastard who happens to be a King. Not only is he named King in the North but he also has the rightful claim to the Iron Throne.

> **Moral Reformer.** His watch—that is, his primary ethic—is deeply concerned with unifying humanity in love of neighbor and stranger, such as the Wildlings, for the sake of fighting a common enemy: Death. And of course Death has many slaves, whether that's Jon's defeat of Ramsay Bolton in the "Battle of the Bastards" or everyone's hopeful expectation that he will finally defeat the Walkers (which turn out to be men corrupted by fear and power).

> **Jon has died, Jon is risen, Jon will come again.** He is betrayed by those he's trying to protect and killed for the threat he poses to their power and hatred ("Mother's Mercy"). And on the third episode following his death ("Home"), he rose again.

Moral Reform

The main lesson I want to draw from Jon's role as *Game of Thrones*'s primary Christ figure is his *minority moral reform*. Minority moral reform is a historical ethical theme whereby an individual or small community committed to moral principles opposed to the dominant moral perspective attempt to exert moral change. The kind of change they hope to achieve is not only to *persuade* the dominant culture of an alternative moral knowledge, but to *reform* the moral agents of that dominant moral perspective. Jesus, Gandhi, and Martin Luther King, Jr. are all considered minority moral reformers.

And this is what is so significant about Christ figures in real life or in *Game of Thrones*: In order to be a successful minority moral reformer, it's not enough to talk the talk. You need to walk the walk. Incidentally, this is included in the ancient conception of philosophy (though it has largely been lost): The philosopher isn't simply concerned with knowing wisdom or truth, but living and exemplifying it. For Jesus, Gandhi, and MLK, moral reform required martyrdom.

The Christ story handed down through Christianity is the story of moral reform: humility and love subverts power, fear, suffering, sin, and death. In the moral horror of *Game of Thrones*, we're drawn to the dim light of Jon Snow. But that dim light has the substance of subversive goodness that offers us the only hope that the *Game of Thrones* world is redeemable.

If there's any redemption at all, it must come through an extremely small minority, and by the means of moral *exemplification*. This subversive goodness must be embodied in a complete life, as Aristotle would say. Jon's moral character—his humility, his love of neighbor, his value for unity, his identification of common human dignity, and his deep sense of justice—are inert without taking shape in the contours of his life and community. His particular context is a moral wasteland, making it all the more important that his moral principles find expression in his very agency and actions, and not merely in principles or rules.

Jon's being an allegory of Christ only goes so far; but it goes far enough to substantiate and justify his pursuit of moral reform and redemption for the broken world of *Game of Thrones*.

Looking in the Mirror

When Melisandre looks in the mirror in "The Red Woman" she sees her true self—not the beautiful woman she falsely projects to the rest of the world, but the older-than-you-ever-wanted-to-be grandmother of Gollum. Suppose each of us took off our magic necklaces and took a long look in the mirror. I'm sure we'd find more than a few wrinkles.

You are what you watch. What you see, you become. And the people in our lives—moral agents—are mirrors of our selves. Their virtues or vices give us our own way of being, for better or for worse.

But this perhaps reveals some of the moral utility even of vice; the redeeming force of Martin's gleeful forays into blood and gore. We have a deep desire to understand ourselves, and the fact about us is that we are broken. Life in human society is largely dystopic.

Like the Known World of *Game of Thrones*, in our contemporary reality poverty prevails, violence is a sure form of power, and even our most beloved leaders are susceptible to moral decay and atrocity. Our world is also a world of horror. *Game of Thrones* is the mirror that reveals our true selves. It's not a pretty picture. Thankfully, there are still moral exemplars—those few beacons of dim light—that we might look to for guidance through our own night's watch.

8

Brienne and the Struggle for Recognition

PAUL GILADI

Central to both George R.R. Martin's epic fantasy *Song of Ice and Fire* novels and their adaptation into the fantasy-drama TV series *Game of Thrones* are various characters who represent explicit challenges to the current recognition order of Westerosi society.

Brienne represents a specific struggle for recognition, insofar as Brienne explicitly challenges various long-standing attitudes towards women: she does so by embodying as far as is reasonable the value-system and physical capacities of the chivalrous knight, where such a value-system and physical capacities can only be possessed by men according to Westerosi society—for example, she becomes Kingsguard to Renly Baratheon; she pledges oaths of loyalty to Catelyn Stark and Sansa Stark; she is able to overcome Sandor Clegane in brutal combat; she exercises judicial authority on Stannis Baratheon; and she confronts Melisandre for her role in the death of Renly Baratheon.

That Brienne is often mocked and denigrated—either by having sexualized comments levelled at her, or by being threatened with gang-rape as a way of preventing her from maintaining her autonomy (as was the case when she and Jaime Lannister were captured by Bolton banner men)—indicates the great extent to which she represents a powerful challenge to the current recognition order and its corresponding metaphysical as well as moral commitments.

All my life, men like you have sneered at me. And all my life I've been knocking men like you into the dust.

—"The Prince of Winterfell"

In clear contrast to the traditional narrative of depicting women in medieval society either as docile and completely oblivious to social and political states of affair, or as damsels in distress entirely dependent on a virtuous male knight to rescue them, Martin invites readers and viewers to radically re-think various preconceptions about women in Westerosi society: Daenerys Targaryen, Cersei Lannister, Catelyn Stark, Margaery Tyrell, Olenna Tyrell, and the adult Sansa Stark are all central figures in their individual family lives and significant political power players in Westeros; and Yara Greyjoy, Arya Stark, Osha, and Meera Reed are hardly shrinking violets.

While, of course, each character here represents a specific challenge to the moral and political order of Westerosi society concerning what women can do and what women ought to do, arguably the most interesting and powerful challenge to the Westerosi recognition order comes from Brienne of Tarth: she embodies as far as is reasonable the value-system and physical capacities of the chivalrous knight, thereby explicitly rejecting the notion that such a social category is naturally male-gendered.

Brienne Becomes Kingsguard to Renly Baratheon

Let's look at the scene where Brienne becomes a Kingsguard.

Catelyn and her escorts arrive at Renly's camp, where a tournament is held: Loras Tyrell fights another knight. Loras is armed with an axe, while his opponent uses a flail. Renly and his queen Margaery are watching. The crowd cheers for the opponents, mostly for Loras. Margaery stands on her feet and cheers for her brother.

MARGAERY TYRELL: Loras! Highgarden!

Loras knocks his opponent's shield away, then the flail. The other knight charges at Loras, grabs him by the waist and knocks him to the ground. The crowd boos in disapproval.

Loras's opponent opens his visor and holds a dagger near his unprotected face.

LORAS TYRELL: I yield! I yield!

Margaery sits down, disappointed at her brother's defeat. The winning knight stands and sheathes the dagger. Loras stands and quickly moves away from his opponent.

RENLY BARATHEON: [*claps his hands*] Well fought! Approach.

Loras removes his helmet. His opponent approaches Renly and bows.

RENLY BARATHEON: Rise. Remove your helm.

The knight rises and removes the helmet. Catelyn and the rest of the crowd are surprised to see it is a woman—Brienne of Tarth.

RENLY BARATHEON: You are all your father promised and more, my lady. I've seen Ser Loras bested once or twice, but never quite in that fashion.

Loras is visibly annoyed to hear that!

MARGAERY TYRELL: Now, now, my love. My brother fought valiantly for you.

Renly smiles at his queen.

RENLY BARATHEON: That he did, my queen. But there can be only one champion! Brienne of Tarth, you may ask anything of me you desire. If it is within my power, it is yours.

BRIENNE OF TARTH: [*bows gracefully*] Your Grace, I ask the honor of a place in your Kingsguard.

The crowd gasps, for this is an unprecedented request.

LORAS TYRELL: [*quietly*] What?

BRIENNE OF TARTH: I will be one of your seven, pledge my life to yours, and keep you safe from all harm.

After long moment of silence, Renly answers:

RENLY BARATHEON: Done! Rise, Brienne of the Kingsguard.

Renly claps his hands, and Margaery joins him. The crowd applauds, but rather feebly. Brienne stands. Catelyn and one of her escorts approach.

What I take to be so significant about this scene is how Brienne's physical prowess and her commitment to the chivalrous station of the Kingsguard appear to receive rather muted and bewildered responses from both men and women watching the tournament.

Rather than positively acknowledge and admire Brienne's athleticism and her sincere wish to be a moral knight bound by duties of protection, the crowd appear perplexed that not only was Brienne physically stronger than Loras, but also that she demonstrated both the disposition and the will to request a social role that was deemed as necessarily only one that men can and ought to take on.

Their failure to properly recognize and afford Brienne the respect she merits is an act of injustice, not in the sense of depriving Brienne of goods and resources in favour of distributing those goods and resources elsewhere, but in the sense of depriving Brienne of a progressive social environment in which the respect afforded to her plays a significant role in both enabling and fostering her self-confidence and her quest for personal authenticity: societies are gauged by the degree to which all individuals have equal opportunities for self-realization afforded to them by the intersubjective structures of recognition.

Actions require an accommodating social environment from which those actions derive their sense and purpose, and within which those actions fit into a cooperative scheme of social activity.

As such, inclusion and individuation represent formal conditions that can be shown to serve as necessary conditions for individual and societal flourishing. That Brienne is not adequately recognised is a damning indictment of Westerosi society on the grounds that its social structure and moral grammar fail to encourage the quest for personal authenticity and self-realization and thereby leaves individuals who are prejudiced against in a state of self-alienation.

Now let's look at the following scene from "The Prince of Winterfell," which perhaps best instantiates Brienne's struggle with the social structure and value-system of Westeros:

Jaime Lannister and Brienne on Their Way to King's Landing

Jaime keeps teasing Brienne while she leads him to the river:

> JAIME LANNISTER: It's a long way to King's Landing. Might as well get to know one another. Have you known many men? I suppose not. Women? Horses? Aha!

Jaime winces in pain when Brienne forces him to kneel down near a boat, because she spotted people passing nearby on a bridge.

> JAIME LANNISTER: I didn't mean to give offense, my Lady. Forgive me.
>
> BRIENNE OF TARTH: Your crimes are past forgiveness, Kingslayer.
>
> JAIME LANNISTER: Why do you hate me so much? Have I ever harmed you?
>
> BRIENNE OF TARTH: You've harmed others—those you were sworn to protect, the weak, the innocent.
>
> JAIME LANNISTER: Has anyone ever told you you're as boring as you are ugly?

Once the passing people disappear from view, Brienne roughly pulls Jaime back on his feet.

> BRIENNE OF TARTH: You will not provoke me to anger.

Brienne drags Jaime to the river bank.

> JAIME LANNISTER: I already have. Look at you. You're ready to chop my head off. Do you think you could? Do you think you can beat me in a fair fight?

BRIENNE OF TARTH: I've never seen you fight.

JAIME LANNISTER: The answer is no. There are three men in the king-doms who might have a chance against me. You're not one of them.

Brienne pushes the boat into the water.

BRIENNE OF TARTH: All my life men like you have sneered at me. And all my life I've been knocking men like you into the dust.

JAIME LANNISTER: If you're so confident, unlock my chains. Let's see what happens.

BRIENNE OF TARTH: Do you take me for an idiot? In.

Brienne gestures Jaime to enter the boat. He complies.

JAIME LANNISTER: I took you for a fighter, a man—oh, pardon—woman of honor. Was I wrong? You're afraid.

BRIENNE OF TARTH: Maybe one day we'll find out, Kingslayer.

In this scene, we immediately notice how Brienne both talks and acts as a chivalrous knight. However, Jaime Lannister's principal response to her moral nature and sincere commitment to the values of chivalry is not simply one of irritation at any kind of putative moralism on Brienne's part, but crucially one which attempts to mock her by remarking about her sexual appeal.

This is particularly harrowing for Brienne, not because she's upset at being deemed ugly rather than attractive, but because by sexualizing her in the context of a philosophical disagreement about their duties and responsibilities in certain social roles Jaime robs Brienne of her status as a rational enquirer in a conversation, thereby creating an unequal and asymmetrical cognitive environment in which she is not deemed Jaime's conversational peer.

To understand why the failure to regard Brienne as a conversational peer is so important, imagine if Ser Barristan Selmy had been in her place having the philosophical discussion with Jaime about the duties and responsibilities of a Kingsguard:

SER BARRISTAN SELMY: You've harmed others—those you were sworn to protect, the weak, the innocent.

JAIME LANNISTER: Has anyone ever told you you're boring?

Like Brienne, Barristan Selmy is an exemplary instantiation of the chivalrous knight. However, unlike Brienne, it's improbable that Jaime's response to Barristan would involve sexualizing him: yes, Jaime would certainly deem Barristan to be tedious and preachy, but his critical remarks would unlikely go beyond the hedonistic rebuke of the alleged austere and ascetic life of the chivalrous knight. For all of his disagreement with Barristan, Jaime would still deem him his conversational peer.

This shows that the reason why levelling sexual insults at Brienne is harrowing is that such activity negatively affects Brienne's basic and foundational self-confidence as a rational agent with cognitive competency: she is made to think she's not worthy enough to be a participant in a conversation with someone who regards her as their peer.

Arguably, though, the most distressing and explicit way in which Brienne's integrity and basic self-worth is violated as a way of reacting to her desire for recognition is in "Walk of Punishment," when Locke and Bolton banner-men attempt to gang-rape her: they do so, in order to prevent her from maintaining her autonomy as a human being and stultify her aim of realising her potential.

That Brienne is mocked and denigrated indicate the great extent to which she represents a powerful challenge to the metaphysical as well as moral commitments of the Westerosi recognition order: she explicitly challenges various long-standing attitudes towards women, by embodying the value-system and physical capacities of the chivalrous knight, thereby explicitly rejecting the notion that such a social category is naturally male-gendered.

Furthermore, because this is such a radical individual struggle for recognition with immense theoretical and practical consequences for the concept of gender in Westerosi society, Brienne encounters terrible reactionary forces designed to deaden her aim to be genuinely authentic as a human being.

III

**Power Is
Power**

9
Varys's Riddle—Where Does Power Come From?

JASON IULIANO

"Three great men sit in a room—a king, a priest, and a rich man. Between them stands a common sellsword. Each great man bids the sellsword, 'Kill the other two'. Who lives? Who dies?"

While sharing a drink with Tyrion in the Red Keep, Varys posed this riddle ("What Is Dead May Never Die"). Without thinking twice, Tyrion responded that it "depends on the sellsword."

"Does it?," Varys probed. "He has neither crown, nor gold, nor favor with the gods."

Not one to cede his position, Tyrion countered, "He has a sword—the power of life and death."

But once again, Varys pushed back, "If it's swordsmen who rule, why do we pretend kings hold all the power?"

Tyrion slumped back in his chair and admitted defeat. "I have decided I don't like riddles."

With this puzzle, Varys has captured the entire series. Kings, priests, and rich men vie for control, and at the center stand the commoners. Each claimant to the Iron Throne believes that he will be able to command the Westerosi people by wielding the one true power—be it the status of the crown, the allure of gold, or the favor of the gods.

So, what is the answer to Varys's question? Who lives, and who dies? Well, it appears that the riddle's setup is an exercise in misdirection. Varys leads us to focus on characteristics that are irrelevant to the solution. The winner will not survive because of his status as a king, a priest, a rich man, or even a sellsword. The victor will be the person who recognizes the illusory nature of power. This knowledge is worth more than all the armies and gold in Westeros. For you see, real power lies neither in force, nor faith, nor wealth. It lies in knowing the rules of the game of thrones.

Amongst an entire warring continent, Varys is one of a small number of people who perceives this truth. As he explains to Tyrion, "Power resides where men believe it resides. It's a trick, a shadow on the wall, and a very small man can cast a very large shadow." In other words, kings, priests, and rich men are only powerful because others believe they are powerful. Strip away this faith, and the illusion is exposed.

Although Varys is speaking of Westeros, his riddle applies equally well to modern political struggles. In fact, Varys's conception of power serves as the basis for every Western legal system in existence today.

Varys's riddle gives us two contrasting theories of legal authority. The first theory—endorsed by Varys's three great men—is known as the "command theory of law." This understanding of law was famously laid out by John Austin and says that law is a command by the sovereign backed by the threat of force. By focusing our attention on the centrality of the sellsword, Varys sets us up to view power in these terms.

Varys, however, supports another theory. According to him, legal authority resides where men believe it resides. Although his conception of power may have little traction in Westeros, it has garnered substantial support from modern legal theorists. But before we examine this theory of law, let's first dispel the myth endorsed by Varys's three great men.

What Is Law?

Power is power.

—Cersei Lannister

What is law and who holds the authority to make laws? Since ancient Greece, philosophers have grappled with this question. Until fairly recently, almost all philosophers who considered the issue did so from the perspective of natural law. Natural law is a theory that posits that the authority of legal standards is derived from the morality of those standards. The Christian theologian Augustine summarized this approach best, when he said, "An unjust law is no law at all."

In the nineteenth century, John Austin proposed an entirely new conception of law. He was the first legal philosopher to view law as an object of scientific inquiry. Whereas Austin's predecessors treated law as a prescriptive enterprise (asking: What *should* the laws be?), he treated law as a descriptive enterprise (asking: What *is* law?).

Through his analysis, Austin advanced two groundbreaking ideas: 1. morality and legality are not intertwined and 2. it is possible to develop a theory that explains law in all possible worlds. Although Austin himself did not name it as such, this scientific approach to law later became known as "legal positivism." Today, legal positivism has supplanted natural law theory as the most widely accepted theory of law.

In his work, Austin worked to develop a principle that he hoped would distill law into its essential components. This theory focuses on a sovereign—a person Austin defines as someone within a political society who receives habitual obedience from others but who, himself, does not habitually obey anyone else. According to Austin, a law is any command by the sovereign backed by the threat of force. Although the sovereign is frequently equated with the king, this need not be the case. In the riddle, Varys's three great men are all vying to be the sovereign. Each maintains that his given power demands habitual obedience from the sellsword and, by extension, all the people of Westeros.

In "The North Remembers," there is an exchange between Cersei and Littlefinger that brilliantly captures Austin's Command Theory of Law. In this scene, Cersei—upset at the disappearance of Arya Stark—approaches Littlefinger and implores him to find her.

Not wanting to waste his time, Littlefinger suggests that she seek out Varys. This rebuff, however, annoys Cersei and leads her to pick a fight. First, she grabs Littlefinger's sigil— the mockingjay around his neck—and offers a backhanded compliment. But when this fails to get the desired response, Cersei insults him by commenting on Littlefinger's poor beginnings and unrequited love for Catelyn Stark. "I heard a song once, about a boy of modest means . . . found his way into the home of a very prominent family. He loved the eldest daughter. Sadly, she had eyes for another."

Littlefinger takes the bait and makes a veiled criticism of her relationship with Jaime. "When boys and girls live in the same home, awkward situations can arise. Sometimes, I've heard, even brothers and sisters develop certain affections. And when those affections become common knowledge, well . . . that is an awkward situation . . . indeed, especially in a prominent family."

If Littlefinger had seen the hatred in Cersei's eyes, he would have stopped there. Alas, he was too amused by his own cleverness and blundered on. "Prominent families often forget a simple truth . . . knowledge is power."

Seething at this point, Cersei turns to her guards and commands: "Seize him . . . cut his throat."

At the last second, Cersei orders the guards to stop. She laughs and informs Littlefinger that "Power is power." And just then, it seems as if she's right.

This scene is a strident attack on Varys's theory of power. Littlefinger defends the claim that knowledge is power and, within seconds, is almost killed. Is there any way to reconcile this exchange with Varys's theory? Let's try.

Power Is an Illusion

Austin is undeniably one of the most influential legal thinkers in history. His development of legal positivism has had lasting effects that exert a profound influence over every legal system in existence today. That said, his more specific understanding of law has fallen on hard times. No one has more widely discredited Austin's command theory of law than H.L.A. Hart.

In his influential book, *The Concept of Law*, Hart asks us to imagine a gunman at a bank. When the gunman orders us to do something, we are likely to obey. However, we do so not because we feel inclined to respect the gunman's commands but rather because we fear being shot. Hart argues that Austin's sovereign is no different than the gunman. We obey the sovereign's orders because we are *obliged* to do so, not because we are *obligated* to do so. Hart argues that this distinction is vital. Law is not an essentially coercive institution that obliges us to obey through threat of force. Rather, law is a social institution that generates rules that we are duty-bound, or "obligated," to obey. Because Austin's command theory fails to recognize this point, it is fundamentally flawed.

Hart next proposes his own theory of law. He begins by breaking legal systems into two sets of rules. First, there are primary rules. These rules directly influence our actions. Statutes prohibiting murder and regulations setting speed limits are two straightforward examples.

In addition to primary rules, there are secondary rules. These rules are procedural in nature. They dictate how laws are made within a given society. For Hart, the most important secondary rule is the "rule of recognition." This rule specifies the ultimate criterion of validity within a legal system. In other words, it allows someone within the legal community to identify valid and invalid laws.

Hart emphasized that the rule of recognition comes into existence by means of social practice and custom. This means that people must collectively consent to it. They can't be forced to accept it. This point is the key distinction between Austin and Hart. Whereas Austin maintained that law's authority is derived from the power of the sovereign, Hart argued that law's authority comes from societal acceptance.

According to Hart, if people reject the sovereign's right to govern, then the sovereign has no power to make laws. The sovereign may continue to issue commands. But these are not laws. They are nothing more than orders backed by the threat of force. In such a situation, Austin's sovereign would be the same as the gunman. As Hart observes, we may be obliged to obey for fear of death, but we are not legally obligated to obey.

Now, let's return to the scene between Cersei and Littlefinger. Cersei is just like Austin's sovereign. As such, it's not surprising that she relies upon force to back up her command. Littlefinger is under no obligation to follow her order. Indeed, we could not blame him if he had refused. Nonetheless, Littlefinger feels obliged to follow her order for the simple reason that he fears death awaits him should he choose to do otherwise.

This exchange between Cersei and Littlefinger proves that the Lannisters are nothing more than gunmen writ large. Their claim to rule is based not upon social acceptance of their position but upon brute strength. Accordingly, the Lannister's position is precarious, and that is precisely why Cersei became so angry when Littlefinger told her that "knowledge is power." She knows that if this truth is revealed, her family's power risks being exposed as an illusion.

To see what happens when the illusion is shattered, consider an event that transpired during the Battle of Blackwater Bay. When the tides turned against the Lannister forces, Sandor Clegane retreated into the Red Keep ("Blackwater"). Joffrey ordered him to go back and fight. Instead, the Hound shook his head. "Fuck the Kingsguard. Fuck the city. Fuck the king." Clegane knew he was under no obligation to obey the king. And given Joffrey's inability to enforce his orders, Clegane was also not obliged to obey the king. Instead, the Hound merely walked away, confident in the knowledge that Joffrey had no authority over him.

Winning the Game of Thrones

If all it takes to defeat the great men is to show that their power is nothing but "a trick, a shadow on the wall," then why do they remain so great? There are two reasons. First, many of the people who know the truth have much to gain by perpetuating the illusion.

Recall the scene in which Joffrey tells Tyrion that he plans to feed Sansa the head of Robb Stark ("Mhysa"). When Tyrion responds by threatening Joffrey's life, Joffrey shouts, "I am the king! I will punish you!" At this point, Tywin Lannister intercedes and tells Joffrey that "Any man who must say, 'I am the king' is no true king." Tywin clearly knows that true power can only be conferred by others. However, he has much to gain by maintaining the illusion and everything to lose by tearing it down.

The second reason that the illusion persists is because most people are disdainful of knowledge and wisdom. They prefer the illusion to truth. This theme is straight from Plato's Allegory of the Cave—a philosophical story that Martin was certainly familiar with when he began writing *A Song of Ice and Fire*.

In this allegory, Plato tells us of a cave where people have been imprisoned since birth. These prisoners are chained so that they cannot move their heads or limbs. They are forced to look straight ahead at a wall. The only illumination comes from a fire behind them that they cannot see. At times, people from outside the cave come in and place puppets in front of the fire. The prisoners cannot see the puppets. All they observe are the shadows cast on the wall. Plato argues that, for the prisoners, these shadows seem to be the only reality.

Next, Plato asks us to imagine that one prisoner is freed. When this prisoner turns to look at the fire, his eyes will burn and his vision will blur. If he were told that the fire and puppets before him are more real than the shadows on the wall, he would refuse to believe it. And if given a choice, the prisoner would opt to go back to the safety and comfort of the shadows.

Suppose, however, that someone else were to drag the prisoner outside. When the prisoner emerges from the mouth of the cave, the sun would blind him. At first, this new reality would be overwhelming, but eventually, his eyes would adjust, and he would be able to see plants and animals and other people. In time, the prisoner would come to prefer this reality to the illusion in the cave.

Finally, suppose that this man returns to the cave to free the remaining prisoners and share his knowledge with them. Upon entering the cave, the man would find himself blind again. Having grown accustomed to the reality outside, he would no longer be able to navigate through the shadows. The remaining prisoners, observing the man's blindness, would conclude that his journey out of the cave had harmed him. Accordingly, the prisoners would refuse to leave and would go so far as to kill anyone who tried to force them out.

In Westeros, the common folk are the prisoners in the cave. They may despise their current situation, but they are even more fearful of knowledge and change. Quite simply, the Westerosi prefer the known illusion to the unknown reality. And for this reason, it will prove almost impossible to rally them to the cause of truth and wisdom.

By his riddle, Varys has urged us to think about the nature of power. Is it nothing more than brute strength, and does it, as John Austin contends, confer the authority to rule? Varys points us in this direction, but it is clear that he, himself, favors a different view. Like H.L.A. Hart, Varys maintains that power is an illusion.

As the Game of Thrones plays out, pay close attention to which theory of power prevails!

10
How to Be Free

LAUREN O'CONNELL AND ROBERTO SIRVENT

In the world of *A Song of Ice and Fire* we find two groups of people who appear to be a lot of things, but "free" is definitely not one of them.

The Faceless Men of Braavos and the Unsullied of Astapor are tied to servitude. They're servants. Some would even say slaves. So how could any philosopher, philosophy, or philosophy *book* (!) consider them free?

For the Stoic philosopher Seneca (4 B.C.–65 A.D.), true freedom results from the ability to detach yourself entirely from the passions and desires of the world. This kind of detachment reaches its climax when we abandon the most natural desire of all—the desire for self-preservation.

To cling to life is to be enslaved to it. So, at least in Seneca's mind, it is only after we give up our fear of death that our souls can truly be free.

All Men Must Die

In Seneca's *Moral Letters to Lucilius*, Seneca shares his reflections on life with his dear friend Lucilius. Seneca doesn't keep the subject matter light. He talks about slavery, worldliness, and death. How should a person approach death? What does it mean to have mastery over death?

We're glad you asked. Seneca thinks it's perfectly natural to fear death (phew!) but that we're irrational to do so (damn!). Death itself, as Seneca writes in *Letter LXXXII On the Natural Fear of Death*, is neither good nor evil. It's just inevitable. And

79

it's silly to spend our lives fearing something that we have no way of preventing. In *Letter XXIV On Despising Death*, he has us entertain a depressing thought: to be born at all is to embark on a journey towards death. Each day of life is just another step in the gradual process of dying. Fear of death is irrational, time-consuming, and sucks the happiness out of the time we *do* have to live. As the Faceless Men say, "All men must die." It can even be a gift, but it is certainly inevitable.

Death, of course, is not all we fear, and it is not the only thing that enslaves us. There are other fears (of pain, of sickness, of the unknown) and attachments (to possessions, to loved ones, to life in general) that hold us captive as well. Fear of death is fear of losing all these attachments and succumbing to all these worldly concerns. So for Seneca, to let go of these concerns is to lead a life filled with happiness and freedom.

According to Seneca's understanding of freedom *any* person—slave or free—can live freely as long as they abandon all desire and fear. In *Letter XLVII On Masters and Slaves*, Seneca sets out his position on the true meaning of slavery. While he favors kind treatment of slaves, he also points out that slavery really has nothing to do with who gives the orders. For Seneca, everyone can be enslaved or free when it comes to desire and fear.

Seneca writes with admiration about two very different people who exercise this kind of freedom. One example is a general who would rather kill himself than be seized by his enemies at sea. Through suicide the general refuses to grant ultimate power over his life to his would-be captors. Seneca recounts a similar story of a slave boy who rejects his master's first command by killing himself, thereby taking back his freedom by conquering his fear of death.

These stories not only show Seneca's great admiration for freedom at any cost, but also the freedom found by any person who abandons her fear of death and puts herself in full control of the situation. Death for these people actually *released* them from certain threats: imprisonment, sickness, and servitude, just to name a few.

Death also stripped away any burden they might have encountered by remaining alive. When it comes to battle, Seneca is clear on who has the upper hand: "He is lord of your life that scorns his own." Power and freedom therefore belong to those who can willingly and at any moment abandon everything and embrace death.

Seneca tells us that with the right practice and contemplation any person can come to live freely, even beyond the enslavement he attributes to life itself. For Seneca, life itself is a form of slavery "if courage to die is lacking."

All Men Must Serve

Both the Unsullied and the Faceless Men have strong connections to enslavement: the Faceless Men began in the slave mines of Valyria (*A Feast for Crows*) and the Unsullied are born slaves, chosen for an existence as duty-bound soldiers (*A Storm of Swords*). We can see why assassins and soldiers might be studied alongside a philosophical meditation on death. But freedom?

However, if freedom comes from detachment, then we can begin to see why the Faceless Men and the Unsullied are excellent illustrations of Seneca's Stoic philosophy. What makes these groups uniquely suited to their service is their training programs, which result in detachment. An assassin who clings to a past identity or a soldier who prizes a brothel over a battle is less than ideal. So if you're training for the most dedicated service in the world of *A Song of Ice and Fire*, much more is demanded of you. It means cutting all ties and eliminating all fears.

The Unsullied seem to embrace Seneca's wisdom. As one of the most renowned fighting forces in all of Essos, the slave soldiers of the Unsullied go through a training process that produces results Seneca would appreciate. While the means by which their attachments and fears are eliminated are extreme, those who make it through the rigorous training get the freedom Seneca promises.

When Kraznys mo Nakloz presents the Unsullied for sale to Dany in *A Storm of Swords*, he boasts of their absolute discipline, loyalty, and fearlessness. In the episode "Valar Dohaeris" Jorah Mormont questions this lack of fear, stating, "Even the bravest men fear death." Kraznys responds condescendingly, "The Unsullied are not *men*. Death means nothing to them." These soldiers are also impervious to pain. Even when Kraznys cuts the nipple off one soldier, he's left unfazed. They own nothing but weapons. They have no permanent names. They have no possessions, no loved ones, and no individual identities. What they have is freedom from earthly attachments.

The Unsullied's ruthless training begins when they are young boys chosen from the strongest and fastest slaves. They're made eunuchs—not just undergoing castration, but total removal of *everything*. The removal of their genitals removes another factor that Seneca argues enslaves men—lust. The Unsullied are also detached from their own identities, having a different name chosen for them each day, a name whose sole purpose is to remind them that individually they are nothing. From the day they're cut, they drink the wine of courage to dull their senses and render them fearless in battle.

The training methods only get more extreme. On the day they are cut they are also given a puppy to raise for the year, at the end of which they must strangle their pet. At the end of their training, each is forced to slaughter an infant in front of its mother and to pay her master for the privilege. Again, the goal is for the Unsullied soldiers to detach themselves from any feeling whatsoever. To be fair to Seneca, these training techniques are likely *not* the kind Seneca would embrace, but they do have a similar result.

In *A Dance with Dragons*, Tyrion considers the Unsullied to be the best of any soldiers, mainly because they are ignorant of life outside of their slavery and therefore desire nothing but to serve. They have no care for their own lives and no fear of losing them. This absence of fear should, according to Seneca, leave them a kind of freedom that transcends their earthly captivity.

We see the reversal of this for Grey Worm in the episode "Kill the Boy." As he describes his near-death to Missandei in the battle with the Sons of the Harpy he admits his shame, saying, "I am ashamed because when the knife go in and I fall to the ground, I am afraid." Missandei responds, "All men fear death," to which he replies, "No, not death. I fear I will never again see Missandei from the Island of Naas." This exchange illustrates what happens to a soldier's fear (and Seneca's version of his freedom) when he acquires an attachment.

At the House of Black and White

Seneca's prescription for freedom is also hard to overlook in the Faceless Men. We first witness the results of the Faceless Men's training in "Valar Morghulis" when Arya bids farewell to Jaqen H'ghar. The man she had come to know vanishes before her eyes, explaining, "Jaqen H'ghar is dead." He shows no fear or distress at the passing of this identity, but simply takes on a new one, complete with a brand new face.

Identity for the Faceless Men is as fluid as the Blackwater Rush. It is only later that we see closer details of the training and learn how a person can transform her face at will. As the kindly man explains to Arya, in order to come into the service in the House of Black and White, a prospective assassin must give up *everything* to the Many-Faced God.

In the episode "The House of Black and White," Arya arrives at the headquarters of the Faceless Men and is asked to declare her identity many times. With each identification of herself and suspected lie about her past, she is smacked with a stick. When she insists that 'a man' is Jaqen H'ghar, he corrects her, explaining that he is actually "No One, and that is who a girl must become."

After relinquishing her every worldly possession (except Needle, which she buries), a man asks her in "Unbowed, Unbent, Unbroken," "Is a girl ready to give up her eyes, her nose, her tongue, her hopes and dreams, her loves and hates, all that makes a girl who she is, forever?" He then determines, "No, a girl is not ready to become No One." Only through careful training and practice, can those who are dedicated enough to abandon all attachments to their previous lives and to their very *selves* be rewarded with the power to be instruments of the god of death. This kind of detachment sets up its adherents for the greatest freedom of all (at least by Seneca's standards): freedom from the fear of death.

As Arya spends more time with the Faceless Men, their attitude towards death becomes clear. Even before any training begins in *A Feast for Crows*, the priest asks Arya the all-important question, "Do you fear death?" Her reaction—not only kissing the skull on his 'nose' but also eating a worm from his eye socket for good measure—ensures her place at the House of Black and White. To be fair, overcoming fear of death at the House of Black and White is probably easier than everywhere else, since death is given as a 'gift' to those who seek it. They drink from a cup dipped into the pool and die peacefully, without pain.

Death at the House of Black and White is a sweet release (as Seneca argues, neither inherently good nor evil). In the episode "Oathbreaker," we also see Arya's progress when a man asks her to blindly drink from a mysterious cup. He encourages her saying, "If a girl is truly No One, she has nothing to fear." She takes it and drinks, showing that she no longer fears the release of death that the cup might very well bring.

The mantra of the Faceless Men, 'Valar morghulis' ('All men must die'), points to the inevitability that makes fear of death irrational. The consistent repetition of the phrase is a reminder of this inevitability and aids in bringing the Faceless Men to indifference concerning death. This practice is much closer to the kind of contemplation that Seneca would advise in attempting to 'free' the soul than some of the more brutal tactics used by the Faceless Men (and the Unsullied, for that matter).

But as a group of assassins in the service of the Many-Faced God, the Faceless men are sometimes charged with bringing the 'gift' of death to those who do not seek it, such as when a rival actress hires Arya to kill Lady Crane. An indifference to death and freedom from all attachment allows the Faceless Men to properly live out these duties to their god; after all, 'All men must serve.' It would again seem, however, that Seneca would frown upon such behavior.

The Starks Are Always Right Eventually

Both of the groups in *A Song of Ice and Fire* that best fit Seneca's definition of freedom are groups bound in servitude. But being unafraid of death allows for a more important kind of freedom, even for those living as slaves. The Stoic philosophy of Seneca helps one to find freedom in the most unlikely of situations.

Even though the Unsullied and the Faceless Men are duty-bound, they can enjoy a kind of freedom beyond their circumstances. Ironically, it is the same freedom from fear of death that allows them to so masterfully perform their respective duties. While much of their training and its consequences (beatings, drugging, murder) would likely *not* be appreciated by Seneca, freedom from fear of death could come in very handy for them—particularly in a world where even the lives of the most beloved characters are at best precarious. And where the biggest threat (arguably) comes from the Army of the Dead.

11
The Iron Bank Will Have Its Due

JEFF EWING

Supernatural entities like dragons, shadow assassins, and White Walkers often seem to be the major factors that will 'win' the 'game of thrones' for whichever faction controls them.

At the same time, one far less sexy factor may be the *real* determinant of who wins—and keeps—the Iron Throne: money.

On the one hand, financial issues like the costs of wars and various economies form the background of many tactical considerations in Westeros. Accordingly, many powers in Westeros have slogans with fiscal themes, from the Lannister's unofficial "a Lannister always pays his debts" to the Iron Bank of Braavos's "the Iron Bank will have its due." In Westeros, finance dominates politics.

Money Is King

Now we've got as many armies as there are men with gold in their purse.

Many different forces are employed in the war to gain the Iron Throne. Many factions try and take the throne by force—raising armies and building weapons in the name of taking King's Landing. Others try using supernatural forces—spawning shadow assassins to kill alternate contenders or raising dragons to conquer Westeros. One of the often unacknowledged sources of power behind the Iron Throne, however, is money. As Petyr Baelish explains, "Gold wins wars, not soldiers" ("A Golden Crown").

In Westeros, money is King—as evidenced everywhere from the rise of Petyr Baelish from rags to riches to the unacknowledged power of the Iron Bank of Braavos. Nowhere, however, is the power of money in Westeros more evident than in the history of the Lannisters and Tyrells.

House Lannister is seated in Casterly Rock, a castle which overlooks the Sunset Sea. The fortunes of the Lannisters had been built on the shrewd political instincts of Tywin Lannister. His father Tytos had lost the family's esteem at court and their family wealth on bad investments. Tywin's machinations saved the family's fortunes by restoring the profitability of their gold mine—the most productive gold mine in the Westerlands—making them the wealthiest family in Westeros until the War of Five Kings.

Tywin's efforts even enabled the family to control the Iron Throne through securing his children Jaime, Tyrion, and Cersei, in various positions of power. Cersei became Queen to Robert Baratheon and her children became heirs to the throne, before Cersei ultimately became sole monarch herself. Even Robb Stark recognized that wealth is the source of Lannister power:

> If we take Tywin's castle from him, the lords of Westeros will realize he's not invincible. Take his home, take his gold, take his power. ("Rains of Castamere")

The story of the Lannister rise to power historically hinges on Tywin's tactical efficacy backed by the Lannisters' primary asset—their fortune.

House Tyrell of Highgarden is another of the Great Houses of Westeros, and rules over the Reach, a large and fertile region. While it was recently headed by Lord Mace Tyrell, his mother Olenna Tyrell was the family's real leader. The notably populous Reach was granted to the Tyrells by Aegon Targaryen. The Tyrells are a cunning and wise house, with strong family ties to each other. In short, they are more tactical than the Starks and more honorable than the Lannisters. Ultimately, their primary strengths rest in their agricultural surplus and their large population, guaranteeing them great wealth via taxation. Their large population also enables them the capacity to amass a large army at a moment's notice. Their power in agriculture, population, and money was keenly displayed in a discussion between Olenna and Tyrion over contributions to Joffrey and Margaery's wedding:

> LADY OLENNA TYRELL: I can't think how it slipped my mind. What is it, twelve thousand infantrymen the Tyrell family has supplied? Eighteen hundred mounted lances. Two thousand in support. Provisions, so this city might survive the winter. A millions bushels of wheat. Half a million bushels each of barley, oats, and rye. Twenty thousand head of cattle. Fifty thousand sheep. You don't have to lecture me about wartime expenses, I'm quite familiar with them.

> TYRION LANNISTER: And we are so grateful for your contributions, which are necessary for the preservation of the realm. ("Kissed by Fire")

Their influence is so great that while they initially supported Renly Baratheon's claim to the Iron Throne, following Renly's death they were able to ally with the Lannisters in supporting Joffrey's claim to the throne on the condition that Margaery becomes queen.

While Robert's rebellion unseated the former Targaryen king from the throne, following his death it was clear that wealth produces power in Westeros. Lannister wealth placed Cersei into the position of Queen and following Robert's death her sons become King. When the War of Five Kings drained the kingdom's financial resources, the Tyrells came to the rescue, enabling Margaery to become the new Queen (before her untimely demise thanks to Cersei).

The two wealthiest families take their places as the heads of Westerosi society and fight over the crown—wealth becomes power. Karl Marx was a notable critic of the impact of wealth on power, including political power. Marxist insights explain the rise of the Lannisters and Tyrells, as well as the power of money over the Iron Throne more broadly.

Exploitation of the Smallfolk

The Master of Coin finds the money, the King—and the Hand—spend it.

The economic system in Westeros is best defined as a variant of late feudalism, with monarch-dominated societies similar to medieval Europe. In contrast is the Eastern continent of Essos, where both nomadic tribes and city-states exist. There is no region with an economy that is industrial, or where economic activity is widely performed by politically free workers (except Braavos)—political power enforces production and distribution relations.

There are also multiple societies within and without the boundaries of Westeros who produce nothing, but rather thrive by conquering those who do produce. The Dothraki are nomadic horse-mounted warriors from the plains of Essos, and they plunder what they need—supplies, slaves, or valuables. While they do not believe in currency, they trade using an honors system.

Similarly, the Free Folk in the North beyond the Wall have historically recognized no inherent political authority and live under general conditions of freedom and political equality, while also living without enforced laws—you keep what you take and defend.

Finally, the Ironborn of the Iron Islands, ruled by House Greyjoy, have a society that values raiding due to a lack of natural resources. Numerous significant societies within and without Westeros have economic systems that rest largely on raiding and coercive acquisition.

Meanwhile, in the rest of the Seven Kingdoms, economic activity is not primarily based around immediate coercion, but political force *still* enforces production and distribution relations. This force can be seen in the relationships between Kings, Lords, and Smallfolk, and in how production and financing occur in the realm. After the Targaryen conquest power was centralized around the Sovereign of the Iron Throne in King's Landing. The Sovereign sits on the Iron Throne as the highest authority in Westeros, claiming ownership of the land and possessing final political authority over the continent. The Sovereign has vassals, the high lords of the Great Houses who control the most important regions of the Seven Kingdoms. In turn, each of these high lords has their own vassals, the lords of their own pledged noble Houses.

Political authority in Westeros follows primogeniture, where designated heirs inherit their parents' lands and possessions. At the bottom of the hierarchy are the smallfolk—they do not own lands or titles, but work the land of their lords. They have no say in the governing practices of the nobility above them. There is no reliable way by which those of a lower class can move into a higher class, though it can happen at a lord's whim.

The maintenance of the economic and political subservience of the smallfolk to the nobility hinges largely on political coercion and fear. As the High Sparrow intimates to Olenna:

> Have you ever sowed the field, Lady Olenna? Have you ever reaped the grain? Has anyone in House Tyrell? A lifetime of wealth and power has left you blind in one eye. You are the few, we are the many. And when the many stop fearing the few . . . ("The Gift")

He insinuates that the real power rests in the many smallfolk and that their subservience hinges only on their fear—the fear of coercion, the political force (backed by gold) that maintains the Westerosi hierarchy.

In Westeros, the economic system rests on the backs of the smallfolk, whose work and taxes support the realm. When such revenue and gold mines prove insufficient, the Crown can rely on loans from the Iron Bank of Braavos or from the wealthier houses. As a late-medieval society, the affairs of state run on money, thus money brings power—it pays troops, lubricates the affairs of state, and secures a seat amongst the powerful and influential.

As we have seen with the Lannisters and Tyrells, wealth in Westeros can buy the power one needs to hold the Iron Throne. Wealth can also limit power—despite her dragons, Daenerys's ability to challenge King's Landing was limited without the revenue to purchase the Unsullied or the ships to transport the Dothraki. Money can even turn the tide in battles in the long run. Jon Snow had all but lost the Battle of the Bastards before Petyr Baelish led the knights of the Vale to aid him. And how did Petyr Baelish become the Lord Protector of the Vale, in a position to turn the tide? Money—money breeds influence, influence breeds power, power can breed the right marriage, and the right marriage grants authority. In Westeros, money is power.

Karl Marx on Westeros

> . . . is not money the bond of all bonds?
>
> —KARL MARX, "The Power of Money," *1844 Manuscripts*

Karl Marx was a revolutionary, economist, and philosopher, and may well be considered *the* pre-eminent critic of capitalism. While Marx devoted vastly more of his energy to the critique of capitalism than to feudalism, his work is defined by disdain for *all* class societies, and he strongly rejects feudal economies just as he rejects slavery or capitalism. Feudalism is a set of political-economic relations, like Westeros, based on traditional land-ownership and territory, and where the rights and duties of every member of society becomes contingent on their traditional kinship relations—power passes along families and so does subjugation.

As in Westeros, feudal laborers are born into families beholden to the lords who control their land, and it is anticipated that the lords will provide some services such as basic protection. In effect, the major property form during feudalism involved the transmission of land with attached serf labor, little division of labor, and mostly pre-industrial agricultural work.

While scholars differ on the exact factors driving the transition between feudalism and capitalism, the relationship between feudal lord and serf started to change once currency become more influential. Lords started to rent lands to tenant farmers, while some serfs began to pay monetary rents to lords instead of customary in-kind benefits. Around this late period, the power of kings began to centralize. Monarchs could acquire mercenary armies and consequently a monarch's power over feudal lords became sturdier in a military sense as it became more dependent in a monetary sense.

In short, money began to rule. Monetary contributions to rulers were provided by the subjugated classes or loaned to the crown. Money held increasing sway over rulers, as it became a source of centralizing power and as sovereign debt became a concern for kings and countrymen alike.

For Marx, feudal exploitation—where serfs were coerced by lords into exploited labor—was terrible just like capitalist exploitation was. As Marx argues in the *1844 Manuscripts*,

Landlords' right has its origin in robbery. . . . The landlords, like all other men, love to reap where they never sowed, and demand a rent even for the natural produce of the earth.

Far from being legitimate, the right of the landlord to extract labor from serfs rests on their coercively maintained power over the territory. As in Westeros, coercive authority maintains exploitation and subjugation, and social relations in late feudalism begin to transition with an increasing imposition of *money* into feudal relations—serfs must contribute monetarily to their lords and the crown, and monarchs maintain authority by monetary means. As Marx says,

> This huckstering with landed property, the transformation of landed property into a commodity, constitutes the final overthrow of the old and the final establishment of the money aristocracy.

Capitalist Victory?

In short, Westeros is a late-feudal kingdom—a centralized political authority, where political rule is backed by money, and where control over money grants a large-scale influence over the war for the Iron Throne. Marxist analysis of the methods of feudal exploitation, and the gradual domination of money over politics, shines a light on the economic underpinnings of rule in Westeros—the Marxist critique of feudal exploitation surely applies to Westerosi society.

Marxist insights consequently reveal one possibility of who may ultimately win the Iron Throne. Ever the materialist, perhaps Marx would predict that the ultimate victor of the 'Game of Thrones' won't win because of dragons, White Walkers, or shadow assassins. Perhaps, after the indebtedness of the kingdom due to war, not even a Lannister or a Tyrell will take King's Landing.

Instead, if feudal history truly inspires the Game of Thrones, then the Iron Throne will go to someone whose political power has emerged from his activity as a *capitalist* employer. It will go to someone whose tenure as Master of Coin indebted the crown to House Lannister and to the Iron Bank of Braavos—putting existing Westerosi feudal hierarchies under the influence of capitalist financial power. In short, perhaps the final person to sit on the Iron Throne will be the deadly and tactical Lord Petyr Baelish.

12
Margaery for Queen!

Tim Jones

Margaery could have been the greatest Queen that Westeros had ever known and I hope before her inevitable death Cersei realises how much harm she's done to the Seven Kingdoms by blowing her to pieces with the Sparrows.

Or could she *really* have been so great? You're probably thinking that I'm yet another halfwit who got taken in by her charm offensive and that I should get over her death and move on. And sure, you might just have a point—she did have some troubling qualities, now that you mention it! We should probably take a look at the evidence for and against my claim if we want to get a proper picture of who Margaery really was . . .

The Prosecution

Okay, so Margaery was a bit of a selfish egoist, whose main ambition was personal power. TV show Margaery makes her ambition to be Queen pretty clear to us during her conspiratorial chat with Littlefinger following Renly's murder. There's little if any emotion over the recent and brutal death of her husband—not that she seemed to care either about him or his preferring her brother Loras's company to her own.

Her lack of attachment to Renly is followed two seasons later by how quickly she moves from Joffrey to Tommen. It's like these guys aren't really people to her, but just stepping stones on her way to Queenhood. And these strikes against her aren't mitigated by her ambition coming from any improvements she longs to make to the fortunes of the people. Little seemed to move or motivate her beyond her cold drive for power, both for herself and the Tyrells as a whole. Perhaps, the truest thing she said during her false conversion to the Sparrows' religion was that she had been very "good . . . at seeming good."

Speaking of Tommen, Margaery's relationship with him shows her at her most coldly manipulative. She sneaks into his bedchamber at night, uses a very calculated mix of talking to him like the young kid he is and stoking his sexual curiosity with kisses on the forehead, and then gets him to promise that her visits will remain their secret. She takes care throughout to ensure that he'll imagine that everything that happens between them is entirely his decision, rather than a part of Margaery's play for power. It's the first step in a plan for making Tommen emotionally dependent on her, through convincing him that they share a special bond and isolating him from his family.

Once they're married, Margaery's behavior becomes even more manipulative and controlling. She helps Tommen feel like he's finally becoming a real man through their relationship moving to the next level, before putting the thought in his head that he'll never fully be able to call himself a man while his mom's hanging around.

Margaery's insincerity is made clear by how smoothly her expression switches from one of innocent young love to one of crafty indifference, once her back's to him and she begins to broach the subject of Cersei's exile. And if you still think she has real feelings for him, look at how angry she gets once he fails to magic Loras out of prison. While it's in her rights to be upset by her brother's incarceration, her sheer contempt for Tommen's anxiety shows us how their relationship is only a means for her to improve the position of the Tyrells.

You might even think that Margaery's treatment of Tommen is the most morally problematic aspect of all her behaviors. The media blog *The Fan Meta Reader* has put a pretty strong case for calling Margaery no less than a child abuser for the way she controls him. Sure, she isn't sleeping with Tommen for her own sexual gratification as its end goal, but, since it's still unambiguously 'sex as a means for the adult to coerce and manipulate the child', the blog's charge can't just be thrown out of court without a pretty close cross-examination.

It's true that the argument for Margaery being a child abuser doesn't allow for any degree of cultural relativity in the way that we might understand such a crime. Countries like America or the United Kingdom, in 2016, have a very different sense of appropriate relationships between adults and minors than not only Westeros, but other countries today and even our own countries throughout their histories.

Sexual consent laws are different across the globe and relationships that we'd quickly denounce now would've been understood as completely normal for centuries. Royal marriages with a vast age gap, in particular, were an utterly standard means for aristocratic families on the periphery of power to maneuver themselves closer to the throne, so Margaery isn't doing anything particularly out of the ordinary. We can see from her marriage to Tommen being clearly endorsed by the state, and their readily being given their own chamber, complete with luxury double-bed, that Westerosi society isn't at all judgemental towards this relationship. Her defense-force could direct us to the clear disgust of the Braavosi brothel owner in "Mother's Mercy" when Meryn Trant repeatedly turns down her girls for being 'too old.'

Even the world of the franchise clearly holds *some* sort of standards regarding sexual relations with minors, which the sheer *lack* of disgust shown by the wedding cortège and Margaery's inner-circle tells us, by its contrast to the brothel keeper, that Margaery clearly isn't breaking. Even the High Sparrow is keen for Margaery to get back into Tommen's bed, and he's probably the most sexually moralistic guy in Westeros.

So if Margaery *is* an abuser, we have to recognise that it's by our society's standards, rather than her own. And yet I'm not entirely convinced that this should get her relationship with Tommen entirely off the hook. . . . Sure, this would be judging her from a twenty-first century American perspective, but don't we do this pretty readily whenever we look back at, let's say, our own Antebellum history and declare that slavery was morally wrong? I'd say that we've recognised that slavery was always objectively wrong, rather than thinking that it suddenly became so the moment it was made illegal and was entirely fine up to that point—the law was just catching up with a prior truth that we'd not yet developed as a society enough to acknowledge.

And the cultural relativity argument leads us down some paths that could be more directly dangerous for young people in our own society. Some abusers today claim that sex with minors is only wrong because the law says that it is, and that survivors only experience negative after-effects because they're repeatedly told by the culture surrounding them that they've been subjected to an evil. I wonder if waving away the troubling relationship between Margaery and Tommen with the argument that it's clearly fine by Westeros isn't actually supporting these people's point, by agreeing that abuse is only abuse when it happens inside a culture that says that it is.

While my point stands that she's definitely sexually manipulative, whether or not this makes her an abuser too is a tricky question that I'm going to have to get you to decide on for yourself!

The Defense

So let's return to my claim that Margaery could have been the Greatest Queen of All Time. Right now I know it's not looking too good. All of the solid and the hypothetical black marks I've put against her name need acknowledging. And if we focus on them over other considerations, she doesn't really seem like the sort of person you'd want in charge. She's a selfish egoist whose primary concern is that of achieving power for its own sake. She's cold, emotionally and sexually manipulative, and just possibly even an abuser. You might be thinking that Cersei and her wildfire actually did the Seven Kingdoms a favor.

Yet look at what she actually *did* on her road to power. During her engagement to Joffrey following the Tyrell intervention at Blackwater, she's the restraining force who helps him show a benevolent side to his people. And she's utterly selfless when she steps out of her palanquin on the way back from the Sept of Baelor to distribute money, food and clothing to the city's poorest kids—in the very same streets where the royal procession was attacked by a mob just weeks earlier!

It's easy to see, then, why Margaery is so beloved amongst the Flea Bottom smallfolk. These are people who struggle to get enough to eat day-to-day and whose lives will have been made easier by Margaery's charity. They're not likely to give a damn what she does behind closed doors. A Queen is either good or bad depending on what they actually *do* as Queen, rather than why they got there in the first place.

Whether or not her ambition to be Queen is entirely selfish, these steps she's taken to get there would make the same material improvement in the lives of her people. While she even admits that she acted charitably purely so that she could be *seen* to be charitable, this fact does nothing to change the effects of the charity. And as long as her rule would have depended on her keeping this image intact, the charity would have continued flowing.

Margaery can want to be Queen for the wrong reasons and yet still be a wonderful Queen to the vast majority of her subjects, purely because she's crafty enough to know that the best way of securing the position is to keep the people on her side— and the best way to do *this* is to create a material improvement in their conditions.

We can separate the private Margaery, who we see conspire with Littlefinger, manipulate Tommen and show indifference about the deaths of her previous husbands, from the public Margaery, whose identity is the sum total of the good deeds she performs to the people. It might then look like the coldness of the first Margaery doesn't actually do anything to counter or reduce the benevolence of the latter. She *is* a selfish egoist, but the means she pursues to achieve her selfish, egoistical aims tend to promote the common good. The people of Flea Bottom aren't going to feel the effects of her charity any the less because it's her personal ambition, rather than a genuine kindness, that fuelled it.

The Alternatives

So there's nothing inevitably incompatible between the cold ambition of a selfish egoist and a benevolent rule that genuinely furthers the common good, and the sort of craftiness enjoyed by Margaery is what actually bridges the two. Margaery suggests that the best ruler of all isn't necessarily the genuinely kindest, but the one who combines the biggest drive to succeed with the shrewdness to recognize that you need the people onside to stay where you want to be. I'm not saying that egoistical ambition, shrewdness and benevolence will always go hand in hand like they do for Margaery—or even that they're likely to!—but this just makes her own combination of these qualities the more special.

Just look at some of her Seven Kingdom competitors. Ramsay Snow (sorry, Bolton!) is just as keen to get to the top, but he's more likely to flay his people alive in order to get there than show them any charity—and Roose was right that this would make whatever level of rule he achieves pretty short-lived. There's an organized resistance to his occupation of Winterfell when he's barely had a chance to take his cloak off and none of his surviving soldiers care enough to lift a finger to help him when Jon Snow is smashing his face in. The people just don't warm that easily to the sort of guy who leaves mutilated corpses hanging alongside the main thoroughfares.

At the other extreme from Ramsay, I reckon we can put Ned Stark. I don't think it's contentious to say that he's one of the least corrupt and most benevolent characters in Westeros. I bet he'd get them all on side not because he had to, but because he genuinely wanted their lives to be as fulfilled as possible. And yet it's this lack of calculation that seals his fate and ensures he'll never have the opportunity. Whatever you may think of Margaery, the moment she finds incontrovertible evidence that could cause Cersei's inescapable downfall, the last thing she's likely to do is arrange a meeting and politely warn her.

So Margaery is as ambitious as Ramsay, but much less likely to torture her subjects to death; and she has as much of a will as Ned probably does to improve the lot of the people, but is much less likely to be executed for stupidity before getting to actually do much. My point here might sound mean to Ned, but all the plans he might've had for the betterment of the people are completely irrelevant, since he never sustained a position where he could do anything about them.

You might protest that Margaery didn't sustain such a position herself for all that much longer, since barring an off-screen escape she's currently splattered all over the ruins of the Sept of Baelor. You might think that my Margaery super-fandom is making me stretch a little too much here, but it isn't her *own* stupidity that leads to her being stuck in the Sept, but that of the High Sparrow and his followers. She's canny enough to work out in perfectly good time that Cersei's got a devious masterplan—she's only doomed by the fact that the people around her don't share her shrewdness!

And as for any other alternative rulers? Stannis isn't actively cruel like Ramsay, or terminally stupid like Ned, but going by Ser Davos's example, he'd likely run a thorough search into the backgrounds of every pauper or beggar in Flea Bottom before allowing them a crumb. You can imagine him handing out a bread-roll and then hauling the recipient off to the Red Keep before he has a chance to eat it. His complete lack of nuanced sympathy in understanding people's individual situations probably wouldn't help him much when engaging with the dispossessed whom Margaery non-judgementally embraces.

And Joffrey? The only time he experienced the true love of his people was when Margaery was directly beside him, showing him exactly how it's done, which I think proves my point.

The Best Bet

However much we might prefer to see a strong case for the wonderful effects that true virtue and pure motives can have upon the world, Margaery suggests that in a place like Westeros, genuine good might arrive via an altogether murkier path. She's a cold, manipulative egoist . . . and perhaps much worse. But all that some of the most dispossessed and poverty-stricken citizens of the Seven Kingdoms are likely to care about is that she's the woman who gave them both the time and the food that everyone else in a position of power never gave them.

Perhaps all this just underlines how hard and unfair life in George R.R. Martin's world can be—in a place where life is so cheap, the intrigue so thick, and the enemies around those vying for the Iron Throne so numerous, if you want to see any improvements in the lives of its people, a woman like Margaery, with the right combination of hunger for power and shrewdness, might be your best bet.

I only hope that the common folk won't suffer too much from losing her and that whoever ends up displacing Cersei has a similar blend of qualities.

13
Bran, Hodor, and Disability in Westeros

JEREMY PIERCE

Game of Thrones has several important characters with disabilities. Jaime Lannister pushes Bran Stark from a great height, and Bran survives but will never walk again. Jaime himself, a Kingsguard, loses his sword hand. Aemon Targaryen in his old age can no longer see, and Arya Stark loses her sight for a time. Tyrion Lannister is a dwarf, with diminished stature and misshapen features. Doran Martell cannot walk because of gout. Theon Greyjoy, Varys, and Greyworm have lost their sex organs, two in childhood but one after becoming known for his sexual exploits. Hodor has severely diminished linguistic capacities and is (mistakenly?) believed to have diminished cognitive abilities. King Aerys Targaryen II was severely mentally ill and is remembered as the Mad King.

Our society classifies all these conditions as disabilities. What do they have in common? A sensory disability like Aemon's blindness, a physical disability like Jaime's missing hand or Bran's paralysis, a cognitive or linguistic disability like Hodor's, and a mental illness like that of King Aerys appear to be very different conditions. Why do we put such diverse conditions in this category?

The Medical Model and the Social Model

Some people see a life with disabilities as not worth living, sometimes even to the point of saying helping people with disabilities is a waste of resources. The social model of disability responds by arguing that there's nothing wrong with having a disability. Its proponents contrast their view with what they call the medical model. If disabilities are problems, they are social rather than medical problems and have social rather than medical solutions.

According to the medical model, Aemon Targaryen is disabled because his eyes don't function properly. If he lived in our world, the medical model would seek to improve his vision with cataract surgery. He doesn't have that option in Westeros, where not being able to see is even worse than in our world, although he manages to serve his own function well in the Night's Watch. But the difference between the two worlds reveals something important. Why is it worse to be blind in Westeros? One reason is our technology that makes it easier for people who can't see. We have tools that make it easier to accommodate many disabilities.

Advocates of the social model argue that the real disability is not based in the inability to see but instead in the failure of society to accommodate a lack of sight. If I lose my sight but can "watch" *Game of Thrones* by listening to a narrator describe it, then I can do something I wouldn't be able to do without that technology. Even in Westeros, Aemon can have Sam Tarly read to him. He doesn't need audiobooks. The social model says disability is only the result of a society that doesn't accommodate. To the extent we accommodate, there is no actual disability.

Our society has eyeglasses for people whose vision would otherwise be diminished. We have sign language and interpreters, wheelchair ramps, elevators, and extended time on exams. The one-armed drummer for Def Leppard uses foot pedals with his drum kit to replace what he would have done with his missing arm.

But despite all these accommodations, isn't there really still a disability? Someone with a learning disability who gets extra time on exams still can't achieve the same results without extra time. Someone who uses a hearing aid can't hear voices at their usual volume without it. People who use wheelchairs, ramps, and elevators can't get where they're going as easily without them. In Westeros, they might be bedridden or carried by Hodor.

The social model holds that all there is to the disability is the social element, the refusal of society to accommodate. If we say that's all there is to the disability, something is missing from our account. We don't have an explanation for what needs to be accommodated. Isn't the disability the reason we need to accommodate? Isn't something in some sense diminished, not functioning well, or incomplete, apart from how they're being treated? It doesn't seem that disability can just be lack of accommodation.

Impairment versus Disability

The social model responds to this objection by distinguishing between physical impairment and disability. Not being able to see well is an impairment. Not being accommodated with eyeglasses is a disability. Not being able to move around on your own is an impairment. Not having a wheelchair and accessible ways into and out of places is a disability. An impairment makes accommodation necessary, while the disability is socially caused. Even if Bran had technology to get him around anywhere he wanted, he would still have an impairment. His legs don't function the way most people's do. But he wouldn't have a disability if he could still get around.

Many people, however, use the word 'disability' to refer to what the social model calls impairment. It's good to make clear distinctions, setting apart two concepts to show how they're different, using language clearly. Even so, once we've clarified our terms, we have to remember that not everyone has been taught these nuances. A lot of people use the word 'disability' to mean what social model calls impairment.

One might wonder if the dispute between the social model and the medical model can be dissolved by just being clearer in our terminology. Isn't the impairment still medical, even if the disability is lack of accommodation? Philosophers call this a verbal dispute. But there is still a debate to be had.

Disability, Impairment, and Well-Being

Some versions of the social model also hold what I'll call the "mere difference" view. According to this view, having an impairment is different but not worse in any way. An impairment is a mere difference. For example, a lot of deaf people don't think an inability to hear makes them worse off. They have language. They just don't need to hear to use it. As long as those they come into contact have learned sign language, they can communicate. If everyone learned sign language, deaf people could communicate with everyone (though not in the dark). According to the social model, I'm the one who's disabled if I'm around people who speak only sign and I don't.

Imagine what someone's life would be like in Westeros if they couldn't hear. If Westeros lacks sign language, wouldn't they be worse off? But many deaf people think that, in a society with sign language, they aren't any worse off than being left-handed. To the extent that society doesn't accommodate left-handed people, lefties might have it worse. But if society accommodates, then being left-handed isn't a problem. We have left-handed desks, scissors, guitars, and so on. Being left-handed is a mere difference, not a difference that in itself makes someone worse off. Philosophers would say being left-handed is not intrinsically bad. It's not bad in itself. It's only bad if the environment you're in makes it difficult for people who are left-handed.

Is this true for disabilities? Sign language can accommodate communication, but it doesn't accommodate everything someone without hearing might be unable to do. They can't hear noises that others can hear and thus avoid a life-threatening accident, although they might feel some sound. They can't hear music, which most people think adds value to their lives, even if they can feel it and dance to it. Isn't that a sign that deafness makes someone worse off?

Local and Global Harm

But, wait! A condition might make someone worse off in one sense but not in another. Suppose Jorah Mormont has his arm amputated because of his Greyscale infection. The loss of his arm in that case is beneficial, but doesn't it also make things worse for him in other ways?

Philosophers distinguish between local and global harm. Something harms me locally if it makes me miss out on some good I could otherwise have. But it doesn't necessarily harm me globally, because there might be some more important good that I care more about having. Having two arms isn't worth becoming a Stone Man. If we care more about life or some aspect of life than limbs, we might be willing to give up our limbs to keep living. Jaime might be worse off without his hand since he received no benefit from losing his hand, but if removing my hand prevents me from becoming a Stone Man, then it's a global good despite being a local harm.

Some disability theorists think something similar occurs with disabilities in general. Often people lose a limb, a sense, or a capacity, and they say they're not worse off. While that could be a coping mechanism, many who say such things seem honest about it. They think their lives are not worse globally just because they've got a disability. In some cases, they've gained other things that compensate for the local harm.

Deaf people enjoy the signing community. Some attribute moral or spiritual growth to dealing with their impairment. Sometimes there's even a sensory increase in other senses, when the disability is sensory. Conditions like autism involve deficits in some areas but increased abilities in other ways. Bran gained a prophetic ability after his accident. Varys gained a valuable immunity to sexual manipulation. How one should compare the relative value of the local harm of a disability with the local good that can also accompany it is at least an open question.

Mere Difference and Teleology

Sometimes when people assert the "mere difference" thesis, they mean that people with disabilities aren't worse off globally, even if they're worse off locally. But sometimes they mean something more radical. They mean that even the local difference doesn't involve a loss. It's merely a difference, not a difference that's bad. Why would someone think this?

The answer goes back to an ancient debate. Aristotle (384–322 B.C.E.) believed in something philosophers call natural teleology. Teleology is purpose or goal. When Jon Snow committed himself to serve in the Night's Watch, he did it for particular reasons. Those are his purposes. We might ask what brought him to the Wall, and he could give a literal answer. A horse did. But that kind of explanation answers how he got there, not why. Teleology is about purposes or goals we possess, the reasons we do things.

What is natural teleology? Aristotle believed in goals and purposes in nature itself. That idea makes sense if you believe in God. If there's a benevolent being who oversees the universe, who wants certain things to happen at certain times, who guides things along toward those purposes, then much of nature conforms to God's purposes. But while Aristotle's ultimate explanation of the universe, the "Unmoved Mover," is intelligent and perfect, it merely explains the universe and enjoys its own perfection. It doesn't care about us the way God does in some traditional religions.

So why did he believe in purposes in nature? Aristotle might answer that there are purposeful patterns in nature. Teeth are for chewing. That's what they're for. Leaves are for photosynthesis. They're for absorbing light and using it to help the plant grow and be healthy. Legs are for walking, among other things, and eyes are for seeing. That's their purpose. Sex organs have at least one natural purpose, which is reproduction, and most people would add pleasure and perhaps uniting with another person.

Varys and Theon were robbed of something naturally good when their organs were cut off. When he experienced his future death, Hodor lost a good that he once had, the ability to communicate linguistically. Some people never possess the capacities that others consider normal. If Aristotle is right, then it makes sense to see disabilities or impairments as harmful, at least locally. But some have argued against Aristotle. In the ancient world, one such philosopher was Lucretius (99–55 B.C.E.), who belonged to the Epicurean school of thought.

Lucretius gives the following argument. Teleology makes sense when you have purposes that someone intends. When Robb Stark marries the woman he loves rather than the woman arranged to marry him, it makes sense to say there's a purpose behind that event. But when structures form biologically without any guiding mind behind them to give them a purpose, why think they have a purpose?

If Lucretius is right, the "mere difference" thesis follows. Your brain could be in any number of neurological states. Some allow higher-level thought. Others would make you like Hodor, or you could have a stroke and be able to form intentions to speak but not able to produce the words. If Lucretius is right, none of these brain states are intrinsically worse or better than any other. There are no purposes internal to them. They only have the purposes we choose for them. If we want to do algebra or philosophy, then we want brains like the ones we have. Direwolves have no such desires. If someone wanted them to do algebra, their brain doesn't suit that purpose. But that doesn't make it intrinsically worse, just not suited for that purpose.

Aristotle's alternative view is to take those differences as having intrinsic value. He wouldn't say someone is a worse person if they have a disability, but he would say our bodies have certain functions. If we can't perform those functions, it's bad for us. We're worse off. We're lacking in well-being in the local sense. In this respect, Jaime's missing his hand makes him worse off. There are purposes a hand is properly suited for that he can no longer achieve. Aristotle would say some of his natural purposes are frustrated. Lucretius would counter that the state of having a hand and the state of not having one are just two different states. Neither state is better or worse until you add a chosen purpose. There is no purpose in nature.

But for Aristotle nature contains purposes. Trees have purposes for their leaves even if we don't choose it for them. Leaves are for photosynthesizing. A tree needs no intelligence to have that goal. If that's right, then plants and animals have intrinsic functioning. If those functions are prevented, they're worse off. If Aristotle's right, the "no difference" thesis is wrong. The states we call disabilities or impairments really are locally worse for us, not because of what we intend but because of what's naturally good, what natural purposes we have, and what functionality it is natural to have. Someone might or might not be globally better off with their impairment.

Even if the "mere difference" view is wrong, it doesn't follow that people with disabilities have a worthless life or that we should refuse to accommodate them. It just means something is intrinsically unfortunate about the way they are. That motivation for the social model doesn't require the "mere difference" thesis.

So where are we left after all this? The "mere difference" view holds that no condition is any better or worse than any other, even locally. We might instead think we're worse off if our natural purposes get frustrated by what happens to us (whether we think natural purposes come from a Creator or in the Aristotelian way).

I don't intend to settle this disagreement, but I hope thinking about it sheds some light on the philosophical dispute about disability and intrinsic value. In any case, as *Game of Thrones* has repeatedly shown, characters like Bran, Hodor, Varys, and Jaime have great significance despite their disabilities. Their value should never be underestimated. Their abilities should never be underestimated. They can be as heroic as any other character.[1]

---

[1] Thanks to Winky Chin for very helpful comments on a draft of this chapter.

IV

The Things I Do for Love

14
The Gods Hate Incest

ADAM BARKMAN

"The gods hate incest," says a nameless knight in the fictitious land of Westeros (*A Clash of Kings*, p. 157). That the knight is nameless is important since his sentiment is nearly universally acknowledged in *A Game of Thrones*. People as diverse as Stannis Baratheon, Tywin Lannister, and Catelyn Stark all agree that consanguine unions, incest, or, crudely, a sexual union between near relatives is an *"abomination"* (p. 158), a "disgusting" thing (*A Storm of Swords*, p. 265), and "a monstrous sin to both old gods and new" (*A Clash of Kings*, p. 497).

While all of the gods of Westeros and Essos seem fairly regional, limited and imperfect, the fact that everyone seems to think that the gods are opposed to incest suggests something important: The consensus that incest is morally repugnant implies that undergirding this incest taboo is a broader fundamental moral reality.

This fundamental morality reality has been called different things by different people in our world: Confucius calls it the Mandate of Heaven; Plato, the Good; the Stoics, *Natura*; Christians, Natural Law; the Egyptians, *Maat*; the Zoroastrians, *Asha*; and the Hindus, *Rta*.

All of these people and thinkers, moreover, would agree not only that it is morally wrong for humans to commit incest, but also that people should feel repulsed by this and can know that this is in fact wrong. So, it's likely that this is true of the people of Westeros and Essos as well.

Nevertheless, given the popularity of Freudian psychology, relativistic ethics and the countless cases or hints of incest in *A*

Game of Thrones—from Jaime and Cersei, to Caster and Gilly, Viserys and Daenerys, Arnolf and Alys, Walder and his brother's wife, Theon and Asha, Loras and Margaery, and a host of others—many will still find it hard to believe that there's anything like a *natural* instinct against, and a *natural* command forbidding, incest. This, then, is what will need to be shown.

Jaime, Freud, and the Westermarck Effect

Jaime and Cersei Lannister are full-siblings and lovers. Born twins, they saw in each other their own reflection and their own other half: "You are me," Cersei says to Jaime, "I am you" (*A Feast for Crows*, p. 179). From their earliest days, they pushed the boundaries of gender and sex norms, cross-dressing "for a lark," (*Clash of Kings*, p. 849), imagining themselves of the opposite sex—"If I were a woman," says Jaime, "I'd be Cersei" (*Storm of Swords*, p. 294)—and even in their early childhood expressing erotic feelings for each other:

> As children, they would creep into each other's beds and sleep with their arms entwined. . . . Long before his sister's flowering or the advent of his own manhood, they had seen mares and stallions in the fields and dogs and bitches in the kennels and played at doing the same. Once their mother's maid had caught them at it . . . he did not recall just what they had been doing, but whatever it was had horrified Lady Joanna. She had sent the maid away, moved Jaime's bedchamber to the other side of Casterly Rock, set a guard outside Cersei's, and told them they must *never* do that again. (pp. 286–87)

However, once Jaime and Cersei's mother died, the two were free to continue to explore their increasing erotic attraction toward each other to the point where they eventually became full-blown lovers. Indeed, their young adult devotion to each other was so intense that Jaime gave up his inheritance as the future lord of Casterly Rock to be part of the Kingsguard so that he could be closer to his sister, who had then become Queen of the Seven Kingdoms.

The infringement of sexual norms (cross-dressing and incest) led to another—adultery—which in turn led to Jaime attempting to murder seven year-old Brandon Stark, and which also led Cersei to have a hand in murdering Eddard

Stark. Subsequently, this led to civil war and, among other things, tens of thousands of lives lost. In the midst of this, Jaime was adamant that he wanted to wed his sister ("Marry me, Cersei," he says in *A Storm of Swords*, p. 852), yet eventually he discovered that she had been unfaithful to him, having had another incestuous affair with their cousin Lancel while Jaime was imprisoned. Never once did either Lannister imagine incest to be morally wrong. As Jaime says, "I'm not ashamed of loving you, only of the things I've done to hide it" (*Storm of Swords*, p. 1002).

Sigmund Freud would have loved this odd take on the Lancelot-Guinevere story. The famed Viennese psychotherapist is renowned for reducing other forms of love, such as *storge* or affection, *philia* or friendship, and *agape* or sacrificial love, to *eros* or sexual attraction.

Building on the assumption that all norms are only social constructs (meaning that norms forbidding consanguine unions can be overturned if desired), Freud argued that people are largely sexual beings who only control their sexual urges to keep society working, and not because there is anything inherently wrong with any sexual act or relationship. In particular, Freud believed that sons have a "natural" sexual desire for their mothers (the Oedipus Complex), that daughters feel likewise about their fathers (the Electra Complex), and so on.

As he says in *A General Introduction to Psychoanalysis*, "psychoanalytic investigations have shown beyond the possibility of doubt that an incestuous love choice is in fact the first and regular one" (pp. 220–21). Jaime and Cersei couldn't agree more.

Nevertheless, nowadays we know that Freud's theory was, as he himself often hinted, driven more by autobiographical experience than fact: "I have found, in my own case too, falling in love with the mother and jealousy of the father, and I now regard it as a universal event of early childhood" (*The Psychopathology of Everyday Life*, p. 265). Though Freud's theories are popularly known, few psychologists and philosophers accept his theory of incest, and this fact is largely due to the research of Edward Westermarck.

In a nutshell, Westermarck argued that inbreeding has deleterious consequences (high rates of genetic disorders), and that because of this, many species, including human beings, have natural aversions to sexual relationships with early childhood associates:

> The attempts to prove the harmlessness of even the closest inbreeding have not shaken my opinion that there is convincing evidence to the contrary. And here I find, as before, a satisfactory explanation of the want of inclination for, and consequent aversion to, sexual intercourse between persons who from childhood have lived together in that close intimacy which characterises the mutual relations of the nearest kindred. We may assume that in this, as in other cases, natural selection has operated, and by eliminating destructive tendencies and preserving useful variations has moulded the sexual instinct so as to meet the requirements of species. (*Three Essays on Sex and Marriage*, pp. 158–59)

This principle, "the remarkable absence of erotic feelings between people living closely together from childhood" (*A Short History of Human Marriage*, p. 80) is sometimes known as the "Westermarck Effect."

Thus, where George R.R. Martin would have us imagine Jaime and Cersei's incestuous relationship as *developing* from early childhood instincts, Westermarck would say that this is extremely unlikely, and he's backed in this view by two important studies.

First, primatology has shown that there is indeed a natural instinct in apes and others to avoid incest, especially when those related are sexually mature: "Nonhuman primates provide abundant evidence for an inhibition of sexual behaviour among closely related adults. . . . The primate data supports Westermarck's theory that familiarity during immaturity is a major reason for this avoidance" (*Inbreeding, Incest and the Incest Taboo*, p. 71). Insofar as our DNA is very similar to apes, we should expect that many of our *instincts*, including our sexual instincts, would be similar to those of the apes.

Second, studies conducted of Taiwanese *simpua* ("little daughter-in-law") marriages, where a girl is adopted by her future husband-in-law's family and raised alongside her future husband, show 1. that out of five hundred and fifty *simpua* marriages studied, these marriages had a 40% lower fertility rate than other marriages; 2. that such couples were three times as likely to end up divorced; and 3. that spouses were twice as likely to have extramarital affairs (*Inbreeding*, p. 77). If the couple had been raised together before the age of three, the Westermarck Effect was extremely noticeable, if they were raised together before the age of eight, the tendency was still very strong, and if they were raised after the age of eight, the effect gradually became less sensitive, though was by no means absent. This means that because Jaime and Cersei were raised closely since birth, readers should probably conclude either that that the twins are instinctually malformed or that their relationship is unconvincingly written.

Yet whatever conclusion you prefer, there are other incestuous relationships in *A Game of Thrones* that are more convincing given the Westermarck Effect. In the case of parents and children, we know that parents who spend quality time with their young children and participate in raising them also develop natural sexual aversion to their offspring, though for parents this is strengthened not merely by strong affection or *storge* from birth but also by a natural caregiver instinct. Thus, if a parent is absent a lot or, for whatever reason, has little affection for his or her child, the Westermarck Effect is weakened and incestuous relationships become much more likely: "Incest occurs, overwhelmingly, in grossly disturbed families in which neglect, abandonment and physical abuse are also common" (*Inbreeding,* p. 171). So, when Black Walder took his brother's wife, even while he was alive, this, instinctually speaking, is fairly believable since Black Walder was, in addition to being an evil man, neither raised alongside, nor raised, his brother's wife. Likewise, when Littlefinger passionately kissed Sansa Stark, his wife's niece, his Westermarck instinct wasn't malfunctioning since he was neither raised alongside Sansa nor was he her guardian throughout early childhood.

As with most theories, Freud's has some basis in reality. Nature doesn't always act optimally, meaning that there may be a few couples like Jaime and Cersei who are born with malfunctioning instincts. And incestuous dreams do occur, but probably have nothing to do with repressed sexual desire. A few mothers are sexually aroused while breastfeeding—perhaps Lysa Arryn would be a candidate ("The Pointy End").

And then, most children are naturally attracted to people who are similar to their parents since studies in "optimal outbreeding" have shown that children unconsciously choose mates who are a balance between what is familiar and yet still different. While inbreeding causes an unusually high number of genetic deformities, excessive outbreeding has its own problems as well. If a man with a big jaw and teeth married a woman with a small jaw and teeth, it's possible that their grandchild might end up with a small jaw and big teeth, which could cause problems.

And finally, though an instinctually malformed or simply an evil parent or sibling could take advantage of a child or a younger sibling sleeping in their proximity, studies have shown that *storge* is *storge* and *eros* is *eros* and that "Contrary to expectations, children who coslept with their parents were *less* likely to have been treated in a mental health clinic for emotional and behavioral problems" (Erickson, p. 179).

Natural Commands and Natural Roles

But do we have a universal, *moral* command forbidding incest? The near universal agreement in Westeros, Essos and Earth makes this a possibility. Combining the general moral prohibition "Do no harm," the general moral principle "Take care of the weak," the general moral precept "Respect your superiors," and the general moral principle "Favor your family over others," an incest prohibition, which is generally and universally binding, is readily deduced in at least three ways.

First, it didn't take knowledge of advanced genetics for people to discern that inbreeding often results in unhealthy children who suffer and thus cause their parents and society to suffer: the ancient Arabs knew "the seed of relations bring forth feeble fruit" (*Marriage Ceremonies in Morocco*, p. 55), and the Toradjas warned that such children "will be weak, sickly or idiotic and quickly die" (Adriani and Kruyt, *The Bare'e-speaking Toradja*, p. 11). Dwarfism is a common result of incest, though we have no reason to suspect that Tyrion the imp is a product of this! Whatever the case, inbreeding is usually harmful and has little benefit, and so in most cases it unnecessarily harms everyone considered and is thus unjust.

Second, if endogamy or marriages in a small group were the norm, then society would be further harmed since it would prevent the glue of marriage from bonding people into the larger society. If the Lannisters didn't marry the Baratheons or the

Starks the Tullys, then there would be less solidarity in the seven kingdoms. Indeed, even the wildlings know, "A true man steals a woman from afar, t' strengthen the clan. Women who bed brothers or fathers or clan kin offend the gods, and are cursed with weak and sickly children" (*A Storm of Swords*, p. 365). Extreme endogamy also does unnecessary harm to society and is thus, in most cases, unjust.

Third, recent findings in psychology confirm what many have longed believed, namely, that the nuclear family—one father, one mother and their children—is the natural organization of human beings. The goal of the family from the point of view of evolutionary biology is primarily to breed and raise optimally healthy children. Since the notion of a natural family presupposes natural *roles* within the family, each family member must be aware of his or her role. Because a basic moral principle teaches the strong to take care of the weak and the weak to respect the strong, parents—here, the strong—are aware of a natural moral command to take care of their children, and children understand it as quite natural to obey their parents.

Moreover, since most people also know that they ought to prioritize their own family over others to some degree, parents understand that they have a very strong obligation to help their children, and children to obey and respect their parents. But since incestuous relationships confuse roles and expectations in the family, domestic happiness is impaired: sons who sleep with their mothers might see themselves as their fathers' equal in position and authority and fathers who have sexual relations with their daughters betray their daughters' natural expectation for parental care (Turner, *Incest*, p. 41). For these reasons, incest should be seen as harmful, unnatural, and generally unjust.

But what about cases where incest is encouraged such as with the Targaryens of Westeros and Essos, who wed brother to sister to keep the "bloodlines pure"? (*A Game of Thrones*, p. 485). Baelor married Daena for this reason, and Daenerys was expected to do so with either her brother Rhaegar (*Storm of Swords*, p. 587) or her brother Viserys (*Dance with Dragons*, p. 73). Yet there is also an irony in this practice. Inbreeding leads to the weakening of bloodlines. Indeed, we are told that the Targaryens are plagued by a "taint" of madness (*Dance with*

Dragons, p. 153), which, when it runs its course, can ultimately end up destroying the bloodline. Thus, the preservation of bloodline argument is flawed, and the practice of incest for this reason is still immoral and unnatural.

But even more sinister and unnatural is the hint that the Targaryens, like the Greek gods, Egyptian pharaohs and Japanese emperors, simply thought themselves above the Natural Law and all derived injunctions against incest. Catelyn Stark believes that the Targaryens practiced incest since they "answered to neither gods nor men" (*Clash,* p. 498), and Jaime wants to marry his sister, thus showing "the realm that the Lannisters are above their laws, like gods and Targaryens" (*Storm,* p. 287). This arrogance and blasphemy is immoral and unnatural and incest on this basis can't be justified.

Abominations Born of Incest

Incest is, by and large, unnatural, and we can be aware of this through both natural instincts and reasoning from the Natural Law. If not "in defiance of *all* the laws of gods and men" (*Dance with Dragons,* p. 247), it's certainly in defiance of *most.* Nevertheless, what needs to be added is that children born of incest—children such as Gilly's baby, Joffrey, Tommen and Myrcella—aren't quite the "abominations" that they're often thought to be.

It's true that biologically speaking, many children born of incest will be deformed and in this sense "abominations," but what is also true is that such children didn't choose to be born thus and it would be wrong to judge them as if they had. Joffrey, for instance, is an abomination, not because he was born of incest, but rather because of his choices to act against a higher moral reality.

15
Joffrey on the Couch

JAMES WILLS

Hands up, who hated Joffrey Baratheon? I bet if you asked a bunch of people that question, you'd get a fairly high hand-count; I'd even wager it very easily could be every hand.

But why has the Boy King of Westeros been so vilified? Is it because he ordered the beheading of Ned Stark in "Baelor"? Is it because he forced Sansa Stark to look upon the severed head of her father in "Fire and Blood"? Or is it even when he had innocent people executed in "The Old Gods and the New" because a protestor threw cow excrement at him?

If you type "bad things Joffrey has done" into any Internet search engine, you'll get countless "Top Ten Worst Things He Did" lists that have been compiled in honor of the Boy King of Westeros. And in May 2012, as Season Two was being aired, James Ellaby of *The Huffington Post* asked the very question many of us had been thinking when watching *Game of Thrones*: "Has there ever been a more fundamentally loathsome character on television than Joffrey Baratheon?" Ellaby also claimed that Joffrey's actions were, along with a handful of the small screen's vilest characters, so utterly detestable, there is a "separate level of TV hell reserved" for him.

When you consider what he does on *Game of Thrones*, we should probably all be lining up to throw Joffrey into "TV hell," chucking away the key while we're at it. All this begs a couple of questions though: Why is Joffrey bound to such villainous behavior? And more importantly, why do we vilify him, taking such endless pleasure in compiling twisted versions of his "greatest hits," then posting them across the Internet? I believe the answer lies in where Joffrey comes from, as well as the carnal desires that created him. This answer too says an awful lot about our own impulses, and indicates it is probably in our interest to hate Joffrey Baratheon. To help me make my point though, I first need a little help from Sigmund Freud . . .

Freud and the Real "Problem with Incest"

At the beginning of the twentieth-century, Sigmund Freud (1856–1939) was writing about the unconscious and our primal urges, although that is précising somewhat . . . In 1913, he published *Totem and Taboo*, a lengthy study about primitive peoples in which, amongst other things, he analyzed the concept of the taboo; particularly the one we all try not to talk about: incest.

Here's the basic idea: Freud wrote about the earliest peoples on our planet; people we in our modern world might call uncivilized savages. These primitive groups created societies based on a concept called Totemism, which organized both their culture and their behavior. Each tribal group would select a totem, which was often a carefully chosen animal or object; these totems would then come to represent a "tribal family," who lived under its rules and laws. And one of these laws was (you guessed it): it was strictly forbidden to have sexual contact with anybody who lived under the same totem. In other words: don't have sex with anyone from the same "family" as you.

But here's the really interesting bit, which has real significance when we think about the hatred that has been directed at Joffrey Baratheon. Freud makes the claim—which I think is pretty valid—that, if you create a law to prohibit people from sleeping with other members of their family, then there must have been the desire to do it in the first place.

Freud is being rather clever here: in harking back to the most primitive forms of society, he is showing us what we used to be like, stereotyping early people as the savages we often tell ourselves they were. In doing that, he also moves things forward to the present day by suggesting these incestuous thoughts are, in most people, successfully repressed (I'm sure we've all heard of the Oedipus Complex . . .).

Joffrey's Beginning

Like Freud's *Totem and Taboo*, *Game of Thrones* is set in the past, but it uses that past to tell us things about the present. It certainly doesn't take a genius to work out that Westeros isn't real, but is depicting a medieval world of savagery and brutality that wouldn't have been so out of place five or six centuries ago.

But it's a world fully aware of the barbarous acts of modern warfare and totalitarianism in the last couple of hundred years too, so David Benioff and D.B. Weiss are never shy in showing us how utterly brutal Westeros is. The fact that it's set so far in the past means we're able to distance ourselves from its brutality, just like Freud did in *Totem and Taboo*. That past savagery is *not* us; we surely don't have any kind of urge to murder or rape the innocent, or sleep with our family. We are civilized now.

It won't have escaped your notice that there's plenty of incest in *Game of Thrones*: we see it as early as the end of "Winter Is Coming", when Cersei and Jaime Lannister are caught in an amorous tryst by Bran Stark. Early in the first season too, it also becomes no secret that Joffrey Baratheon is *not* the son of King Robert and Queen Cersei: he is, in fact, the product of incest; of a carnal desire between brother and sister. But incest in the Lannister family doesn't end there: below is just a small segment of the Lannister Family Tree, where italics indicate offspring as a product of incest (or at least alleged incest).

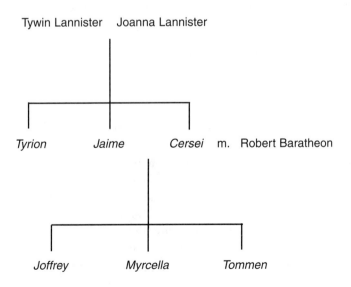

Freud would say the Lannisters have well and truly broken the rules of totemism here. In summary: Tywin and Joanna are cousins, who have three children, two of which—Jaime and Cersei—produce three more children. Joffrey therefore, is the product of a kind of "accumulative incest"; his grandparents are cousins and his parents are siblings. Basically, this is one hell of an incestuous web, and Joffrey is caught right in the middle of it. For the audience, this sexual depravity is pretty much designed to make our stomachs churn, bringing on those inevitable feelings of nausea.

Loving to Hate the Boy King

Let's say something obvious: Joffrey Baratheon is vile. Let's then point to some evidence that supports such a statement. He has Ned Stark beheaded, despite telling Sansa he would let him go; he orders the execution of hundreds of peasants because he has cow excrement flung at him; he orders the death of any of Robert Baratheon's illegitimate children at King's Landing; he abandons his men at the Battle of Blackwater, and runs to his mom; he casually kills Ros with a crossbow in "The Climb," impaling the prostitute several times to the frame of his bed; he cruelly tells Sansa "he is her father" upon her marriage to Tyrion in "Second Sons," knowing full well he killed her actual father. I could have added plenty more, but you get the gist: Joffrey Baratheon is beyond detestable, and you'll get no argument on that particular point from me.

So he's vile, and his actions are entirely appalling. But why does he act in this way? Does his past, and the sexually deviant backdrop he is born into, account for (at least some of) his deplorable behavior?

Joffrey Baratheon is a heady combination of cruelty and aggression mixed with naivety and petulance; then again, the Lannisters are hardly a family devoid of what we might call "negative character traits." Joffrey certainly suffers from megalomaniacal delusions, feeling he deserves nothing but devotion from his subjects, despite his utter ineptitude as a ruler; then again, Cersei Lannister has obviously spoilt her son from the moment he was born, which goes some way to explaining his ludicrous sense of entitlement, but also seems to hint at some kind of incest—after all, she does have a "strange connection" to her eldest which she doesn't have with her other children. Joffrey has no self-control and acts only according to twisted, perverse impulses; then again, remind me of how he was conceived . . . twisted and lacking in self-control seem to fit nicely into Freud's incest theory, don't they?

I'm not saying Joffrey is a good guy: far from it. I'm just trying to get to the bottom of his character; trying to work out why it is we love to hate him. And you don't need to look very far to find people who are pretty good at loving to hate Joffrey Baratheon. Here are three musings on the Boy King of Westeros, and it isn't hard to spot a recurring theme:

> We all know that Joffrey Baratheon—or should we say Lannister—is a bastard in more ways than one. Just one look at that smug little face is enough to make us want to rip his eyes out. (Roth Cornet, April 2014)

> Joffrey is arrogant, cowardly, cruel, murderous, sadistic, spoilt, tyrannical, whiny and a pathological liar with delusions of grandeur that he has consistently failed to back up with his actions. And that's on a good day. (Tim Liew, April 2014)

> One of the most hated characters on television in his prime, King Joffrey was our go-to guy for on-screen cruelty. He was a petty, vicious little sadist, and therein lies his saving grace: he thought small. (Gene Bathurst, June 2015)

And when the time came for him to die in "The Lion and the Rose," some fans were actually a little disappointed; it seemed a merely horrendous death by poisoning at your own wedding wasn't enough. Here's just one example of the many of its type, posted in the comments section of Roth Cornet's article, quoted earlier:

> I feel like his death wasn't horrible enough… I wanted him to be slowly disembowelled and his entrails shoved into his mouth as white hot fish hooks were shoved under his nails. (Posted by *TeeZen*, April 2014)

What these reactions show, without the shadow of a doubt, is there are a lot of people who love to hate Joffrey Baratheon. Of course, there are a few fans and critics who see different sides to his character, but the majority of musings tend to be variations on the themes present in the comments above. Questions still remain though: what is responsible for this kind of reaction? And where does this vilification come from?

The Taboo in Vilifying Joffrey

Freud would have been very interested in the characterization of Joffrey Baratheon, but he would have been even more interested in reactions to the Boy King of Westeros from fans and critics of *Game of Thrones*. So, while not trying to speak *for him*, the following is how I believe Freud might write up "The Case of Joffrey Baratheon, Boy King of Westeros":

> *Game of Thrones* is a fantasy drama, set in the distant past, deliberately detaching itself from today's "modern world." Westeros itself is designed to mirror the brutal and visceral urges of humanity, where prohibition is left to individuals, and Kings often win their throne in fits of anger, fury, and bloodlust.
>
> When you consider Joffrey Baratheon's immediate family, he was clearly a spoilt child. He was also the product of, what I would call, a broken taboo: his grandparents were cousins and his parents were siblings. These incestuous acts would completely break the societal taboos that were enacted in the earliest stages of humanity. So, against this backdrop of sexual deviancy, Joffrey Baratheon is conceived and raised, clearly making him prone to similar acts of sexual depravity and violent aggression.
>
> The reaction to Joffrey Baratheon and his behavior in *Game of Thrones* is therefore, in my opinion, one of projection. The audience knows that incest is prohibited; the earliest peoples of the human race made this very much "the law." However, the carnal desire to break taboos remains strong in our unconscious; it's just that most of us are able to successfully repress these urges, redirecting this energy into more morally acceptable behaviors and actions.
>
> I believe the reaction to Joffrey Baratheon is consequently a way of successfully continuing this tradition to repress the unconscious desire to break incest taboos. The Boy King of Westeros was created and conceived through the breaking of a taboo, twice over, and becoming accumulatively more "direct"—that's to say, his grandparents' sexual depravity, being cousins, is then made worse by his parents, who develop this "web of incest," being siblings.

This would have a profound impact on an audience, principally because incest is strictly prohibited in modern society: it is, after all, probably still the *ultimate* taboo. However, a paradox resides in the fact this unspeakable taboo is one which, deep in our unconscious, we actually have an impulse to break. As a result, labeling Joffrey Baratheon as a "vile bastard," suggesting his death wasn't "satisfying enough" or reserving him a "separate level of TV hell" are all ways of successfully repressing these taboo urges.

I would like this to be quite clear: if you, like *TeeZen*, have written on an Internet message board about how vile Joffrey Baratheon was, or compiled one of those meticulous lists of reasons why you hated him, it *doesn't* mean you want to sleep with your brother, sister, or cousin (you can breathe that sigh of relief now . . .). I also want to make it absolutely clear that Freud would likely think in exactly the same way too.

Instead, the almost universal hatred of Joffrey is merely an unconscious projection of these urges, rather than the means to want to live them out in reality. By doing this, *TeeZen*, along with everyone else, is "successfully repressing" these desires, creating a defense mechanism to maintain our sense of societal decency.

Benioff and Weiss, George R.R. Martin before them, and Freud before that, are clearly very aware of the darker side of the human psyche. Despite this analysis of Joffrey Baratheon, some things don't change: his behavior is still vile and deplorable. But the crucial difference is, this "behavior" subtly reminds us of those dark drives and desires Freud thought lived within us all. And because these dark urges are so vehemently prohibited, our hatred of the character becomes a way to successfully channel these desires. Joffrey becomes a place to project them, keeping them securely out of our conscious thought, leaving us safe in the knowledge that our lives will never be like "The Case of Joffrey Baratheon, Boy King of Westeros."

16
Hope for Bastards and Sand Snakes

AURÉLIA DESVEAUX

The *Game of Thrones* story focuses upon the bloodlines of powerful families, or Houses. The members of these families deal with each other according to alliances and grudges inherited from previous generations.

Filiation, the legal system of the transmission of familial recognition, is the concept that determines who belongs to which House, gives social status, and confers a destiny. This legal concept helps us make sense of the *Game of Thrones* story. Never saying its name, filiation is, nevertheless, written all over the story. It shapes, helps, and hinders the personal development of the characters and establishes the landscape the social order.

The beauty of the *Game of Thrones* show comes from its rhythm, which is depicted in terms of contrasts: contrast between the bastards and their 'legitimate' families and the contrast between the wealthy elites and the plebs.

Filiation Rules

It's the family name that lives on.

—TYWIN LANNISTER

Marks of family identification are everywhere in Westeros. Items like sigils, flags, costumes, jewels are made visible in order to show that the social order of filiation is above individuals. Filiation operates as a silent law directing characters. Even the range of colors individuals wear are used as a visual key to identify them with their family.

Marks of filiation on the person run deep and shows itself in genetic characteristics. Hair color is one sign, among others, of this belonging: platine for the Targaryens, brown for the Baratheons, black for the Starks, blond for the Lannisters . . . Any exceptions are meaningful: if Sansa is not black haired, she is the Stark who desires to join another family . . . Cersei and Jaime's children are all blond: an important clue giving mysterious and indirect evidence of their incestuous filiation, a clue which will not be missed by the masses of the people exhausted by the abuses of their leaders.

The system of justice is based on filiation. In the world of *Game of Thrones*, respecting the law is no joke. Because the show depicts all kinds of corruption and deviance, the contrast has to be clear. The very beginning of the show sets the tone: a lad, escaping the Night's Watch, totally scared out of his wits by what he had seen beyond the wall, is caught by Ned Stark's soldiers . . . Ned cuts his head off because he has to enforce the law with these words: "In the name of the King Robert of Baratheon, the first of the name, Kings of the Andals . . . I, Eddard, of the House of Stark, lord of Winterfell, and governor of the North, sentence you to die."

The accusation does not allow any defense: "He swore an oath, law is law, my lady," Master Luwin says . . . The weight of the law is huge and even children like Bran are expected to watch the execution.

Bastard Freedom

Let me give you some advice, bastard. Never forget what you are.

—Tyrion Lannister

The family names of bastards in *Game of Thrones* demonstrate their lack of civilized familial commitment, by suggesting an identification with uncivilized nature: *Snow* is the bastard name in the frozen north and *Sand* is the name at Dorne.

It looks like the bastard's past is covered by an immaculate layer from nature, the snow or the sand is like virgin ground, giving them the freedom to write their own story. This allusion in their name could mean that they belong to Nature itself, in opposition to "Civilized Culture" . . . and the Law of filiation. The figure of the Bastard demonstrates the effects of the concept of filiation, precisely because bastards are deprived of legal family, legitimacy, and social standing.

Consider Jon Snow, the beautiful. His story is so touching, because he is so authentic. We can say that he is not a phony, who is trying to fit in with a familial style but truly embraces a sense of his destiny through the story of his birth. His choice to join the Night's Watch benefits him since it gives him a family to join, one where even his bastard status is wiped away. His freedom of thought comes from the fact that he's unbiased. He's not hindered by the interests of a House. He chooses his own masters. Open-minded, he is able to drive people towards another vision and recognizes new solutions, such as his alliance with the wildlings.

The relationship between Jon Snow and Catelyn Stark is another great dramatic feature. The severity with which she treats him raises a question: how can such a remarkable, fair, loving woman treat him so harshly? The answer could be that she is not free . . . she belongs to an order. The law of filiation requires shame and silence concerning the fact that her husband came back from war with another woman's baby. Accordingly, she has to suffer. She tells Robb's wife, Jeyne Ouestrelin, of the moral battle she experienced when this child entered her circle.

In a complete opposite way, we see another bastard character, Ramsay Snow, who fits the most extreme negative stereotypes concerning bastards. Confusing his imagination with reality, unable to stand in his own skin, and rejecting his bastard status, Ramsay steals the skins of others . . . Somehow, insanity crosses the road of filiation law . . . Furthermore, he ultimately is legitimized by royal decree. His bastard condition will end. Yet, why is he given this opportunity? What accounts for this sudden nobility? This dignity is conferred by Tywin Lannister as a reward for Bolton House's help in the trap of the "Red Wedding" . . . This moment is a critical point. Filiation is clearly in the backdrop of this scenario.

Similarly, the Sand Snakes, the eight bastard daughters of Prince Oberyn Martell are an interesting example because Dorne is not Westeros. Its social values differ. People are "free lovers," meaning that different rules direct social expectations concerning childbearing and the legitimacy of descendants. There is no shame in having or being a 'bastard' in this society.

Symbolically, their nickname "Sand Snake" is an echo of their father's name: "Red Viper" . . . as bastards, they don't wear the name of the House Martell, but have the symbolic part of the name of their father . . . a great wink! They still take pride and honor in their family—but with a difference: the loyalty of the Sand Snakes is to their father himself, rather than to his house. And they're determined to avenge his brutal death. They are free to have their own commitments and not be absorbed into a system.

And last but not least, Tyrion offers a great counter point of the figure of Bastard. He confesses to Jon: "All dwarves are bastards in the eyes of their fathers . . ." This time, bastardness is expressed physically. George Martin is playing with the idea of filiation at many levels!

Jon Snow, Ramsay, and the Sand Snakes: somehow their psychological issues are based on their history with their parents. Outsiders from legitimate filiation, they show the significance of this concept: the alliances, honor, security that accompany filiation . . . But the scenario also shows those who have no familial standing. The common people. The plebs. Here, filiation marks the frontier between two categories of people, the heirs and the other.

No one weeps for spiders or whores.

—LORD VARYS

Behind the social order of filiation is the question of how sexual relationships without descendants to be treated, or relationships consummated without any family ties.

Theon Greyjoy doesn't want to pay Rose, a prostitute he loves, because paying hurts his feelings. She replies: "If you don't get married, you pay." We see that there's no space between a heavy official-political wedding and paid sexual intercourse. These are the only relational options in the civilized order. This lack of freedom undergirds much of the story: Tyrion is obliged to hide his beautiful Shae, while Jon is discovering free love with Ygritte, a wildling, who belongs to another system.

The whores, who are seen in a great many scenes, are strong figures in this fantastic world. In this depiction of society, sexual commerce is a normal part of social life, and whorehouses are a normal part of cities—at least until the High Sparrow gets his way.

In contrast with filiation issues, all seems possible, no rules limit individual fantasy . . . the freedom to contract agreements is wide open, with the risk that persons may suffer heavy abuses and became goods to be sold. Even slavery is practiced as part of this social system.

As usual, the show bluntly explores even the most extreme consequences of this situation. When no social or legal limit exists power or money can drive everything. Joffrey can torture and kill prostitutes if he wishes.

The rules of the games are clear. From one side, there is an over-weighted moral order intended to preserve legitimate families. On the other side, there is a free and risky market where people themselves can be sold, without any legal rules to protect them . . . and what divides this order is the concept of filiation!

Filiation in Our World

In today's world, the symbols of filiation, like blazons or seals, used in Europe for centuries by aristocratic families are hidden, stored in drawers, or museums. They have become amusing artifacts of the past. Tribunals are no longer busy with cases of filiation: endless hearings in order to establish or to contest a filiation claim.

Until some decades ago, the consequences of filiation were huge: in terms of social status as well as in terms of heritage. The result of such a trial could change an entire life. Today, this question is hardly discussed anymore in courts of justice.

Today, the law enforces equality between people and forbids discrimination. The evolution of our values drove us toward more social justice. Nowadays having a child in or out of wedlock is legally irrelevant (at least in France, since 1972), and half of the children are born out of wedlock. Fortunately, children are no longer punished for the fault of their parents, when they were excluded from their family just because of the lack of legal bonds between their parents. The moral order does not penalize such innocent ones, as it once did, as depicted in *Game of Thrones*.

Meanwhile, the tremendous worldwide success of *Game of Thrones* reveals a nostalgia for those social constructions built on the sense of honor and acceptance of each person's allotted place. This is far removed from where we are in today's western societies, seeking absolute freedom, translated through our fascination with the power of money, bringing any issue down to the question of paying. By the way, what is the Lannister's maxim? "A Lannister always pays his debt." Here we are.

Game of Throne shows us some features of our civilization as the negative of a photograph: the violent gap between the heavy burden of traditions and the lack of basic rules protecting the human person from abuses drives us to question our own blind quest for individualistic power.

It's no surprise that traditional religions are, unfortunately, returning with a vengeance! Now once again, we need to better establish universal laws to protect people from the cruel ravages of social conformity.

17

Sex, Consent, and Rape in Westeros

Lori J. Underwood

> What is honor compared to a woman's love? . . . We are only human, and the gods have fashioned us for love. That is our great glory, and our great tragedy.

When Maester Aemon speaks these words to Jon Snow in *A Game of Thrones*, they're discussing the importance of the vow of chastity taken by the Brothers of the Night's Watch. The meaning of his words, however, is far more profound. We are social creatures who are drawn to others of our kind.

"The gods have fashioned us for love," but the disposition to love does not comprise the extent of our nature. There are also drives to power, vanity, honor and duty. Taken in sum, we become beings for whom the need for love can be "our great glory, and our great tragedy."

The glory and tragedy of love play out on a grand scale throughout the *Song of Ice and Fire* and its corresponding television series, *A Game of Thrones*. Certainly one of the most tragic events in an intimate relationship is rape. There are at least three central relationships in the *Game of Thrones* series in which the issue of rape arises. These relationships occur

between Sansa Stark and Ramsay Bolton

between Daenerys Targaryen and Khal Drogo

and

between Cersei and Jaime Lannister.

There are two distinct kinds of consent that must be considered in regard to the determination of rape. While in the modern era, there is a tendency to focus more exclusively on legal consent, it was not nearly so complex in the medieval world upon which the *Game of Thrones* universe is based. *Game of Thrones* source material suggests that its legal standards for consent are consistent with those of the fifteenth-century period on which it is based.

In the fifteenth century, under the Church "doctrine of conjugal debt," a wife's body belonged to her husband, and she had no right to refuse him sex. This doctrine of Canon law was incorporated into legal codes throughout Europe well into the twentieth century. It gained its authority from biblical descriptions of the marital relationship. "The husband should give to his wife her conjugal rights, and likewise the wife to her husband. For the wife does not rule over her own body, but the husband does; likewise the husband does not rule over his own body, but the wife does" (1 Corinthians 7:3).

Given this description of spousal dominion over the marriage bed, legal consent is easily defined. Drogo did not, at any point legally rape Daenerys, nor did Ramsay legally rape Sansa. On the other hand all of the sexual interactions between Cersei and Jaime, however mutually desired, were legally impermissible. Just as all spouses had a legal right to one another's bodies, so to have sex with another man's wife was a crime. To have sex with your sister was the additional crime of incest. To have sex with the king's wife was treason. In sum, there was no legal standing for Jaime and Cersei to have sex with or without consent. In fact, Cersei had no standing to consent.

The Moral Standard of Consent

Having established the boundaries of legal consent in *Game of Thrones*, we can look at the far more complex question of moral consent in these relationships. Whereas standards for legal consent evolve and change with societal standards and alterations in legal codes, there are fundamental standards for moral consent grounded in basic standards of human dignity and agency and the moral obligations that follow from those standards and the recognition of that agency.

Here are a few key points about the complex issue of moral consent.

1. Moral consent covers actions that it would not be practically feasible to cover under legal consent. Given the standards of a society, there are numerous means of obtaining sex that, while perfectly legal, are nonetheless immoral. For modern society, these include sex obtained through fraud or coercion that does not rise to levels that would constitute a legal infraction of consent. In his book, *Consent to Sexual Relations* (2003), Alan Wertheimer provides some excellent examples to illuminate this distinction. Consider a Gynecologist who tells a patient that he is inserting a medical instrument into her vagina, but instead inserts his penis. This is a case of sex by fraud that is not only immoral, but also illegal. Contrast that with someone who says he is in love so a young lady will yield to sex (she is otherwise unwilling and he is not in fact in love with her). She consented to sex on the basis of fraud, but it would not be reasonable to prosecute such cases.

2. Moral consent may concern compromises of the dignity and autonomy of victims of sexually immoral acts rather than solely physical and psychological harm.

3. Moral consent allows us to distinguish between the wrongfulness of actions and the harmfulness of actions. Some believe that these pick out the same sorts of actions (others don't), but the concepts themselves are nonetheless distinct. An action's wrongfulness consists in its violation of a moral rule. An action's harmfulness consists in its effects on a member of a moral community.

First consider the example of sex obtained through fraud or coercion that are immoral but would not be illegal. Fraud is used to lead Sansa to consent to marry Ramsay, which makes her vulnerable to sexual assault. In this case, the fraud does not come from Ramsay himself, but from the negotiator of the marriage contract. She is convinced to marry Ramsay by Littlefinger, who has 'rescued' her from King's Landing and has promised to protect her. She later realizes that he must have known what would happen to her.

Did you know about Ramsay? If you didn't know, you're an idiot. If you did know, you're my enemy. Would you like to hear about our wedding night? . . . Maybe you did know about Ramsay all along. ("The Door")

In a society like Westeros, would it be illegal to arrange a marriage for a woman and not tell her that the groom was a known sociopath? Strictly speaking, no it would not. Is it immoral? Such fraud by omission is demonstrably immoral under any viable moral theory.

As for the two other couples, fraud and coercion play differing roles. Dany feels strong coercion to 'please' Drogo in order to fulfill her family duty and her brother's wishes. Viserys convinces her that they cannot return home without her being offered to Drogo in exchange for an army. "So tell me, sweet sister, how do we go home? . . . We go home with an army. With Khal Drogo's army. I would let his whole tribe fuck you, all forty thousand men and their horses too, if that's what it took" ("Winter is Coming"). So, while fraud does not play a key role in the Dany-Drogo relationship, coercion does.

While fraud is a key component of Jaime and Cersei's relationship, neither fraud nor non-physical coercion plays an important role in their sexual interactions. Their fraud is a shared endeavor, and is directed outwardly to hide rather than facilitate their sexual relationship.

Disregarding Consent

An example given by Alan Wertheimer illustrates both the issue of compromise of autonomy and the wrongfulness-harmfulness distinction. Suppose that B is a quadriplegic who cannot express her wishes regarding sex. B very much desires for A to engage in sex with her, but makes no performative indication thereof. A has no way of knowing whether or not the act in which he is engaging is consensual, and, based on his behavior, it does not appear that he cares. By most reasonable accounts, his action is wrong. Why? He completely disregards the status of her consent. It is this disregarding that leads to harm.

Is his action harmful, given that B desires for A to engage in sex with her, and it is simply a physical limitation that prevents her from behaviorally showing that consent? This is a more complex question. In the context of the harmfulness traditionally associated with rape and particularly in terms of a violation of consent (and separate from the wrongness of A not taking consent into account), it does not seem that B was harmed by having her autonomy violated.

The question of her dignity is more complex. It is a violation of her dignity that A does not take her consent into account, because A does not account for B's assent to sex. The key issue is not his violation of her consent, but rather his disregard of her right to grant it. A acts as if B is merely an object for his desire rather than also being a subject in herself with moral agency and corresponding moral rights to self-determination in her choices, including her choice to engage in (or refrain from engaging in) sexual congress.

Mutual Recognition

Reciprocal subjectivity, the recognition that each individual engaging in a behavioral exchange (in this case a sexual one) is a moral subject, and not merely an object is a necessary but not sufficient condition for a sexual act to be morally permissible. The harmfulness in the quadriplegic example lies not in B's desire, but in A's total disregard of her dignity and subjectivity. She is a complete object for him. Her consent, were she able to express it, would be meaningless to him precisely because he does not regard it as an important factor in deciding upon his course of action.

Some may argue that a person has the right to consent to be objectified, but that is different. I may consent to be an object of someone's desire if I am also a moral subject for that person, for I can be both things simultaneously. I cannot, however consent to be something I am not, a being devoid of moral agency. Why reciprocal subjectivity? It is important that the subjectivity be reciprocal because each must recognize the moral worth of their partner and their own moral agency. It is necessary that consent be given, received and acted upon for a sexual act to be morally permissible.

How, then does this necessary condition apply to *Game of Thrones*? The easiest case in which to apply this standard is that of Sansa and Ramsay. It's clear from his behavior that Ramsay considers Sansa to be nothing more than an object. On their wedding night, Ramsay forces Theon/Reek to watch as he rips Sansa's clothes from her body and forcibly has sex with her. "Oh, no, no, no. You stay here, Reek. You watch. Do I need to ask a second time? I hate asking a second time. Reek. . . . I told you to watch. You've known Sansa since she was a girl. Now watch her become a woman" ("Unbowed, Unbent, Unbroken").

It's later revealed that Ramsay has beat, cut and violated Sansa in every possible way he could think of without harming her face because he needs her face to make his claim on Winterfell and the North. As Sansa told Littlefinger, "He never hurt my face. He needed my face, the face of Ned Stark's daughter. But the rest of me, he did what he liked with the rest of me as long as I could still give him an heir" ("The Door"). Ramsay's words and deeds make it clear that he sees Sansa only as an object. Thus their sexual relations are, in all cases, rape.

The dynamic between Drogo and Daenerys is complex and changes quickly. At the beginning of their marriage, evidence suggests that Drogo sees Daenerys as an object. He refuses to look her in the face during sex, and he does not attempt to communicate with her in any way (though the language barrier explains some of this).

Her willingness or unwillingness to engage in sex seems to hold no meaning to Drogo whatsoever. This attitude is consistent with the Dothraki world-view. Therefore, it's reasonable to conclude that although there is legal consent, morally, the early sexual interactions between Drogo and Daenerys are rape (based on lack of reciprocal subjectivity).

Daenerys learns from a slave how to be intimate with Drogo in a way that will compel him to see her as a subject. She insists when they are intimate that he look at her, that he see her as a person, as a subject fully capable of participating in a relationship with him. "No. No. Tonight I would look upon your face" ("The King's Road"). The results are transformative of their relationship and of the moral status of their sexual relations.

At one point, Daenerys is saved from a near assassination by Jorah. Drogo's reaction demonstrates that he has come to love Daenerys and view her as a subject of intrinsic value. "Moon of my life. Are you hurt? Jorah the Andal, choose any horse you wish. It's yours. I make this gift to you for what you did" ("You Win or You Die"). Daenerys becomes beloved to Drogo, and he is willing to demonstrate his love for her. When they are together, she legally and morally consents to their union.

Rape within a Love Relationship

The issue of moral consent is, perhaps, most complex for Jaime and Cersei. Leaving a multitude of moral questions aside, let's focus on the issue of reciprocal subjectivity. In most of their relationship, this condition seems satisfied. However, there is one instance that must be addressed. This, of course, is the infamous scene by Joffrey's body. Jaime and Cersei are devastated by his death. Cersei blames Tyrion and wants revenge, and Jaime goes into a rage at her cruelty and forces himself on her. "Jaime: Why have the gods made me love a hateful woman? Cersei: Jaime, not here, please. Please . . . Stop. No. . . . (*Crying*) It's not right, . . . Jaime: I don't care" ("Breaker of Chains").

Jaime admits that he hears Cersei withholding her consent to sex, but he doesn't care that she does not consent. At the same time, he professes his love for her. This is a rape, for it is sex in the absence of moral consent. It is not however, a violation of reciprocal subjectivity. Cersei is not a mere object for Jaime. He loves her. Yet he is so angry with her that he is willing to act in a manner contrary to that love. He is willing to violate her dignity and autonomy to demonstrate his anger. While reciprocal subjectivity is necessary for a sexual act to be morally permissible, this example illustrates why it is not sufficient.

No one ever claimed that life, or death, are easy in the *Game of Thrones* universe. Just as the politics are complex and dangerous, so are the intimate relationships. One issue that inevitably arises when politics and intimate relationships are mixed is the issue of consent. We've seen that not only must there be the presence of consent in the mind of both parties, both parties must also regard one another as subjects. In other words, not only must there be consent, the person receiving the consent must view their partner's consent as morally significant and necessary.

This in no way resolves all the debated issues about consent, but it is a step in the right direction. If it is true that "the gods have fashioned us for love," then to behave as if we are merely objects to be used and disposed of surely sows the seeds for tragedy rather than glory.

V

I Swear before the Old Gods and the New

18
Gods and Beetles

KODY W. COOPER

The World of Ice and Fire is religiously pluralistic. As Salladhor Saan reports, "I've been all over the world, my boy, and everywhere I go, people tell me about the true Gods. They all think they've found the right one" ("The Night Lands").

There is monotheism, as in the Faith's belief in the Seven as various expressions of One God. There is polytheism, as in the North's belief in the Old Gods. Yet, for all its pluralism, there is a common belief animating most of the people in this world: there exists a more-than-human source of meaning and existence, and this entity or entities is or are related to the world in a causally significant way.

But is Westerosi-Essosi theistic belief justified? Here's a standard objection to theistic belief, expressed by Jaime Lannister.

As Jaime sits imprisoned, Catelyn confronts him. She declares that he will rot in the lowest of the seven hells for his crimes, by the just judgment of the Gods. Jaime mockingly replies: "What Gods are those? The trees your husband prayed to? Where were the trees when his head was getting chopped off? If your Gods are real and if they are just, why is the world so full of injustice?" ("Fire and Blood").

Jaime expresses a classic objection to theistic belief voiced by philosophers from Epicurus through David Hume, to J.L. Mackie: How could beings sufficiently good and powerful to merit worship as God or gods exist in a world rife with evil? For, if these beings were entirely good, they would want to prevent evil in the world; and, if they were all-powerful, they could prevent it.

In the World of Ice and Fire we can uncover three solutions to the problem of evil that correspond to three pictures of divine causal relation to the world: Manichean divine patronage, voluntarism, and humanism. Let's first consider the reality of evil before turning to these various responses to it.

Evil in the World of Ice and Fire

There is evil in the World of Ice and Fire. Evil has two dimensions from any particular individual's perspective: events *outside of* and events *under* that person's control.

History suggests that there has always been evil *outside of* any individual's control. When King Robert speaks wistfully of the halcyon days of his youth, Renly rhetorically asks which days precisely were so rosy?

> The ones where half of Westeros fought the other half and millions died? Or before that, when the Mad King slaughtered women and babies because the voices in his head told him they deserved it? Or way before that, when dragons burned whole cities to the ground? ("A Golden Crown")

The stability of the king's peace quickly dissipates after Robert dies. Meanwhile, there are ominous prophecies and evidence of a coming Long Night, when winter, darkness, and death will cover the globe.

Joffrey, Ramsay, and Littlefinger are alike in that they seem to have no remorse for their sundry evil acts, which were *under their control* to do or not to do. On the other hand, Catelyn, Ser Jorah, Jaime, and Tyrion express remorse for their sins in a way that presupposes free choice and accountability. As Tyrion puts it in a public confession: "My crimes and sins are beyond counting. I have lied and cheated, gambled and whored" ("A Golden Crown").

Those repentant of the evil they have committed seek redemption through honorable works. Some join the Night's Watch, an order closely tied to religious belief. Jon and Sam say their vows before a weirwood tree, calling upon the Old Gods to "Hear my words, and bear witness to my vow" ("A Golden Crown"). Sam reminds Jon of these words when he seeks vengeance for Ned Stark, and Jon realizes that Ned would rather have him honor the gods and his promise.

Others seek redemption through The Seven. Catelyn weaves a prayer wheel to the Seven in supplication for her sons, and seeks forgiveness for having hated and shunned Jon Snow. Even the Hound comes to find healing and peace by joining a cloister of holy brothers of The Seven, who seek penance through prayer, work, and silence (*A Feast for Crows*).

Hence, religion practically functions as a balm to heal the broken and as a sanction to live honorably. But sometimes it fosters fanaticism, as in the cases of Lancel Lannister and Selyse Baratheon who follow the High Sparrow and Melisandre, respectively. Let us turn to consider how the Melisandre's faith responds to the problem of evil.

Manichean Divine Patronage

The divine patronage view holds that God favors and protects a specific temporal-political order. Divine patronage is given to the members of the client city on the condition that they perform the proper religious rites. Divine affliction is then visited upon the enemies of the client city. This view is expressed by Melisandre, who sees herself as an agent of divine justice. The divine patronage view thus adopts a *punitive* interpretation of evil—hardship, suffering, and death are seen as the just deserts of the sinful enemies of the client faithful.

In the faith of R'hllor, Divine patronage is Manichean. Manicheism is a dualistic philosophy that attributes evil to a malicious deity in eternal war with a good deity. The theory of Divine patronage is not always Manichean, but it often is, and it is in the faith of R'hllor.

Melisandre repeatedly reminds us of the reality of evil in the world. "The night is long and full of terrors." R'hllor, the Lord of Light, protects his faithful from the darkness. Hence, all other gods are false idols, and Melisandre ritualistically burns effigies and worshippers of the Seven, calling on R'hllor's blessing in return.

Melisandre believes that Stannis—and later, Jon—is Azor Ahai reborn, a deliverer anointed by R'hllor to save his people. She explains R'hllor's patronage to Davos: "There's only one God ... and he protects *only those who serve him*" ("Garden of Bones").

Melisandre frames the choice for or against R'hllor as a choice between good and evil, between R'hllor and the Other who must not be named. The red priestess thus clarifies that hers is a *dualistic* religion, in which there are *two* gods: "a god of light and love and joy and a god of darkness, evil, and fear. Eternally at war" ("Lion and Rose"). This is a Manichean theology.

Yet, as St. Augustine (354–430) demonstrated, this would be impossible, supposing the all-powerfulness and complete benevolence of God. For, since all things were created by God (omnipotence), and since only good things can come from God (omnibenevolence), it follows that evil is not a substance—not its own created thing—and therefore cannot *be* a rival god. Evil is rather a corruption in the creature. Hence, Melisandre has either misunderstood the true nature of R'hllor and evil, or she has admitted that R'hllor lacks omnipotence or omnibenevolence.

To lack these qualities, Augustine says, would be to fail to be worthy of highest praise and devotion. Moreover, Augustine points out that afflictions are not necessarily punishments, for sometimes the afflicted are actually innocent, as in the case of Shireen. Additionally, as Lady Olenna points out to the crusading High Sparrow, half the population deserves punishment for breaking the sacred laws. The punitive model is incapable of equitable application. Manichean divine patronage fails to be rationally satisfying.

God's Freedom

A second theological response to the problem of evil is that of voluntarism. In contrast to Manicheism, this view maintains the absolute uniqueness and power of God. In the history of philosophy, this view was formulated by William of Ockham (1287–1347), who critically responded to St. Thomas Aquinas's (1225–1274) attempt to reconcile Augustinianism (which tended to emphasize God's power over nature) with Aristotelian rationalism (which tended to emphasize the autonomous order of nature).

Ockham thought that Aquinas's synthesis would shackle God. He argued that God is radically omnipotent and therefore radically free of any constraint—so free that God, by his command, could make it virtuous to perform evil deeds.

A hint of this view is apparent in Selyse Baratheon's claim that "No act done in service of the Lord of Light can ever be a sin" ("Kissed by Fire"). But, as we have seen, the Lord of Light is not really omnipotent, if the Other is truly independent of R'hllor. The voluntaristic understanding of the divine is voiced symbolically by Tyrion to Jaime as he sits in his prison cell, wrongfully accused of regicide.

Tyrion reflects on his impending trial by combat: "Deciding a man's guilt or innocence in the eyes of the gods by having two other men hack each other to pieces. Tells you something about the gods." Tyrion recalls their cousin Orson Lannister, who had been left "simple" after being dropped on his head as an infant. Orson spent all of his days smashing beetles, punctuated only by grunts of "Kuh!" and "Smash the Beetles!" Tyrion was driven by a curiosity: why did Orson smash all of those beetles? As Tyrion observed Orson, he became convinced that Orson's beetle-smashing was not mindless, but reasoned and purposive. Tyrion became obsessed with Orson and his beetles:

> It was horrible that these beetles should be dying for no reason . . . It filled me with dread. Piles and piles of them. Years and years of them. How many countless living and crawling things . . . In my dreams I found myself standing on a beach made of beetle husks stretching as far as the eye could see. I woke up crying, weeping for their shattered little bodies. ("The Mountain and the Viper")

Tyrion is allegorically expressing his metaphysical wonder about divine causality and evil in the world in the person of Orson (God) and the beetles (all creatures). Tyrion's trial by combat is one of countless truthmakers of Jaime's claim that "Every day around the world, men, women, and children are murdered by the score" ("The Mountain and the Viper"). People stand in relation to God as the beetles do to Orson—we are completely at his mercy.

Tyrion explicitly maintains that it is very difficult to believe that everything is meaningless. The history of the world is like a book. Even if, like Davos, we struggle to read it, that does not mean that the scribbles on the page are meaningless. But this implies an orderer of history, an Author of the story. But then it seems to follow that this Author slaughters creatures by the score, purposefully.

We find ourselves questioning the Author further: why? And we find that this question is unanswerable, and that the Author's purposes are radically mysterious. Hence voluntarism's solution to the problem of evil. As a radically omnipotent Being, God's affliction of persons can neither be understood nor morally blamed.

The problem with this picture is that it is open to a devastating objection, voiced by Tyrion: "The Lord of Light wants his enemies burned, the Drowned God wants them drowned. Why are all the Gods such vicious c—ts?" ("The Prince of Winterfell"). Tyrion's moral sense is too strong to be persuaded by voluntarism. In a less vulgar way, this was essentially the response of the Thomists to Ockham. As Francisco Suarez (1548–1617) argued, the idea that God can command us to commit evil acts is absurd, because it is incompatible with God's goodness. For the most evil thing God could command is that we hate Him. But, it is impossible to command someone to hate that which is intrinsically the most loveable thing in the world, goodness itself.

But Suarez's reply assumes that God's existence as all-powerful and all-good can be vindicated. Tyrion's beetle story suggests precisely the opposite. The rampant evil in the world indicates the irrationality of belief in divine goodness and therefore any divine order at all. Tyrion tells Jorah he has chosen disbelief ("Unbent, Unbowed, Unbroken").

Humanism and the Free-Will Defense

Consider the humanistic response to evil, expressed in various ways by Tyrion. The humanist believes that the world is what *we* make of it, by our free choices, not the gods. Humanists tend to order their lives by unaided reason. In their view, evil is just the result of dumb or depraved choices made by persons. The job of the humanist on this view is to mitigate evil as much as he can. This is an *existential* response to the problem of evil, dramatized in the greatest literature written on the subject, from the Book of Job to *The Brothers Karamazov*.

In his choice to travel to Meereen, Tyrion seeks to do good *independent* of faith and religious orders. Similarly, Jaime chooses to help Brienne; Jorah decides to follow Dany; Theon decides to help Sansa and Yara (Asha). The important thing about these decisions on the humanist account is that *they were truly free choices*. The humanist affirmation of free will provides the key premise that can answer Jaime's challenge.

In response to Jaime, Catelyn—who like Ned and Jon is a religious humanist—replies that evil exists *because of men like you*. This is *not* an affirmation of determinism. For Catelyn asks Jaime to choose a different path, the path of honor, and return her girls from King's Landing in exchange for his freedom. This request only makes sense given the belief that human beings truly have freedom of choice.

Hence humanism in its believing and nonbelieving expressions provides the crucial premise to answer the problem of evil. This is a classic argument rooted in Augustine and recently developed by philosopher Alvin Plantinga. The argument is that the world is, on the whole, better off if its creatures are significantly free. But they cannot be significantly free if they do not have the capacity to choose evil. For, God wills our fulfillment, flourishing, happiness, our moral good. But the moral good *can only come through free choice*, and the will is not really free if it can't choose evil. Hence, the only way God could ensure there would be no evil in the world would be to create automatons who lack the capacity for free choice, for genuine love, and therefore genuine happiness.

Still, Jaime's objection could be pressed, in light of his point that scores of *children* suffer daily. As the atheist Ivan Karamazov argued, the free-will defense seems only to suffice to explain the suffering that attends *adults* in their wanton choices. Ivan recounts stories of sadistic cruelty inflicted on Russian children that would make even Ramsay Bolton blush. From the murder of the Targaryen babes to the suffering of the Starks, *A Song of Ice and Fire* is a story deeply concerned with the problem of children suffering and dying like Orson's beetles. Ivan's objection is that no greater good of the whole could be justified by the suffering of a single innocent child.

Humanism offers an *existential* response to this objection, in a political and personal mode. The political seeks to use power to mitigate the suffering of the innocent as in rule of the Starks, Tyrion, Dany, and the Martells. The very cornerstone of Dornish domestic policy (before the Sand Snakes' rebellion) was: "We don't hurt little girls in Dorne."

Tyrion provides an example of the personal existential response in how he uses his knowledge and power to help the weak. When Bran lies in a coma, a child victim of adults' evil choices, Cersei and Jaime remark that the suffering of the maimed is senseless. Tyrion replies that "only the gods know for certain" what the outcome of suffering will be. Tyrion is more hopeful for the grotesques—bastards, cripples, and broken things—because "Death is so final, whereas life . . . Life is full of possibilities ("The Kings Road"). Bran lacked the will to live; but through the encouragement of Tyrion and help from his friends, he turns the evil of his deformity toward the good end of joining the Three Eyed Raven in the war against evil.

These existential responses mirror those of Ivan Karamazov's deeply pious and humanistic brother, Alyosha. Alyosha effects a reconciliation with a terminally ill child and his estranged friends, sharing in the burden of their suffering and communicating good through acts of self-giving love.

Justified Theistic Belief

Theistic belief for religious humanists is not defeated by the reality of evil. Although the existence of children in a cruel world enhances the poignancy and urgency of the objection, it poses no *logical* contradiction to the existence of a omnipotent and omnibenevolent God.

On balance, are there positive reasons enfolded in the story of the world to believe in the divine? Or is it a tale "told by an idiot, full of sound and fury, signifying nothing," as Shakespeare's Macbeth puts it?

Some skeptics in the World of Ice and Fire come to change their mind on this point. Jorah tells Tyrion that he used to be a skeptic like him—until he saw Dany and her three dragons miraculously emerge unburnt from the flames: "It's hard to be a cynic after that" ("Unbent, Unbowed, Unbroken"). Dany (or the resurrected Jon Snow) might be Azor Ahai, the divinely-sent hero and deliverer prophesied across many religious traditions.

For humanistic believers in a Transcendent Source of meaning and existence, who see the miracles as evidence that the divine has sent prophets and saviors into the world, Qyburn is wrong that religious belief is "the death of reason" ("Hardhome"). For religious humanists, faith and reason are seen as partners in the existential response to the problem of evil: to respond to cruelty with love.

19

Prophetic Foreknowledge in *Game of Thrones*

STEPH RENNICK

Gorghan of Old Ghis once wrote that a prophecy is like a treacherous woman. She takes your member in her mouth, and you moan with the pleasure of it and think, how sweet, how fine, how good this is . . . and then her teeth snap shut and your moans turn to screams. That is the nature of prophecy, said Gorghan. Prophecy will bite your prick off every time.

—*A Feast for Crows*, Chapter 45

When we consider stories that contain prophecies, it's often assumed—by characters and ourselves—that if someone knows the future, this means the future is somehow fixed or inevitable: it is predestined (we need only make two—generally uncontroversial—assumptions about knowledge: that knowing something entails you believe it, and you can only know something that is true).

We like to think of the future as open, as something we can mold or shape, and this seems incompatible with the possibility of true prophecy. While we're normally happy to accept that we can know things about the past and that this knowledge merely reflects the way the past was (it does not confine the past), it would be different—we think—to know the future. The past, after all, is over and done with (or at least beyond our control, as Bran discovers in his weirwood visions). The future, on the other hand, is still up to us. We're free to do something about it, and it is this very freedom that true prophecy seems to threaten.

151

You Will Do It but You Didn't Have To

What we mean by 'free' is a matter of great philosophical debate: it might require the ability to act otherwise than we in fact do (as the Libertarians and New Dispositionalists suggest), having the right kind of control over our actions (as in Agent-Causation and Event-Causation theories), acting in accordance with our desires and our values (Mesh theories) or responsively to our reasons (Reason-responsive accounts). It doesn't matter which of the main schools of thought about free will you prefer—true prophecy, at least of the kind in *Game of Thrones*, is no threat to any of them. To demonstrate this, we need to make an important philosophical distinction, between something that will happen, and something that must happen (keep in mind that many of George R.R. Martin's prophecies are even weaker that this; they describe events that merely might happen). In *A Game of Thrones*, prophecies aren't magical fates woven by their very utterance (except, perhaps, in the self-fulfilling cases we'll get to shortly). The prophecies describe future events; they don't dictate them. This distinction is crucial.

For instance, if it is foreknown that you will buy this book, then you will buy this book, and no one or nothing will prevent this from occurring. After all, one can only know something if it is true. However, you did not *have* to buy it, and had you chosen otherwise, it would not have been the case that you bought it (and the person who claimed to know you would, would have been mistaken, or instead would have known that you would not buy it). The same goes for the rebirth of Azor Ahai, the fate of Jon Snow, and all the other prophetic dreams and visions in *Game of Thrones*. To see how this works—and why it's not a problem for free will—let's consider nonmagical, non-prophetic foreknowledge, the kind we often take ourselves to have.

You Know Some Things, Jon Snow

You might know that you will watch Season Seven of *Game of Thrones* (because you intend to), that your best friend will watch Season Seven (because they told you so), or that the show's theme tune will remain the same (because it has done so reliably thus far, just like you know the sun will come up tomorrow). Unlike prophecies, these sorts of ordinary cases don't worry us: it seems clear that your knowing the sun will come up will not fix it so that it will be the case that the sun comes up. Nor does it prevent the sun not coming up. Similarly, your knowing that you will watch Season Seven does not mean that you could not have done otherwise. Of course, your claim to know might be right—it might report something true about the future—but it didn't have to be. Your watching isn't an inevitability.

Generally speaking, accounts of ordinary knowledge are fallibilist. A person's beliefs don't have to actually be true to be sufficient for knowledge (along with whatever other criteria your preferred theory of knowledge requires, such as strong evidence or justification). For example, if you believe you will watch the next season, and satisfy the other required criteria, and then come the premiere you do watch, we would be inclined to say that you knew you would: you had ordinary foreknowledge. Yet, you could have been proven wrong (by, for instance, the start of a zombie apocalypse and resulting lack of television), even though as things turned out, you weren't.

Prophecies and Visions

But prophetic foreknowledge seems more troubling. Often in these prophecies, the seer has direct access to the future, they can witness it—such as Melisandre looking into the fire, or Jojen and Bran's green dreams. Rather than the seeming 'guesses' or 'predictions' of ordinary foreknowledge, such prophecies reveal knowledge gained through senses and experience—the seer sees the future as it unfolds.

But does true prophecy lead to the sort of irksome inevitability that makes us worry about our freedom? Does it mean that we couldn't have acted otherwise, that our actions are out of our control, or that our reasons and desires have no power? No more than knowledge of things going on around us right now! Just as in ordinary foreknowledge cases, the seer's knowledge does not fix events in a certain way, or prevent them happening differently: it just reports how things happened to occur.

So in Season Three, when Jojen Reed sees Jon Snow surrounded by the wildlings, it is not that Jojen's dreaming the events means that they must have occurred, but rather that Jojen just so happened to see those events because they occurred. They might not have—Snow might have acted differently, or made different choices—and if they had not, Jojen would have seen something else; after all, it is Snow's actions that determine the content of Jojen's visions, not the other way around.

Also notice that many of the prophecies in *Game of Thrones* are fallible, either because they are misinterpreted or they depict something that may yet be averted: when someone claims to know that something will occur, they could have gotten it wrong. For instance, Melisandre confuses Alys Karstark with Arya Stark in a vision, and Jojen sees the Stark boys dead at Theon's feet.

A particularly striking example is the Dothraki prophecy about The Stallion Who Mounts the World, which is thought to apply to Daenerys's son Rhaego, and thus can seemingly no longer come true. If a seer makes a true prophecy, then the events foretold will come true. But no prophecy has to be true, it just happens to be, and if it is, then no one did (as opposed to could) make it otherwise. If the prophecy is false, then the seer does not know what will occur, either because they are mistaken in their vision, or because they prophesy something different after all.

In other words, while it is true that if a prophet knew a future event would come about, then it will come about—such as Jojen foreseeing the deaths of several men at the hands of the Ironborn—there is nothing necessary about the prophecy being true: it didn't have to be (Bran recognizes this when he tries to avert it). Likewise, when I read a history book, if it's true, then the events it describes did occur.

But its being a true description doesn't fix or constrain the past; true history books don't have some special power to make the past a certain way—they just report the way the past was. Likewise, true prophecies don't fix or constrain the future, they just report the way it happens to be (and it could have been different, and the prophecy have been false—or describing a different future). This is a common response—in the actual world—to worries about God's foreknowledge; it's not that you have to do what God knows you will, but rather that God knows whatever it is you (freely) decide to do.

We might think that prophecies entail something stronger than this, that if future events are known, they are necessary; they must happen, rather than that they merely will happen. Perhaps we think that Jojen Reed isn't exaggerating when he claims that his visions always come true, maybe he's infallible and we're doomed to be unfree—we can't do otherwise than he foretells, our reasons and desires are irrelevant to what comes about. It might very well be the case that the world of *Game of Thrones* is such that certain events will happen no matter what, that events are fated in freedom-depriving fashion. But in that case, what difference does the prophecy make? Events would be fixed no matter what, and the characters would be unfree either way. Unless we think of prophecies as magical causes that set the future in stone—and given that visions of the future are treated the same way as visions of the past in *A Song of Ice and Fire*, for instance Bran's weirwood visions, this would be rather arbitrary—they shouldn't have any impact on our free will. This would be cold comfort for those who value free will, as your fate would be inescapable, prophesied or otherwise.

You Did It Because You Knew You Would

But what if characters act differently having heard the prophecy than they would have otherwise? Take Azor Ahai. It is prophesied that he will be reborn amidst salt and smoke, and wield a flaming sword called Lightbringer (in *Game of Thrones*, Azor Ahai and the Prince who was Promised are treated interchangeably, although things are not so clear-cut in *A Song of Ice and Fire*).

According to Melisandre, Stannis Baratheon is the promised one, and she acts to bring this about, enchanting his sword with magical flame (in *Game of Thrones*, she has him pull it from the fire). Thus the prophecy influences events, it is potentially self-fulfilling; if Melisandre had not heard it, or had interpreted it differently, the outcome may likewise have been different. In this case, and repeated throughout the series, the prophecy itself is vague and incomplete, and thus easily misunderstood—it lends itself to two or more possible interpretations and it is potentially this quality that makes it self-fulfilling. While Melisandre's interpretation of the prophecy is that it applies to Stannis, her visions show only 'snow'. Meanwhile, in Volantis, another Red Priestess claims that Daenerys is the savior reborn.

Self-fulfilling prophecies are self-fulfilling because it is the actions of a character upon hearing the prophecy that makes them come true. An interesting feature of those in *Game of Thrones* is that characters are often willing to comply with such prophecies, rather than trying to avoid them (unlike in other popular texts, from *Buffy the Vampire Slayer* to *Kung Fu Panda*, and the classical *Oedipus Rex*). If Stannis really is Azor Ahai reborn, then his filling the role has—at least in part— been caused by him (and Melisandre) hearing and going along with the prophecy. If this hadn't been the case, it's not clear that the events would have come about.

This is particularly worth noting when we worry about free will. After all, it is not solely the existence of the prophecy that causes events to unfold in the way foretold. In self-fulfilling cases, it is characters believing the prophecy which ensures it ultimately comes true. So rather than this being an example of fatalism at work, it is the opposite: rather than future events happening no matter what the characters do, these events occur because of what they do.

Foreknown but Free

Some of the prophecies in *Game of Thrones* are false, and others are true but misunderstood, or only true because they are believed and, presumably freely, acted upon. But what about those that are neither wrong nor misunderstood?

At worst, true prophecies describe the future as it will be, and might influence how it comes to pass (in the self-fulfilling cases). But it still might not be obvious why that's not a threat to our freedom. True prophecy seems most threatening to accounts of free will requiring alternative possibilities—those accounts which require us to choose between different options in order to be free. After all, if someone knows what will happen, how can there be room for choice? If there's only one option—the future depicted in the prophecy—then aren't we destined, or doomed, to take it?

Thankfully not. Alternate possibilities are not precluded by the true prophecy of *Game of Thrones*: it does not follow from something being true that it could not have been otherwise. In other words, if an event is truly prophesied, all that entails is that it comes about, not that it had to do so. It being true that Cersei would be queen, or Azor Ahai reborn, is compatible with the existence of an alternate Westeros in which Cersei ran off with Jaime, or Azor Ahai failed to reappear. Likewise, it being truly prophesied that you will watch the next season of *Game of Thrones* is compatible with the existence of a possible world identical to this one (including its past and its laws) in which you read the books instead.

In the actual world, at the very point that you turn on your television, you have the choice to refrain (that there is a true prophecy describing your choice does not impede this: it just happens to be true that you watch, it is not necessary that you do so; if you decide to read, 'You will decide to read' would be true instead). If a seer has truly prophesied that you will remain a skeptic at the end of this chapter, then you will remain a skeptic. But the prophecy does not prevent your being convinced; indeed, if you had been convinced (come chapter's end), then either the seer would have been mistaken, or prophesied that you were convinced instead.

A true prophecy doesn't fix or determine the future, it doesn't mean that something has to happen, it just describes what happens to occur; just like a history book doesn't fix the past, it just reports it. However, given the vagueness, fallibility, and generally cryptic nature of the prophecies in *Game of Thrones*, it's worth keeping in mind these wise words from Tyrion:

> Prophecy is like a half-trained mule. It looks as though it might be useful, but the moment you trust in it, it kicks you in the head. (*A Dance with Dragons*, Chapter 40)

20
Cersei, Sansa, and the Problem of Evil

TRIP McCROSSIN

Cersei and Sansa experience dramatic and analogous developments over the course of Season Six of *Game of Thrones*. Both successfully escape their Season Five imprisonments, during which they suffered extreme degradation. Both kill their captors, and do so spectacularly. And both rise to political prominence in the aftermath, as Queen of the Realm and Lady of Winterfell respectively.

Nonetheless, they develop as morally polar opposites, Cersei ever more wicked, Sansa ever virtuous by contrast (even in spite of occasionally lying to her brother).

Their divergence develops not only around the problem that evils exist in the world, which Cersei inflicts and Sansa suffers, but around the *problem of evil* more generally. How do we make sense from the point of view of faith or reason, of bad things happening to good people—Sansa—and good things happening to bad—Cersei?

Which is not to say that bad things don't happen to Cersei as well, but they seem only to worsen her moral character. And these two have been diverging for some time, since their first serious conversation, during the Battle of Blackwater Bay.

Merciless Gods

As the battle looms and then rages, Cersei and Sansa are holed up in the bowels of the castle of King's Landing with its cohort of Ladies. Seeing Sansa kneeling with three of them, in silent prayer, Cersei beckons and derides her.

159

CERSEI: You're *perf*ect, aren't you. *Pray*ing. What are you praying for?

SANSA: For the gods to have mercy on us all.

CERSEI: Oh? On all of us?

SANSA: Yes, your Grace.

CERSEI: Even me?

SANSA: Of course, your Grace.

CERSEI: Even Joffrey?

SANSA: Joffrey is my . . .

CERSEI: Oh, shut up, you little fool. Praying for the gods to have mercy on us all? The gods have no mercy. That's why they're gods. My father told me that when he caught me praying. My mother had just died, you see. I didn't really understand the concept of death, the finality of it. I thought if I prayed very, very hard, the gods would return her to me. I was four.

SANSA: Your father doesn't believe in the gods?

CERSEI: He believes in them. He just doesn't like them very much.

Their exchange continues, including the eventual revelation that the reason Ser Ilyn Payne's on hand is to provide a quick death, if the battle is lost, so that none suffer the dire consequences of capture. When the battle appears indeed to be lost, Cersei flees with Tommen for the Red Keep's Throne Room. Sansa moves immediately to reassure those who remain, baldly lying that the Queen had ensured their safety before leaving. Shae convinces her to save herself, which she does. Meanwhile, we find Cersei sitting on the Iron Throne with Tommen, preparing to poison him, presumably in the spirit of Ser Ilyn's supposed mercy.

In the nick of time, Lord Tywin—who she'd just recalled as disparaging the gods—saunters in, declaring the battle won. Visibly relieved, withdrawing the vile of poison from Tommen's lips and emptying it onto the floor, how can the successful defense of King's Landing not confirm her father's disdain for the gods? In this, Cersei follows him in reflecting a certain historical approach to the problem of evil. How to reconcile human suffering with divine mercy, and the power and knowledge to act on it? By denying that divine action, backed by power and knowledge, is moderated by mercy in the first place.

That perspective shapes Cersei's increasingly wicked behavior through the culmination of Season Six, including inadvertently leading Tommen to take his own life in response to her merciless destruction of the Great Sept, and with it his newfound spiritual mentor, the High Sparrow, and his beloved wife Margaery, not to mention a whole lot of his various subjects.

Lord Tywin's successful defense of King's Landing has the added effect of keeping Sansa in Cersei's merciless orbit a while longer. There she develops an approach of her own to the problem of evil, which shapes her persistently virtuous behavior through the culmination of Season Six, including her return to Winterfell and the justice she metes out to her subsequent tormentor Ramsay Bolton.

Gods Old and New, a Problem Old and New

The problem of evil, from its ancient origins up to the Enlightenment, is primarily a theological problem. Human reason has a difficult time reconciling faith in divine wisdom, power, and benevolence—be it that of "the old gods" or "the new"—with regular and conspicuous human misery.

The difficulty is reflected early in the storyline in Jaime Lannister's response to Catelyn Stark's suggestion that he be destined for "the deepest of the seven hells if the gods are just." "If the gods are real and they are just," he quips, "then why is the world so full of injustice?" It's reflected more recently in Jon Snow's response to what destiny Lady Melisandre suggests may await him on the eve of the Battle of the Bastards. The Lord of Light allowed her to bring him back to life, but not to know why. "Maybe," she wonders, "he brought you here to die again?" "What kind of god," Jon wonders in turn, "would do something like that?"

The problem of evil has evolved since the Enlightenment, Susan Neiman has proposed in her 2002 *Evil in Modern Thought,* to recognize a more secular version of the problem as well. With no special preoccupation with the divine, reason rebels at our experience of virtue and happiness diverging at least as often and conspicuously as they converge. This version of the problem arises regularly in the storyline as well.

When Lord Varys visits the condemned Ned Stark in his dungeon cell, he wonders aloud what possessed him to reveal to Cersei his knowledge of Joffrey's incestuous lineage and the resulting illegitimacy of his claim to the Iron Throne. "The madness of mercy," he admits, "that she might save her children." "It's always the innocents who suffer," Varys bemoans, foreshadowing virtuous Ned's very bad ending. The world of Westeros is a world in which, as in ours, virtue appears to be just as easily punished as rewarded.

More recently, we've seen Arya resisting her assigned assassination of Lady Crane, because "she seems like a decent person." "Do you think death only comes for the wicked," Jaqen H'ghar responds, "and leaves the decent behind?" When she's revealed as having purposefully botched the job, another is sent not only to kill Lady Crane, but Arya as well.

We've also seen Gilly, responding to Sam Tarly's mistreatment by his father, "I'm angry that horrible people treat good people that way, and get away with it." And we've witnessed Melisandre's answer to Jon's question above, as to "what kind of god" would bring him back from the dead only to have him killed a little while later. "The one we've got," she says simply, though it's not really so simple, judging from the oddly unhappy resignation with which she speaks.

Neiman has also proposed that in response to both versions of the problem, primarily two competing perspectives arose during the Enlightenment, which are with us still today. One insists that "morality demands that we make evil intelligible." The other insists that instead "morality demands that we don't." Cersei and Sansa appear to be equally willing to make evil intelligible, but to do so in very different ways.

Doing the Gods' Work

Cersei's lip service to The Seven hides her real view of god, which is cut from the same mold as Saint-Fond's cruel god in the Marquis de Sade's *History of Juliette*. "Why did you stray into the paths of virtue?," God asks, because "the perpetual miseries with which I've blanketed the universe, should they not have convinced you that I love only disorder, and that you had to imitate me in order to please me?" Cersei's solution to the problem of evil is that she's just doing the gods' work, emulating their own merciless nature.

She keeps the faith, according to this picture, by concluding that human misery's not bewildering after all, because mercy's not part of the divine equation. If to love a god is to emulate them, then if they appear to be sadistic, she simply must be so as well. This picture brought Sade predictably into conflict with the religious authorities of his day, and so it is with Cersei. She is judged in the Light of the Seven, according to the High Sparrow's interpretation. She is accused of adultery, incest, and regicide, and confessing to the first, accepts the humiliation and degradation of the Walk of Atonement, from the steps of Great Sept to the Red Keep, Septa Unella chanting "Shame!" all along the way.

But while we can't help but see that she suffers, does she suffer shamefully? According to the response to the problem of evil we're attributing to her, no, she would feel no shame. She's godlike, after all, in her mercilessness, which would be the source of all of which she stands accused. Without mercy, the gods do what feels good, regardless of consequences, and this is just what she tells Septa Unella she's done, as she gleefully condemns her to torture and death at the hands of the Mountain. All that she's done—the adultery, incest, dissembling, regicide, mass murder, and more—and all that she ever does, she does because it "feels good."

And now, godlike, she's ascended to the ultimate position of power as Queen of the Realm. But might not the very language of "the old gods and the new," reprised time and again in the storyline, be a harbinger of things to come? The question that's yet unanswered is how the impending wars—over competing claims to rule over the Realm, and in its defense against White Walkers—will turn out. Cersei presents one model for making such evils intelligible—the gods do what feels good, mercilessly indifferent to the human misery that results, and so will she. Sansa presents another.

The Unprotected Life

"No one can protect me," Sansa declares to Jon, who's just promised never to let Ramsay hurt her again, "no one can protect anyone." It's a stunning admission, a sullen summary of who she's grown into, and what she's endured in the process. She's far from the prim, proper, and naive girl who stood with her siblings to greet Cersei and Robert and their retinue in Season One's premiere. She's far from the girl kneeling in prayer during the Battle of Blackwater Bay, incredulous that Lord Tywin might not believe in the gods. When Littlefinger seeks her out after the Battle of the Bastards, finds her by the weirwood tree, and worries aloud that he may be disturbing her if she's "at prayer," she says simply, "I'm done with all that." She's far even from the unsure version of herself we watched stumble through the oath of fealty with Brienne at the beginning of Season Six. She's all grown up now it seems.

She's a noblewoman, Lady of Winterfell. She would be Queen of the North, were she not otherwise inclined to cede leadership to Jon, for the time being at least. She's grown morally, apologizing to Jon for wronging him when they were children. She's also grown into a warrior. "I don't know anything about battles," she admits to Jon, but still she has the persuasive cunning and personal conviction to convince him to retake Winterfell, and the tactical prowess he lacks to avoid underestimating their opponent Ramsay Bolton.

"If you think he's going to fall into your trap," she warns, "he won't, he's the one who lays traps." "Just don't do what he wants you to do," she pleads, but ultimately he does. Ramsay frees their brother Rickon, telling him to run to Jon, killing him with an arrow through the heart just shy of safety. It's meant to bait Jon into risking himself and the battle, and sadly he bites, in spite of Sansa's wiser warning, and proceeds to lose. Wise to warn, wiser still to plan, Sansa sent a raven to Littlefinger in advance to enlist the Knights of the Vale in her and Jon's struggle. The battle all but lost, they arrive in the nick of time, turning the tide and winning, in a manner that can't help but remind us of Lord Tywin's similarly late arrival, at Cersei's behest, to win the also all but lost Battle of Blackwater Bay.

Sansa's come full circle. She wisely allied herself with Littlefinger for the sake of defeating Ramsay. With his help, she reproduced the events of the Battle of Blackwater Bay, so as to right a wrong then set in motion, her eventual subjugation to the abominable Ramsay. Having ensured that she would never relive that particular misfortune, by killing Ramsay, she just as wisely distrusts Littlefinger's subsequent overtures, as her father had tragically failed to do, and so resists reliving his misfortune as well.

What Sansa's circling around is a sort of dread implicit in her rebuke of Jon, that "no one can protect anyone." In the extreme, there's no "else" implicit here, and what she means is that no one can protect even themselves. We have our wits and our moral character, but the former can do only so much, in the face of the frequently unfathomable ruthlessness of our experience. Nowhere is this more evident than Sansa's rebuke of Littlefinger's plea that he'd made a tragic, but nonetheless honest mistake in arranging her marriage to Ramsay. "You freed me from the monsters who killed my family," she accuses, "and then handed me to other monsters who killed my family." Whether we believe in his sincerity, Sansa doesn't, and so experiences betrayal and cruelty destabilizing in the extreme.

If Cersei's response to the problem of evil is in the spirit of Sade's, Sansa's is in the spirit of Kant's. We can't help but hope to be happy in proportion to our virtue. Given the radical contingency of our experience, however, we've no guarantee that our hope will be realized, and indeed we've ample evidence that it likely won't. Unable to protect even ourselves, what we can control is our moral character.

Life is an unprotected business, and so what to hang on to? What Sansa does: family, home, honor, and justice. As the latter's meted out to Ramsay, it's without mercy, but it also seems not vengeful. Rather it's a question of ridding the world of what threatens her most, and about having him pay for his crimes, to the extent that she can, and what better way than to have him be eaten by his own dogs. How such a perspective plays out on a larger scale, that is which approach to the problem of evil prevails ultimately, Cersei's or Sansa's, depends, as it did for Kant, on the ways in which politics and history progress. All we can do now is await the continuation and conclusion of their game of thrones.[1]

[1] Thanks to Azeem Chaudry for so enthusiastically introducing me to *Game of Thrones*, to Sue Zemka for so kindly making sure I kept writing, and to the volume's editors for so patiently waiting, far above and beyond the call, for me to *finish* writing already.

21
Stannis—Knight of Faith or Tragic Hero?

WILLIAM J. DEVLIN

Game of Thrones tells a tale centered on betrayal and the quest to become king. When King Robert Baratheon dies, the War of the Five Kings is underway. One prominent figure in this war is Stannis Baratheon.

His struggle to become king involves many adventures, including assassinating his brother Renly, leading the attack on King's Landing, and defeating Mance Rayder. His campaign, however, reaches a tragic end. With the onset of winter, Stannis's march is harsh and crippling, leading to his army's destruction and his execution.

Stannis maintains that he's the rightful heir not simply because he has a kinship to the former king, but because he believes he's backed by divine decree. Following the religion of R'hllor, Stannis relies heavily upon faith, which culminates in sacrificing his own daughter, Shireen. His dilemma between sacrificing Shireen to save his army and secure victory and saving Shireen while his army perishes, echoes several historical and mythological dilemmas.

The Paradox of Faith

Danish philosopher Søren Kierkegaard (1813–1855) explores such dilemmas in light of the question of faith, arguing that while most characters facing similar dilemmas are *tragic heroes,* some are understood as *knights of faith* who embody the 'paradox of faith'. Is Stannis Baratheon then a tragic hero or a knight of faith?

> There's no man in the Seven Kingdoms more honorable than Stannis Baratheon.
>
> —Davos Seaworth

When Robert dies, several aim to take the throne. Unlike his adversaries, Stannis has a legitimate claim as "the one true king." As Ned Stark explains, since Robert has no trueborn children, Stannis is the rightful heir. Unlike his opponents—such as Renly, Joffrey Baratheon, and Robb Stark—Stannis is not driven by greed and lust for power, wealth, pleasure, or vengeance. He seeks the Iron Throne because it's the *right* thing to do.

Though Stannis is the rightful heir, he lacks the charm to make fans in Westeros. Stubbornly, he refuses to work with Renly, noting that Renly has "men whose allegiance rightly belongs to me" ("The Night Lands"). Unbending, after many of his soldiers die in the Battle of Blackwater, he commands the rest to attack, coldly predicting "thousands" will die ("Blackwater"). Ever pedantic, he even has a penchant for pointing out the proper grammatical use of "fewer" ("Garden of Bones"; "Kill the Boy").

Davos Seaworth—his best friend, Hand, and strongest ally—admits he's "a complicated man" and his tone can be misleading ("High Sparrow"). Renly calls him "charmless, rigid, a bore" ("The Garden of Bones"). Even Ser Loras Tyrell says he "has the personality of a lobster" ("The Wolf and the Lion").

An Honorable Man

While Stannis is hardened to the point of appearing joyless, his critics miss an integral part of his character. He prides himself as a morally good and honorable person insofar as he lives his life by following duty and acting according to the law. As Davos points out, Stannis is an "honorable" man worthy of "loyalty" ("The Night Lands"), "an honest man" ("The Laws of Gods and Men"), and a man who "wants what's right for the Seven Kingdoms" ("High Sparrow").

Stannis adopts a *deontological* approach to morality. Famously presented by Immanuel Kant (1724–1804), deontology is an ethical theory which holds that an action is good or bad regardless of its consequences. Good actions include being honest, helping others in need, and refraining from stealing. A morally good person acts morally, not for the purpose of some great end or personal gain, but for the sake of following the moral laws, which are understood to hold for all people, in all places, at all times.

Stannis embodies deontology in various ways. He acts according to his duty, regardless of the consequences or of his own desires. Even if it's in his best interest to bend the rules, he won't. He refuses to join armies with Robb or Renly (even though he needs their help) since they fail to recognize his kingship. He tells Renly, "The Iron Throne is mine by right. All those that deny that are my foes" ("Garden of Bones"). This isn't due to pride or ambition—he pursues the throne because it's his duty. As he explains to Davos, a man of reason and a self-proclaimed atheist, "I never asked for this. No more than I asked to be king. We do not choose our destiny, but . . . we must do our duty" ("Second Sons").

On the rare occasion Stannis gives in to desire—such as intercourse with Melisandre—he fights against it, telling her "I have a wife, I took a vow" ("The Night Lands"). Once he breaks the vow, he shamefully confesses to his wife, Selyse ("Kissed by Fire"). Furthermore, Stannis is honest, avoiding embellishment. When drafting a letter he removes the adjective "beloved" towards his brother, noting "he wasn't my beloved brother. I didn't love him. He didn't love me" and that such a "harmless courtesy" is "a lie."

He adds that Jaime Lannister should be referred to as "kingslayer" and still be addressed as "Ser" since "whatever else he is, he's still a knight." ("The North Remembers"). Finally, Stannis accepts that his duties are absolute and won't even cut corners for a friend. In "Garden of Bones," Stannis and Davos discuss justice and how Davos saved Stannis's starving army by smuggling onions into Storm's End. For Davos's act of bravery Stannis rewarded him by knighting him. Yet, for Davos's acts of smuggling, Stannis punished him by cutting off four of his fingertips.

Faith and Reason

Stannis Baratheon, Warrior of Light, your sword awaits you.

—MELISANDRE

Though morality is essential to Stannis's character there's another important attribute: faith. In "The North Remembers,"

having converted to the religion of R'hllor, Stannis watches
Lady Melisandre burn the effigies of the "false" gods. Contrary
to both the "New Gods" (which encompass seven deities) and
the "Old Gods" (which include innumerable deities), this religion has two deities, "eternally at war." There's the one true
god, R'hllor—or the Lord of Light—who is the god of fire, "a god
of light and love and joy" that brings life. Then there's the evil
deity, the Great Other, who is the "god of darkness, evil, and
fear" that brings death ("The Lion and the Rose"). This religion
prophesies that a chosen one, the mythical "Prince that was
Promised," will rise. Commonly referred to as the "Warrior of
Light" and said to be "born amidst salt and smoke," ("Garden of
Bones"), it's believed he'll pull his firesword, "Lightbringer,"
from the flames.

Following Melisandre's counsel and use of magic, Stannis's
actions fit this religion and the belief that he's the Lord's chosen. He burns idols and pulls his sword from their flames. He
burns the infidels, including his father-in-law, for refusing to
convert to R'hllor. Melisandre provides Stannis with reasons to
believe in R'hllor. They conceive a Shadow to assassinate Renly,
thereby eliminating one of his enemies. They extract blood
from Gendry, which they offer as a sacrifice of "king's blood" to
the Lord of Light to (seemingly) cause the deaths of Robb
Stark, Balon Greyjoy, and Joffrey. They see visions in the
flames of what's to come. While there's evidence, Melisandre
counsels "you must have faith" and explains, "I've seen the path
. . . but first you must give yourself to the Lord of Light" ("The
Night Lands").

Stannis walks the line between faith and reason. In *Fear
and Trembling*, Kierkegaard explores this line. He describes
faith as a paradox simultaneously containing two contradictory
characteristics. One has subjective, personal, certainty that
what he believes is true *and* recognizes objectively, that one is
rationally uncertain about the belief. Since faith is immersed
in doubt, Kierkegaard notes that real faith is rare and highly
admirable. Referring to a person of faith as a *knight of faith*, he
explains that the knight perpetually makes a leap of faith by
moving beyond reason to believe what's seemingly irrational.

This leap may involve a suspension of the moral laws insofar as it's commanded by God. Furthermore, faith is a direct
relationship and private bond between the individual and God.

Since faith is private and involves moving beyond reason, it's unspoken, instead being a passion and love within the individual. So, the knight doesn't explain his faith to others—he remains silent.

Stannis's relationship to R'hllor makes him a candidate for a knight of faith. Taciturn by nature, Stannis rarely speaks about his faith. Focusing on his duty as a warrior and his role as king, he instead discusses his campaign to take the Iron Throne. Nevertheless, he alludes to the idea that it's his "destiny" to become king, and so relates to the prophecy of the chosen one. Like the knight's suspension of moral laws, Stannis is excused for his act of adultery with Melisandre. As Selyse explains to Stannis, "No act done in service of the Lord of Light can ever be a sin." Rather than be angered by Stannis's infidelity, Selyse "wept with joy" when learning of his actions ("Kissed by Fire").

We can even compare Stannis to Kierkegaard's paradigm of faith—the Biblical Abraham. Here, God promises Abraham a son, Isaac, who'll be a father to future generations. When Isaac is born, God calls Abraham to sacrifice him—the one he loves most and the one necessary to fulfill God's promise that Abraham will be father of future generations. Abraham prepares to do so, but God stops him. As Kierkegaard explains, Abraham's spiritual journey consists of "a double movement" in faith. He simultaneously prepared to kill Isaac while believing that "God could give him a new Isaac, bring the sacrificial offer back to life." He believes this paradox "on the strength of the absurd, for all human calculation had long since been suspended."

Like Abraham, Stannis loves Shireen more than anyone. He commands Selyse to never strike her ("The Lion and the Rose"). When she was dying from greyscale, everyone advised Stannis to send her away. Stannis "told them all to go to hell" and "called in every Maester on this side of the world" to save her ("The Sons of the Harpy"). Selyse laments bearing Shireen, but Stannis sees her as his princess. Like Abraham, his love and allegiance to his duty as father bring forth Stannis's dilemma.

Beset by a depleted army, Stannis is told he must have Shireen killed so that R'hllor can have more "king's blood," thereby assuring his victory ("The Gift"). Stannis is torn between his duty as a father and his duty as a king. Having sent Davos to the Wall, he's unable to consider his future advice: "If he commands you to burn children, your lord is evil" ("Winds of Winter"). Like Abraham, Stannis is alone. Torn between competing duties and faith and reason, he's willing to sacrifice his child under his god's command.

Davos's response to the Lord of Light's call to sacrifice Stannis's daughter is similar to Kant's response to God's call to sacrifice Abraham's son. In *The Conflict of Faculties*, Kant tells us, "Abraham should have replied to this supposedly divine voice: 'That I ought not to kill my good son is quite certain. But that you, this apparition, are God—of that I am not certain, and never can be, not even if this voice rings down to me from heaven'." Davos dismisses the Lord as being evil and so he turns out to follow Kant's morality more closely than Stannis.

Stannis the Tragic Hero

For the night is dark and full of terror.

—MELISANDRE

While Stannis demonstrates several characteristics of the knight of faith, ultimately he falls short. Abraham embodies the paradox of faith through his double movement, but Stannis does not.

Unlike the knight, Stannis *reasons* through his choices, always justifying his actions. When Melisandre advises having faith in his war with a small army, Stannis relies upon calculations: "Faith? In a real war, the side with the greater number wins, nine times out of ten" ("The Night Lands"). As Stannis reasons with Davos, he explains he burned his father-in-law as an "infidel," not because he's unfaithful, but because he refused to obey his king: "I ordered him to tear down his idols. He disobeyed" ("The Lion and the Rose").

As Melisandre encourages Stannis to sacrifice Gendry, he frees Davos—a rational and loyal ally—who acknowledges that "you could have freed me yesterday or tomorrow, but you came to me now before this boy is put to the knife because you knew I'd counsel restraint." ("Second Sons"). Stannis also discusses faith in a logical, scientific, and empirical manner. He has faith only because of what he's seen: "I saw a vision in the flames. A great battle in the snow . . . I never believed, but when you see the truth, when it's right there in front of you as real as these iron bars, how can you deny her god is real?" ("Second Sons"). Clearly, Stannis relies upon reason and duty rather than faith.

Following Kierkegaard, Stannis is better understood as a *tragic hero*. From the Greek mythologies of Agamemnon sacrificing his daughter Iphigenia, to the Biblical story of Jephthah sacrificing his daughter for God, to Brutus, the Consul of Rome, executing his sons for treason—several fathers faced the tragic dilemma of whether to sacrifice their own child. Kierkegaard explains that these tragic heroes are contrasted with the knight insofar as their behavior is rationally comprehensible: "The hero I can *think* myself *into*, but not Abraham; when I reach that height, I fall down since what I am offered is a paradox." We cannot explain Abraham's contradictory beliefs, but we can understand the beliefs of the tragic hero.

Similarly, we can understand Stannis's reasons for sacrificing Shireen. Struggling to march on Winterfell, his army is overwhelmed by the harsh winter: forty horses die, food is running out, and sellswords run away. Ramsay Bolton sneaks into camp, killing hundreds of horses, burning food stores, and destroying siege weapons. Unable to press forward without a thaw and short on food to return to Castle Black, Stannis is in a hopeless situation. Nonetheless, he's committed to following his duty to become king and continues his march: "If I retreat again, I'll become the King Who Ran. . . . This is the right time and I will risk everything. Because if I don't, we've lost. We march to victory or we march to defeat. But we go forward. Only forward" ("The Gift").

Out of options, Stannis follows Melisandre's advice. She explains that she's seen visions of herself in Winterfell with Bolton's banner being lowered, leading Stannis to believe that this is a vision of his victory. Melisandre suggests that "sacrifices must be made to ensure victory." Having already witnessed "the power of king's blood" through Gendry, Stannis accepts the conclusion that given his duty as king he must sacrifice Shireen so that the god can help him march to victory ("The Gift").

As Selyse reasons, sacrificing Shireen is "a great thing. . . . If we don't act, we'll all starve here." Stannis implements a rational course of action. Still honoring his duty as a father, he rationalizes his decision, telling Shireen, "Sometimes a person has to choose. Sometimes the world forces his hand. If a man knows what he is and remains true to himself, the choice is no choice at all. He must fulfill his destiny and become who he is meant to be" ("Dance with Dragons"). In the footsteps of a tragic hero, Stannis justifies his actions, asks Shireen for forgiveness, and burns her at the stake.

Stannis's Demise

We march to victory or we march to defeat.

—Stannis Baratheon

Since he grounds his actions in deontological justifications of duty and since his response to the moral dilemma can be rationalized, Stannis is not a knight of faith, but a tragic hero. While we may disagree with his decision, we can follow his line of reasoning as a last resort to fulfill his duty as king.

However, Stannis's actions lead to his demise. Though the snow has melted, his campaign is mired in tragedy. Ashamed of her part in the death of Shireen, Selyse commits suicide. Half of Stannis's army deserts him, taking all of the horses. Melisandre deserts him. Bolton's army attacks, massacring his dwindled and famished army.

Meanwhile, Stannis himself is executed by Brienne of Tarth as punishment for the murder of Renly (revealed by Brienne in "Book of the Stranger"). When Brienne sentences him to death and asks for his final words, Stannis concludes his tragic story with the fitting words, "Go on, do your duty" ("Mother's Mercy").[1]

---

[1] Special thanks to Mary Lee for her insightful input and assistance in the completion of this chapter.

22
The Many-Faced God and Indian Philosophy

HANS VAN EYGHEN

Arya Stark's trainer Syrio Forel hints at the many-faced God in Season One's "A Golden Crown." In Season Five, the many-faced God gets a more prominent role when Arya Stark is admitted into The House of Black and White by Jaqen H'ghar. Although we do not have a detailed picture of the many-faced God, there are good reasons to believe that his nature resembles a concept of God in Indian Vedanta philosophy and Buddhist philosophy.

> There is only one God, and his name is Death.
>
> —SYRIO FOREL

The many-faced God is worshipped in The House of Black and White which is located in the city of Braavos. His worshippers and priests (the distinction is not clear) are called the Faceless Men. The Faceless Men adhere to the belief that there is only one God but that he is represented in many ways. In the sanctuary at the House of Black and White he is represented as the Stranger, the Drowned God, the Black Goat of Qohor, the Lion of Night, the Weeping Woman and R'hllor. However, the differences in representations are superficial. At root they are all the very same God who has no face of his own.

This view of God is alien to traditional Western religion. The large Abrahamic religions, Christianity, Islam, and Judaism, believe that their representation of God is the uniquely correct portrayal. The belief that there is one God portrayed in many different equally true ways was fairly common in the ancient world and still is in contemporary India. Adherents of ancient mystery religions often had no problem identifying the God or Goddess they worshipped with gods known by other names. Many contemporary Hindus and Sikhs also hold that God can be known by many names, though they will usually insist that the name they use is the correct one.

Becoming No One

All men must die!

—A MAN

An even more striking similarity between the religion of the Faceless Men and Indian philosophy lies in the goal they offer. The religious practices to which Arya is introduced are aimed at letting go of the old self. Arya's stay in the House of Black and White makes it abundantly clear that detachment from the personal self ought to be the primary goal. When she first enters the house the man known as Jaqen H'ghar tells Arya that he is actually "no one" and that she must learn to become "no one" as well.

Throughout her time in the House of Black and White, Arya struggles to leave her old self behind; much to the dismay of the Waif living there. Leaving behind the self is connected to the nature of the many-faced God himself. He is without a face of his own but can adopt many faces if the circumstances require him to do so.

Adherence to the many-faced God and the practices this involves resemble Vedanta philosophy. Vedantists hold that individual selves ("ego" is their preferred term) are illusions that need to be overcome. Any attachment to an individual self stems from ignorance about the true nature of the world. The true nature of the world is that all differences are superficial and reality is fundamentally united as one. This fundamental reality is divine and Vedantists call it Brahman.

As a consequence we as individuals are in our true core not different from this divine Brahman. The Brahman is in itself free from distinct qualities or predicates so it cannot be put into words. Vedantists also believe that the Brahman can take on personal form. This is what most religions believe the nature of God to be. Brahman in its personal form is called Ishvara. The term 'Ishvara' is usually reserved for philosophical discussions. Human selves are in their core nothing else than the divine Brahman or Ishvara.

The ultimate goal of existence according to Vedantic philosophers goes further than letting go of the self. Letting go of the ego is a preliminary step towards identification with the Brahman. The details of how this identification takes place are unclear and it has been interpreted in different ways. For example, some maintain that identification with the Brahman is possible while remaining in a human body whereas others deny this. All interpretations share the idea that the identification is a realization of the truth that true selves of humans are nothing more (but also nothing less) than the divine Brahman.

Though less central in vedantic thought, the identification of the inner self with the divine Brahman implies a denial of any distinct self or robust sense of personal identity that is distinct from other selves. Attachment to the self or the ego needs to be overcome and this implies removing the boundaries between selves and between the self and all of reality. When this is realized, all distinction between individuals also disappears. Arya's struggles in letting go of her old self show that this process is hard and requires time. Her leaving the House of Black and White in "Blood of My Blood" confirms this and shows that such practices are not meant for everybody.

The Uses of Ritual

Who are you?

—JAQEN H'GHAR

The role of Jaqen H'ghar resembles the role Vedantists assign to a guru; a guru being someone who has reached a more advanced stage on the journey towards realizing the identification with Brahman. The journey involves some sort of ritualized action. For Vedantists, these rituals usually involve meditation or yoga. Jaqen H'ghar also subjects Arya to an exercise where he repeatedly hits her whilst asking who she is. The goal of this ritual is to encourage the gradual letting go of the self.

Recently, this effect of such rituals on personal identity was supported by research applying cognitive theory to religion. Anthropologist Harvey Whitehouse distinguishes two ways that ritualized action can alter the experience of the self. In the first way—social identification—the changes are fairly limited. Here individuals can come to have in-group bonds through low-intensity rituals. Whitehouse's examples are the weekly Catholic mass and the Muslim Friday prayer.

A good example from Westeros is the oath new members of the Night Watch must take before being accepted as members. Jon Snow and Samwell Tarly are seen taking the oath in the episode "You Win or You Die" in Season One. Though important for new members of the Night Watch, the ritual is nowhere nearly as demanding as the rituals in the House of Black and White. Rituals of this first kind help to foster group membership but leave most ideas of personal identity intact.

The second way—called identity fusion—is much more profound. Here high-arousal rituals generate a strong sense of oneness with other members of a group. The boundary between the personal and the communal self becomes porous, sometimes to the point that it disappears altogether. According to Harvey Whitehouse, high-arousal rituals have this effect because rituals are causally opaque, meaning that they can be interpreted in many ways.

When people engage in rituals in a communal setting they observe others undergoing the same experience and can imagine them sharing the same rich interpretative process. By sharing personal experiences with a special group of others, rituals can cause the identities of group members to fuse. Identity fusion can lead to profound changes in personal identity but it is not yet clear whether it can also lead to the abandonment of the self at which Vedantists and Faceless Men aim. Removing the boundaries between selves is, however, a necessary step towards removing the boundaries between self and being.

Is God Many-Faced or Faceless?

One issue where the Faceless Men and Vedantists diverge is the facelessness of God. Although Vedantists uphold that Brahman is beyond the sensible and the categories of thought, Brahman still appears to have a "face." In its personalized form, Ishvara, Brahman literally has a face. In its non-personal form Brahman has a 'face' insofar as it can still be the object of human speech and has a certain identity or self.

This 'face' or doctrine of Brahman was attacked by the Buddha in the fifth century B.C. and by subsequent Buddhist scholars. They shared the Vedantists' critique of the ego but expanded it to critique any robust sense of self, including any primordial, divine self. Early Buddhists scholars argued that everything is subject to the law of cause and effect and that it is of no use to talk about a divine Brahman above it. Later Buddhist scholars went one step further and claimed that everything is devoid of essence. The Mahayana school of Buddhist scholars expanded the critique of the self to all phenomena.

Just like the self, everything is without a self-nature or inherent existence. From this principle they developed the doctrine of two truths; the first truth being valid in the realm of daily life and the second being the ultimate truth. The first covers only conventional or superficial truth and here it is appropriate to talk about things or beings as if they had inherent existence. The ultimate truth is beyond all categories of thought and is ineffable.

It's not clear whether the many-faced God is in the end completely faceless. On the one hand, the superficiality of his faces suggests that the many-faced God is beyond human categories of thought but on the other hand the Faceless Men seem to talk about and worship him in a way that is much more in line with the Vedantists' idea of Brahman. Another reason to think the ideas of the Faceless Men are closer to Buddhism is the fact that they strive to become no one rather than realizing their identity with the many-faced God. Also, Syrio Forel's claim that the true God is Death points in the Buddhist direction.

All Men Must Serve

In the House of Black and White the adoption of a self is sometimes considered useful for pragmatic reasons. In the episode "Hardhome" in Season Five Arya Stark poses as a shellfish merchant to prepare for the assassination of the "thin man." In Season Six, Arya takes up yet another role to kill an actress. Taking on this self is, however, only temporary and only to obtain a higher end.

Clinging to a self has no value in and of itself. Taking up an identity for some purpose, exemplified by Arya Stark's taking up the role of the shellfish merchant, resembles the Buddhist idea of conventional truth. It also resembles yet another aspect of Indian thought; namely that of doing one's duty. She is asked to take up this role for a temporary purpose, but at the same time she must not get attached to it.

Something similar is found in the great Indian scripture, the *Bhagavad Gita*. In it a prince named Arjuna is on the verge of engaging in battle. When contemplating the inevitable bloodshed and agony that will result from the battle, Arjuna considers leaving the battlefield. At this point, his guide and charioteer (who turns out to be the God Krishna), urges Arjuna to fight because this is his duty.

Many interpreters insisted that the *Bahagavad Gita*'s main message is to avoid being attached to your role and identity. By considering not fighting, Arjuna shows attachment to his own feelings and thus to his own identity. Throughout the epic, Krishna attempts to convince him to leave this identity behind. We could argue that this results in a paradox because Krishna also urges Arjuna to take up another role, namely that of the warrior, and thus asks him to trade one attachment for another. However, Krishna does not urge him to be attached to his role of warrior either, but asks him to do what is expected of him without any attachment whatsoever.

The *Bhagavad Gita* shows that letting go of your self and identity need not result in the abandonment of all action. Similarly, becoming "no one" can go hand in hand with performing certain actions in the world for the Faceless Men. For Arya Stark, letting go of her identity does not prevent her from acting like the shellfish merchant and performing certain duties. Her failing to perform her duty ultimately shows that clinging to an identity can even prevent you from doing your duty, the possibility that beckoned to Arjuna.

We do not have a detailed account of the beliefs and practices associated with the many-faced God in the world of *Game of Thrones*. Yet, there are remarkable parallels to Indian Vedantic philosophy. The most striking parallel is the importance both put on overcoming your ego or self. Vedantists see this as a preparatory step towards identification with the divine but it is not clear whether the Faceless Men believe something similar.

Both Vedantists and Faceless Men use rituals to attain their goal of altering the conception of the self and recent research in cognitive science provides evidence that intense, high-arousal rituals can indeed accomplish this function. Concerning the nature of the many-faced God, the Faceless Men go one step further than the Vedantists and deny that there is any meaningful way to talk about God as having a self. If this is the correct interpretation of their view, then their ideas resemble those of Buddhist philosophy.

Finally, embracing identities for temporary pragmatic reasons resembles ideas found in the Indian story, the *Bhagavad Gita*, which is also an important source for Vedantic philosophy. The scripture teaches that rejecting attachment to any self or ego need not lead to foregoing all action. Instead, it teaches that action, and especially doing your duty, remains important.

We see something similar when Arya Stark takes up a different identity for a higher goal, even if that goal is something as counter to Vedantic tradition as assassination. As the Faceless Men teach, "All men must serve."

VI

Knowledge
Is Power

23
How Can We Know Anything in a World of Magic and Miracles?

ERIK BALDWIN

The world of *Game of Thrones* is an unpredictable place. You never know how long summer will last or when winter will come. Wargs can take control of the minds of animals and people. The Faceless Men can radically change their appearance. With the re-emergence of Dragons, magic has made a comeback. The powers of the Red Priests and Priestesses of R'hllor, the Lord of Light, have dramatically increased. Magic and the absence of law-like regularities in nature leads us to question whether—and if so, to what extent—people in the world of *Game of Thrones* can know things about the future based on present observation and experience.

It Is Known, Khaleesi

There are three kinds of knowledge:

acquaintance knowledge

competence knowledge

propositional knowledge

To have acquaintance knowledge is to have direct awareness of an object. For instance, when he takes a bite of a freshly-baked Lamprey pie, Hot Pie is directly acquainted with its qualitative features, namely, its spiciness, warmth, and delicious flavors.

Competence knowledge is knowing how to do something and propositional knowledge is knowing facts. Ser Jaime

Lannister, captain of the King's Guard and expert swordsmen, clearly knows how to fight. However, we'll look at propositional knowledge—knowing what is a fact and what is not a fact.

We have propositional knowledge—knowledge of facts— only if what we assert by a sentence is true. For instance, the sentence *Brandon the Builder received help from The Children and The Giants when building the wall* is true just in case The Children and The Giants really did help Brandon build the wall. *That* sentence isn't true in our world. But, it might be true in the world of *Game of Thrones*. And so it is something that the characters in the story might be in a position to know.

According to the traditional analysis of propositional knowl- edge, attributed to the Greek philosopher Plato (427–347 B.C.E.), you know a proposition just in case: 1. you believe it; 2. it is true; and 3. you are justified in believing it. According to this analysis, the first two requirements are met just in case your belief corresponds to the way things really are. Consider the proposition *Daenerys Targaryen is the mother of dragons*. That proposition is true just in case there are dragons and Daenerys is the 'mother' of some of them.

Yet, to meet the final requirement for knowledge that propo- sition can be justified only if you have good enough reason or evi- dence to believe it. For instance, those who saw Daenerys walk into Drogo's funeral pyre with her dragon eggs thought that she was going to die. After the flames died out, those who saw her alive and well holding baby dragons were *justified* in believing *Daenerys Targaryen is the mother of dragons*.

For those who were there and saw it happen, it is known. But people living in Westeros who hear unsubstantiated rumors wouldn't know it. They might believe it and it might be true, but they wouldn't *know* it, because they wouldn't be justified in believing it. Believing something on the basis of a rumor doesn't give you a good justifying reason. In contrast, if one of Varys's spies hears about the birth of baby dragons from a reli- able eyewitness, then Varys's belief in the existence of dragons would be justified on the basis of reliable testimony.

You Know Nothing, Jon Snow

Skeptics maintain that few if any of our beliefs are truly known because we don't have good justifying reasons for thinking they're true. Consider Ygritte, who often tells Jon Snow he knows nothing. Taken literally, she expresses *global* skepticism: Jon has no knowledge whatsoever.

It's doubtful that Ygritte means to go that far. Rather, she seems to be saying that Jon is woefully naive or ignorant about things that are obvious to anyone who grew up north of The Wall. If that is what she means, then what she says seems to be correct. Jon probably should accept a modest skepticism concerning what happens north of The Wall.

Are there reasons for other characters in *Game of Thrones* to be skeptical? Specifically, can they form justified beliefs about the present and future by generalizing from past experience? David Hume (1711–1776) maintains that they can't. Hume argues that for any two events we call 'cause' and 'effect', we can always conceive of one event occurring apart from the other. We don't perceive a casual connection with any of our five senses. Rather, rightly or wrongly, we just assume there is one. So all we can really know about two events is that one occurs after the other.

For example, it's said that "all dragons breathe fire." But we can conceive of a dragon that doesn't breath fire. Perhaps, there is a dragon that breathes lightning or noxious gas instead. So, we can't be sure whether or not the next dragon we see will breathe fire. Consider another example. In the past, when wildfire was shot from a catapult it exploded with great force and produced flames that can't be quenched by water. But there is no real contradiction in supposing that the next jar of wildfire shot won't explode when shot. Perhaps, the next jar of wildfire will be a dud. So we don't really *know* whether or not *this* jar of wildfire will explode. This line of reasoning leads Hume to conclude that since we don't really know whether the future will resemble the past. To use the technical term, we don't have *inductive* knowledge.

Thomas Reid (1710–1796) thought that Hume's skepticism about induction was arbitrary. He points out that when Hume argues that beliefs held on the basis of induction aren't justified, he still presupposes that reason is reliable. Reid maintains that trust in reason and induction are a package deal in the sense that if you think that one is a source of justified belief then you're being irrational if you don't accept the other one as well. He accepts that both are typically sources of justified belief. Reid's 'common sense' position is that we shouldn't doubt beliefs grounded in everyday types of justification *unless* we have some special reason for doing so. And because we usually don't have special reasons to doubt them, most of our everyday beliefs are rationally appropriate.

Yet, whether or not we agree with Reid's response to Hume, it seems that skepticism about everyday inductive claims is appropriate in the world of *Game of Thrones* because there *are* special reasons for them to doubt whether many inductive beliefs are rightly formed and appropriately grounded. There is a startling lack of uniformity of nature in their world. But if inductive knowledge is possible only in environments that exhibit law-like regularities, then they have good reason to be skeptical about many things.

Summers Can Last Decades and Winters a Lifetime

Obviously, the length and changing of the seasons are unpredictable in the world of *Game of Thrones*. People have no idea how long summer will last or how long the next winter will be. In *The World of Ice and Fire*, we read of the Long Night, a winter that lasted so long that people lived and died without ever having seen the spring. We also read that the Maesters of the Citadel tried to predict the procession of the seasons without any success.

Septon Barth argued that the inconstancy of the seasons is due to magic. Based on observations of the stars and the positions of the globe and the sun, Maester Nicol argued that the procession of the seasons might have at one time been regular and predictable. Other Maesters argued that there is no evidence that the seasons ever were predictable. The inability to predict the procession of the seasons generates many practical problems.

The Wolf Dreams Are Better

Wargs can enter into and take control of the minds of animals. Orell of the Free People could control his eagles to spy on The Night's Watch ("Dark Wings, Dark Words"). Bran Stark is not only able to take control of his direwolf, Summer, but Hodor as well ("The Rains of Castamere"). Arya Stark and Jon Snow both have dreams in which they experience the activities of their direwolves.

Wargs can even use their ability to cheat death. As Jon Snow plunges his sword into him, Orell warged with his eagle, continuing to claw at Jon even after the death of his human body ("The Rains of Castamere"). As he was dying, Varamyr Sixskins of the Free Folk warged into his wolf One Eye (*A Dance with Dragons*). For all the characters in the story know, an apparently normal bird might actually be a spy or an old friend enjoying a second life. That such things are genuine possibilities gives them reason to wonder whether that wolf or crow over there is what it seems to be.

A Girl Has No Name

The Faceless Men of Braavos, expert assassins and servants of the Many-Faced God, are able to radically change their physical features to appear as completely different people. The one known as Jaqen H'ghar takes off his face and puts on another right before Arya's eyes ("Valar Morghulis").

Later on, when Arya rejoins the mysterious man at the House of Black and White, the headquarters of the Faceless Men, he first appears as someone else before once again putting on the face of Jaqen ("The House of Black and White"). The Waif, another Faceless Man, appears as a blind young woman ("High Sparrow").

As Arya learns their ways she becomes adept at impersonation. Somehow, the one with the face of Jaqen can make Arya blind ("Mother's Mercy") and make her to see again ("Oathbreaker"). The talents of The Faceless Men are known throughout the world. People, especially those in positions of power, have reason to be suspicious about whether others are who they seem to be, for it is a genuine possibility that a member of the King's Guard is actually an assassin sent by the Faceless Men to kill King Tommen.

The Great Victory I Saw in the Flames, All of It Was a Lie

For some time, the higher mysteries of magic have been absent from the world of ice and fire. But now, along with dragons, magic has returned to the world. It is presumed that there is a causal connection between these events, but no one knows whether magic caused the return of the dragons or whether the return of dragons caused the return of magic. Perhaps some other unknown factor is responsible for the return of both. All that is known for sure is that these events are somehow connected.

Along with the return of dragons and magic, the powers of the Red Priests and Priestesses of R'hllor, the Lord of Light, have dramatically increased. Melisandre has protection from poison and a strong resistance to cold, wearing only light clothing while at The Wall. She also has visions of the future in dreams and when staring into flames. She correctly predicts Davos's plans to kill her (*A Storm of Swords*) and the death of several members of the Night's Watch (*A Dance With Dragons*).

But her visions are somewhat unreliable. She steadfastly believes that Stannis Baratheon is the return of Azor Ahai but when she looks into the flames all she sees is Jon Snow. Apparently, she falsely believed that Stannis would prevail in the Battle of the Blackwater Bay against the forces of King's Landing ("Valar Dohaeris"). She predicted that Stannis would defeat the Boltons at Winterfell, but the battle turned out to be a terrible loss, culminating in the death of Stannis (*A Dance With Dragons* and "Mother's Mercy").

All things considered, Melisandre has a pretty good track record, but many of her visions are unclear or ambiguous in their details and she has a tendency to misinterpret their meaning. Inconsistencies, incongruities, and unexpected happenings give her and those fighting alongside her reason to be skeptical about the accuracy of her predictions.

The Red Wizard, I've Heard that He Has Strange Powers

Thoros of Myr, a less than fully devout priest of R'hllor taken to fighting, drinking, and womanizing, fought in tourneys with his sword set aflame with wildfire (*A Game of Thrones*). Upon King Robert Baratheon's death, he joins Beric Dondarrion and the Brotherhood Without Banners.

During The Battle at the Burning Septry, Thoros set his and Beric's swords aflame using only blood and prayer (*A Storm of*

Shadows). When The Mountain killed Beric in battle, Thoros performed the traditional funeral rituals of his faith. Much to his surprise, after 'the last kiss' Beric was miraculously resurrected (*A Storm of Swords*). Thoros repeated this feat several more times. Later Beric gave his life to resurrect Catelyn Stark (*A Storm of Swords*). Although her methods are different than Thoros's, Melisandre, too, demonstrates that she has this power by raising Jon Snow from the dead ("Home" and "Oathbreaker").

Qyburn, former Maester and member of Queen Cersei's small council, also has power over death. After The Mountain was poisoned with manticore venom by Oberyn Martell during their trial by combat ("The Mountain and the Viper"), Qyburn was able to prevent him from fully succumbing to the poison using unorthodox and unnatural methods involving some admixture of medical experimentation, alchemy, and magic ("The House of Black and White," "Black and White," *A Feast for Crows*).

Most of us believe that dead people stay dead, since one hundred percent of the deaths we experience are permanent. But that's no longer the case for some people in *The World of Ice and Fire*. For those who are aware of Thoros's and Melisandre's miraculous deeds and Qyburn's mysterious experiments, it is an open question whether a person will stay dead or live again.

That's What I Do, I Drink and I Know Things

Because the world of *Game of Thrones* lacks significant law-like regularities due to magic, many inductive beliefs cannot be justified for the people in the story. Given what they know, it is reasonable for them to skeptical. But what do these reflections about their situation have to say to *us*?

They suggest that knowledge, particularly inductive knowledge, requires the world to possess a certain level of regularity. Yet, we can't know whether our world is being co-operative. Is that a problem? Not if Reid is right that it is rationally appropriate to presuppose that our inductive beliefs are rightly grounded. And I think he is right. After all, we don't have good reason to think that the world is generally irregular due to magic. The burden of proof is on the doubter to give reasons to distrust our inductive beliefs rather than vice versa.

It follows that it's reasonable to accept a belief based on induction even if it's not possible for us to prove beyond all possible doubt that the world is being co-operative. Unlike the people living in the world of *Game of Thrones*, we don't have good reason to be skeptical about everyday beliefs formed by induction. Therefore, it's appropriate for us to think our everyday beliefs are justified, unless someone gives us some special reason to doubt them.

24

Samwell Tarly's Renaissance

ARTUR MATOS ALVES

How was Valyrian steel produced? How can the armies of the White Walkers be defeated? How was the Wall built?

In *Game of Thrones*, some of the most interesting technologies and knowledge have been forgotten or fallen into disrepair. Science and technology in *Game of Thrones* either evoke a Golden Age full of lost glories or remain hidden in the secrets of an elite. The emblematic Valyrian steel weapons came to the Seven Kingdoms at an earlier date from old Valyria, brought by the Targaryen conquerors. Other technological achievements, such as the Wall, are the work of great native builders, but they too belong to a distant past.

The setting of *Game of Thrones* and *A Song of Ice and Fire* seems to depict a technologically almost stagnant society. War, then, is the stage where technologies—and magic—come into full display. Knowledge and technology are in the purview of elites, notably the Maesters. There is a general mistrust of innovation, linked as it is to necromancy, magic, or trickery. But what exactly is the connection between magic and science in Westeros?

In *A Song of Ice and Fire*, the characters most devoted to the sciences as a means to achieve concrete solutions are Samwell Tarly and Tyrion Lannister. Samwell, a son of a lord who was sent to serve the Night's Watch at the Wall, is drawn to the large, decaying library of Castle Black. In *A Clash of Kings*, as he gathers information for Lord Commander Mormont, Samwell finds a "treasure trove" of unique documents, which had been almost forgotten in the library. Among the maps and

books, he starts piecing together the original mission of the
Night's Watch, as well as the very different world in which the
first of their brethren lived.

Between Magic and Science

In Westeros, knowledge of magic and science is confined by the
domains of myth and religion, relatively ignored until a new
urgency makes it clear that a practical approach is needed.
Two of the most interesting examples in *Game of Thrones* and
A Song of Ice and Fire are the Maesters of the Citadel and the
Pyromancers of the Alchemists' Guild. Acutely aware of the
thin borders between science and magic, these groups exploit
their monopolies to their own advantage. Outside these limited
groups, science and technology in Westeros are enveloped in
mistrust and skepticism. This skeptical attitude reinforces the
stratified social order of the Seven Kingdoms. In this world-
view, the development of the "practical arts" is a means of
acquiring power for those not born into the upper echelons of
society, which makes it generally suspicious, if not undesirable.

The Maesters are scholars, counsellors, healers, and teach-
ers at the same time. Each Maester has to prove his worth by
learning several disciplines, and forging the links of a chain
worn as a symbol of mastery of a particular subject. A link of
Valyrian steel, tellingly, symbolises mastery of the magical
arts, whereas a silver link testifies to the wearer's competence
in medicine. Grouped in a kind of hybrid of monastic order and
professional guild, the Maesters follow a strict code of conduct
and undertake a lengthy period of specialized, but vast, learning at the Citadel before serving the Seven Kingdoms. They
are the elite of the intellectual arts of Westeros, being specifically tasked to study the seasons and announce the arrival of
Winter.

However, empiricism, which holds that the data we gather
from our senses and our practical activity are the best sources
of knowledge, is alive in Westeros. Tyrion and Samwell represent a more practical approach to the fading power of the
Maesters. The Alchemists represent the other side of technological efficacy in Westeros. Their practical art blends the natural and the supernatural—the fantasy element in *Game of
Thrones*. The Alchemists are best known for holding the secret
of the production of wildfire, a combustible liquid that burns

even in water, much like the Byzantine Greek Fire. The secret is said to involve magic, whose power is purportedly linked to the presence of dragons in the world. Besides tipping the balance of the Battle of the Blackwater (*A Clash of Kings*) in favour of the forces defending King's Landing, wildfire presents a particular way of framing knowledge and science in Westeros. It relies on a mix of myth and science typical of pre-modern forms of knowledge, where practical experimentation, magic, and superstition are intertwined. In the case of wildfire, as in the medieval trade guilds before the creation of industrial and commercial patents, secrecy is essential for preserving a mysterious monopoly.

Technology and magic are both feared and revered in Westeros. The use of the Citadel's knowledge, and above all of Hallyne the Pyromancer's wildfire, is firmly controlled by small groups holding on to the secrets of the trade. Technology and magic are feared because the way they operate is not understood except by the initiated elite. For example, it is only when wildfire is used in battle that most of the characters realize its power. Magic is even more feared and less understood, as it remains intertwined with exotic religions or dragons. Melisandre and Thoros hold the secrets to revive the dead, but not even they are sure why their spells and prayers work. Contrary to our own world, in *Game of Thrones* science, technology, and magic all have some measure of efficacy and, therefore, power to alter the course of events. Not only do they propel the narrative, they compete for influence.

In *Game of Thrones*, we observe an entanglement of the active forces of technology and the supernatural, which is conspicuously absent from our own world. Our modern science is rooted in the pursuit of knowledge through empirical and mathematical methods of enquiry. The divergence between science and magic can be tied to the emergence of these methods and the invention of scientific instruments, which superseded the authority of previous philosophical and mystical traditions. The efficacy of modern technology is underpinned by rational experimentation and replicability, whereas magic and mysticism are empirically sterile.

In Westeros, skills are intellectual territories governed by specific rules of certain groups. The Maesters are suspicious of magic and discourage its study, whereas the Alchemists and the Warlocks do not shy away from using it to disguise their secrets. Valyrian steel, specifically, was produced by a lost blend of metallurgy and magic of fallen Valyria. Magic is fickle and mysterious.

Samwell Tarly and the Fighting Empiricists of Westeros

Finally only the dragonglass dagger remained, wreathed in steam as if it were alive and sweating.

—*A Storm of Swords*, Chapter 18.

In *Game of Thrones*, books are rare and, perhaps, neglected. Rumors and superstition abound. As often happens with heavily regulated institutions, the intellectual situation of Westeros is at a crossroads: facing threats from the White Walkers and hearing the rumors of Daenerys Targaryen's dragons, someone must disentangle magic, superstition, and science.

Samwell Tarly is in the perfect position to link the urgency of the wars against the White Walkers with his first-hand empirical knowledge of the powers of dragonglass and Valyrian steel. In Castle Black's library, Tarly had started to uncover the long lost knowledge of the mission of the Night's Watch. However, his fights with the White Walkers north of the Wall have given him direct, empirical proof of the efficacy of magical weapons in the fight against the Others. It was precisely this kind of investigation, based both on empiricism and on the rediscovery of lost knowledge, which gave rise to Earth's modern science and technology.

Is Samwell Tarly starting a renaissance in the Seven Kingdoms by championing a new synthesis of experience and learning? Or is he, driven by the urgency of the situation, temporarily unearthing answers that will once again be lost when the victory is won? Under urgent circumstances, skeptical attitudes towards science and technology often must give way to practical concerns.

Archimedes was said to have saved his native city of Syracuse from an invasion by focusing sunbeams to burn the enemy's fleet. In addition, even fear of magic can give way before the empirical efficacy of spells: one of the staunchest pragmatists in Westeros, Ser Davos Seaworth, asks Melisandre to apply her knowledge of magic to revive the fallen Jon Snow.

The importance of Samwell Tarly lies in his inquisitive and pragmatic attitude. Driven to action by his oath, he is forced to live outside the confines of the library. This is what allows him to go beyond the dubious authority of old texts and their contemplation, which for everyone else seems to be fantasy, and start creating for himself and his brothers in the Watch a specialized body of knowledge that might ultimately reveal the way to fight the White Walkers. His approach is not mere empiricism. It merges active research with existing knowledge. He wants to learn more, and does not reject the reality of the fantastic in Westeros.

Magical Pragmatism

Given the fantastic nature of Westeros, is it possible to disentangle magic and technology? According to the historian of religion Mircea Eliade, enquiries into supernatural modes of knowledge such as alchemy or astrology existed precisely in the frontier between science and myth.

Alchemists tried to transmute elements—lead into gold, for example—or discover the powerful philosopher's stone. Astrologists looked for meaning in the interplay of celestial bodies. In the sciences of the occult, each object, element or planet was imbued with powers and hidden meanings to be controlled, teased out with incantations, and careful manipulation. Isaac Newton is known to have had a passion for astrology even as he worked on the mathematical foundations of astronomical movement.

The alchemists of our world did not have the advantage of magical efficacy. In Westeros, magic and supernatural powers exist, even if they have fallen from the sight of most characters. Multiple factors can explain the loss of magical efficacy. Dragons are said to fuel magic, but were thought to be extinct. The Children of the Forest and the Old Gods have lost ground to humans and the politicized religion of the Seven Gods. The winters have been mild enough to keep the White Walkers out of sight. As *Game of Thrones* unfolds, we witness these multiple dimensions of a different, fantastic way of life that highlights the importance of the magical arts for developing tools, skills, and methods required to solve the crises.

This fantasy Renaissance will depend on the rediscovery of a Golden Age which is hinted to have prevailed in the past. There is an ancient age of great feats of engineering, conquest, and magic. It was then the Wall was built, Valyria still stood, and humans coexisted with the magical beings of Westeros.

It is that bygone epoch that holds the secrets of a renaissance that Samwell Tarly and the other knowledge-seekers of Westeros are pursuing. But that search for knowledge and technological power is not without its risks. The tale of the Doom of Valyria—a mysterious cataclysmic destruction of home city of the Targaryens—for example, is a cautionary tale. Its story is akin to the fate of Atlantis or other myths of fallen civilizations, where the gods punish those who dare to know or build too much.

Greek, Roman, and Judeo-Christian mythology present us with plenty of cautionary tales of hubris and punishment of our will for knowledge and power. Prometheus, Icarus, Adam and Eve, the builders of the tower of Babel all suffered after piercing the boundaries set to humankind.

Although the fate of Samwell Tarly's voyages and enquiries is uncertain, it brings to light the role of the Maesters in the creation and preservation of knowledge in Westeros, as well as keeping magic in disrepute. In a way similar to the role of monasteries and copyists in Earth's Middle Ages, the Maesters keep records, study, and offer their services to society. Yet, there is still a great need for an inquisitive, empirically tested mind to ignite a new curiosity about the powers of dragonglass and Valyrian steel.

At the time of *Game of Thrones*, the Maesters' monopoly of science and technology shows signs of exhaustion. In their zealous corporatism, lobbying against alchemy and "necromancy," the Maesters hold important knowledge that they do not seek to preserve or transmit. The need for a new understanding of magic and mysterious powers mirrors the crossroads at the origin of modern science, when the experimental sciences and mathematical models successfully confronted mysticism and theology. However, unlike Westeros, our world has no dragons to fuel magical powers.

25
Should Catelyn Have Trusted Brienne?

T<small>YLER</small> D<small>ALTON</small> M<small>C</small>N<small>ABB</small> <small>AND</small> M<small>AX</small> A<small>NDREWS</small>

The continents of Westeros and Essos in the *Game of Thrones* universe present atmospheres of betrayal, alliances made and alliances broken, war, deceit, and ambition where life itself is at stake. As Cersei Lannister warns, "When you play the game of thrones, you win or you die" ("You Win or You Die").

Take the example of The Red Wedding: The King in the North, Robb Stark, made an alliance with Walder Frey in order to cross his bridge over the River Trident. One of the conditions for Robb was to marry one of Frey's daughters though he married Talisa Maegyr instead. Roose Bolton aligns himself with Walder Frey and the Lannisters in an ambitious move to take the North for his own. In "The Rains of Castamere," the Starks are completely unaware that they have sprung the trap set by Bolton and Frey resulting in the death of every Stark present.

Lies and betrayal plague nearly every character. Theon betrayed Robb to win the approval and acceptance of his father resulting in his defeat at Winterfell. Tyrion was maliciously betrayed by Shae in a conspiracy to frame Tyrion for Joffrey's death. The ambitious Petyr Baelish turns against Ned Stark after it became clear that Ned was too honorable for personal ambitions for the Throne. These are difficult situations for knowing whom you can trust.

Brienne's Oath as Catelyn's Sworn Sword

How can Catelyn trust Brienne's loyalty and competence as a sworn sword? When Catelyn is treating with Renly Baratheon to align the Starks with Renly's army, his brother, a Shadow with the face of Stannis, kills Renly in his tent chamber. Brienne had just become a member of Renly's King's Guard and had vowed to protect him. Brienne and Catelyn are the only witnesses to the murder.

As someone who could not uphold her oath to Renly, what good reasons are there for why Catelyn would want her as her sworn sword? What could possibly give Catelyn reason to believe that Brienne will fulfill her vows?

Philosophers have come up with different theories to explain such "reasons to believe." We say that a belief is warranted if there are good reasons to hold it. Warrant is what distinguishes knowledge from true beliefs that are merely lucky. I could for example, have a random feeling that there exist 1,023,042 White Walkers and it could in fact be true. However, a lucky guess isn't knowledge, and this belief wouldn't be warranted. Something more is needed for warranted belief, and philosophers have different theories for what this something more is.

The Spider's Web of Beliefs

Accessibilism is the idea that in order for a belief to be warranted you need to have access to internal reasons supporting the belief in question. Consider what you know already to be strung together like a spider's web where each belief supports the other. Each intersection of the web is a belief that coheres with the rest of the web. How might the belief that Brienne will fulfill her vows cohere with Catelyn's already existent web of knowledge?

> *Catelyn has warrant in believing Brienne will fulfill her vows if and only if Catelyn possesses internal access to enough evidence to believe the fulfillment of vows will occur.*

It doesn't matter *when* Brienne fulfills her vows because the oath never indicates a timeframe, merely that they will be upheld. As Brienne tells Podrick, "Death does not release me from an oath." So, just because Catelyn was murdered at the Red Wedding it doesn't mean the oath has been nullified. When we say Catelyn possesses enough evidence we mean that she has actually accessed it and doesn't merely have the potential to access it. What evidence is accessible to Catelyn that would give her warrant for her belief that Brienne will protect her and her children?

If Catelyn chooses to trust Brienne, then how well does that conform to the evidence?

- **Brienne is an excellent warrior.**

- **Brienne was sincerely distraught by Renly's death.**

- **Brienne couldn't protect Renly.**

- **Catelyn witnessed Brienne's fidelity.**

Catelyn must consider the oath itself and the background knowledge that she already possesses. Is it like having another intersection of the web right in the middle where it fits with ease or is it like stringing up another intersection far from the rest of the web? If Brienne had in fact failed to uphold her oath to Renly in light of his murder, then it seems that trusting her would stretch Catelyn's web of knowledge decreasing the likelihood of warrant.

However, considering that the *Game of Thrones* universe is plagued with magic, something that may understandably cast reasonable suspicion on anything, it isn't reasonable to expect Brienne to do more than any great knight would be capable of doing. After all, what could she do to protect Renly from the magical Shadow offspring between Stannis and Melisandre? Catelyn did not believe Brienne failed in her oath to Renly insisting, "Renly's death was no fault of yours. You served him bravely" ("The Ghost of Harrenhal"). Thus, for Catelyn, Brienne's past loyalty counts as evidence that her current testimony is true.

Suppose all the evidence balanced out as equally probable. Suppose Catelyn had a blue and a red marble in a bag. Without looking or having any evidence as to which marble she may pull from the bag she has a fifty-fifty chance of pulling the blue marble. If the evidence could go either way for warranting trust or distrust of Brienne, perhaps, either option would be rational for Catelyn.

Why should Catelyn follow the evidence? Following the evidence is more likely to lead to the truth. Each strand of the web fits well within the rest of the web. The system of beliefs becomes self-affirming whilst still being able to have warrant for new and contrary beliefs—an evolving web.

What role does intuition play compared to the empirical facts of our sensory experiences for the accessibilist? Most intuitions including moral and social understandings, along with memory and sense experience may be considered as evidence. After all, if Brienne's honor was considered evidence for warrant, what about dishonor? Ethical claims are not experientially verifiable or falsifiable. Can a claim that requires no evidence itself serve as evidence for something experientially? If the accessibilist's need for empirical evidence must be appeased by personal experience, then it follows that the knowledge of certain ethical or pre-experiential truths may certainly be *discovered* via experience.

There seems to be an obvious question for an evidential basis to warrant: if all the objective evidence *seems* to be against Brienne as the one who murdered Renly, then should Brienne respond with, "I must follow the evidence. I thought I didn't murder Renly, but I guess I did!" No! That's why subjective experience and intuition also serve as evidence. *Evidence* must not be limited to empirical facts only.

A proper understanding of the evidence for Brienne's fealty to Renly would include Brienne's own experiences and testimony. A fair consideration of the evidence that Catelyn has access to gives her warrant to trust Brienne to protect her and her children as a sworn sword. Catelyn's good reasons to trust Brienne fit securely within her web of knowledge.

Proper Functionalism

Some philosophers think that having evidence in the way described in the previous section isn't the proper way for a belief to be warranted. Some philosophers take an alternative position called externalism. There are different kinds of externalists, but we will look at a version of externalism called proper functionalism and we will discuss how Catelyn's belief that Brienne will fulfill her oath and faithfully serve her could be warranted according to externalist proper functionalism.

Proper functionalism is the idea that in order for a person to have a warranted belief, 1. the belief needs to be produced by mental faculties or processes that are properly functioning in a context they were designed for, and 2. those faculties need to be aimed toward producing true belief, 3. with the design plan being a good one so that under these conditions it is likely that the belief produced is true. This probably sounds like a mouth full of High Valyrian so let's break this explanation down.

Why must you have properly functioning faculties to have a warranted belief? If beliefs are not produced by properly functioning faculties, then the truthfulness of the belief seems random or lucky rather than properly grounded. Imagine, 'The Mountain' is in the mad scientist Qyburn's new lab when lightning strikes the room and causes a huge explosion with materials in the lab. And even though he is reduced to basic elements from this accident an identical replica emerges. Let's call this replica Labman. It talks like The Mountain and looks like him. Whatever he believed, Labman believes. In fact, Labman even holds the same reasons for thinking those beliefs are true! However, no one could say that Labman's faculties are functioning properly. It isn't as if Labman's mental faculties have been designed by God, evolution, or both. Labman has emerged by complete accident.

But if Labman doesn't have properly functioning faculties, then his faculties have no way in which they should operate. There is no way in which Labman's faculties should or shouldn't produce beliefs. If Labman produces the belief that a White Walker is close by and there happens to be one close by, it still isn't the case that Labman's faculties should produce that belief. It is just a lucky coincidence that they do. There is too weak of a connection between the belief produced from Labman's faculties and the truthfulness of that belief. This would still be a problem even if Labman had internal access to right sort of reasons for its true beliefs or even if it merely got lucky enough to have randomly created faculties that turned out to be reliable.

What about the second proper functionalist condition, the need to have faculties that are operating in the context for which they were designed? Picture yourself going to the peaceful district of Lhazar for the weekend. Since, it is an area filled with pastures and sheep-herders you expect to see all sorts of sheep. However, the village you are in actually has an infestation of dogs that look like sheep and these dogs have scared away most of the real sheep.

If you randomly stumbled upon a sheep in the village and you formed the belief that there was actually a sheep in front of you, then would your belief be warranted? Even granting that your faculties were working properly, being that you would have formed the same belief incorrectly if you had seen one of the 'fake sheep' this context makes your belief forming faculties unreliable even if you happen to get lucky enough to form an occasional true belief. It is like being in a room that is flooded by red light. Most objects would look red whether or not they actually are. Therefore, you could not trust your normal faculty of sight to enable you to distinguish between red and non-red objects.

But according to the proper functionalist having properly functioning mental processes in their designated context still isn't enough. The proper functionalist thinks we also need faculties that are aimed toward truth and the design plan needs to be a good one so that it is likely that beliefs produced under these conditions will be true.

Again, imagine that as a form of punishment the Lord of Light changed the design plan of an unbeliever's intellectual faculties and caused it to generate random beliefs. If among the other random beliefs the unbeliever had she randomly formed the true belief that the Lord of Light had changed her design plan to produce random beliefs, then the belief would still lack warrant. Therefore, in order for a person to have a warranted belief on this view, all three conditions must be met: 1. the belief needs to be produced by mental faculties or processes that are properly functioning in a context they were designed for, and 2. those faculties need to be aimed toward producing true belief, 3. with the design plan being a good one so that under these conditions it is likely that the belief produced is true.

With all of this background information stated, let's return to Catelyn and Brienne. How could Catelyn have a warranted belief that Brienne would serve her faithfully, even in a context that is full of deceptive testimonies? Well, as long as the context is one in which Catelyn's faculties were designed for and her faculties were both properly functioning and truth aimed, then she could have a properly warranted belief. Perhaps, Catelyn might correctly observe that Brienne is a skilled and loyal knight.

Catelyn isn't thinking about good reasons to trust Brienne. Nor is she actively weighing the evidence for and against trusting Brienne. That isn't the way most people normally make decisions. Instead, it just is the case that in light of coming into contact with Brienne and who she is Catelyn naturally forms the belief that she is a trustworthy and gifted warrior.

Now, you might think this all sounds fishy. Even if Catelyn might be initially warranted in her belief, once she considers all of the deception that surrounds her, shouldn't she think that it's more probable that Brienne is deceiving her? No, the proper functionalist thinks that there is such a strong connection between the belief produced from your faculties and that belief actually being true that as long as Catelyn still strongly believes that Brienne is telling the truth, then other considerations be damned; Catelyn would still be warranted in trusting Brienne!

And given Brienne's ultimate success in returning Jaime to King's landing, finding both of Catelyn's daughters, freeing Arya from the custody of the Hound, and her valiant rescue of Sansa from Ramsay Bolton's soldiers, we can see that Catelyn's trust was well founded.

VII

You Think
I Would Trade
My Honor?

26

Horrifying Violence, Gratuitous Sex, and the Truth

Eric J. Silverman

The *Game of Thrones* stories are full of disturbing violence, torture, rape, prostitution, incest, unnecessary nudity, and gratuitous sex. With literally hundreds of on-screen deaths—including many gory, graphically depicted deaths—it may be the most violent television series of all time.

Traditionally, some people have thought that merely viewing art depicting such activities is inherently immoral. One motivation behind such criticisms is that art depicting such activities can propose them to the viewer and make the viewer more likely to engage in similar immoral activities. However, despite whatever moral hazards that may exist in viewing *Game of Thrones*, there are also important morally praiseworthy aspects of the show that can aid in moral development.

Watching from Bad Motives

A man with no motives is a man no one suspects.

—Littlefinger

First, we should realize that some activities are morally neutral in themselves, but are praiseworthy or immoral based upon your motives for engaging in these activities. And so, even if watching *Game of Thrones* is not immoral in itself, there are surely some specific reasons that would be morally dubious motives for watching.

For example, someone might watch the show because they enjoy its occasional torture scenes. While Theon Greyjoy is hardly a sympathetic character, it probably shows vicious callousness towards the value of humanity to enjoy watching Ramsay Bolton torture, manipulate, flay, and dismember him to the point of complete mental breakdown.

And even if justice ultimately requires Ramsay's execution, it's probably immoral to enjoy watching him get devoured alive by his own dogs. Similarly, Walder Frey probably deserves death for the deadly betrayal of his lord Robb Stark, but Arya Stark's delight in assassinating him should disturb us rather than gratify us. If someone watches *Game of Thrones* to enjoy it as a kind of 'torture-porn' and takes delight in the extreme pain and hardships the various characters endure on the show, such enjoyment indicates a vicious and immoral callousness towards human suffering.

Just as it's probably immoral to watch *Game of Thrones* to get sadistic joys from the various characters' sufferings, it may also be immoral to watch it as a form of low-level, socially acceptable pornography. A traditional moral concern claims that pornography objectifies the people that it depicts (usually women), encourages viewers to indulge their baser appetites, and thereby encourages the viewer to treat people as sexual objects rather than inherently valuable persons.

While it may be immoral to watch the show because of these specific motivations, is there a broader reason to think that watching *Game of Thrones* is inherently immoral?

Life Is Not a Song

From the time of Plato's *Republic* one important test concerning the moral value of a particular story has been found in the narrative itself. Does this particular story serve to promote or obscure the truth about reality?

Plato's interest in this issue was not only theoretical. An ancient comedic play entitled *The Clouds* depicted Plato's best friend and mentor Socrates as a bizarre, impious, politically and theologically incorrect heretic who explicitly mocked the socially popular opinions of his day, including the Greek gods themselves. Later, Socrates was actually accused, convicted, and executed for corrupting the youth with his unpopular opinions.

In Plato's *Apology*—his depiction of Socrates's trial—he suggests that Socrates was convicted in part due to the jury's exposure to the slanderous play, although Socrates's repeated insulting of the jury probably didn't help.

As Plato knew first-hand, the lens of narrative stories helps shape the way people view reality. It can shape people's views for the better or for the worse. It can open people's minds to new ideas and facets of reality that they might otherwise overlook. Or it can plant and reinforce inaccurate prejudices in the minds of its audience. For example, if media consistently cast African-Americans in roles of violent, dishonest criminals, then it would be no surprise that watching such shows encourages prejudice against African-Americans. Similarly, if media consistently presents actresses with unrealistic body shapes and sizes, then it would be unsurprising if viewers developed similar unrealistic expectations of women's bodies in real life.

Thus, narratives can bring people closer to or further from reality. By this important philosophical measure *Game of Thrones* tells a refreshingly honest story on many topics. Watching such a show can be morally helpful in several ways.

Violence Really Is Ugly

I choose violence.

—CERSEI LANNISTER

It's easy to criticize the graphic violence of *Game of Thrones*, yet much of this violence is necessary to tell the disturbing truth about war. War is ugly. Death comes to all sides and death is ugly. Virtuous heroes die. Evil villains die, at least eventually. Many innocent and fairly uninvolved civilians are also hurt or killed in war. Even Lord Varys recognizes that it's the innocents and smallfolk who suffer most during war. Narratives that portray war as simply glorious and morally neat and tidy are quite false. Furthermore, they encourage people in real life to embrace naive assumptions about war and to turn to war too quickly.

Just War Theory—a set of philosophical guidelines for morally appropriate warfare that were largely shaped by Augustine of Hippo—warns that even when your cause is just it is important to limit yourself to morally acceptable means of warfare and to distinguish between appropriate and inappropriate targets for military violence. Unfortunately, this is far more difficult than it sounds. Accordingly, even though The Brotherhood Without Banners was founded with an idealistic just mission given by Ned Stark to bring the Mountain and the marauding Lannisters to justice, even they degenerated into an opportunistic band of vigilantes in some ways. For example, they kidnapped and sold Gendry to Stannis Baratheon, nearly costing him his very life.

> How many tens of thousands had to die because Rhaegar chose your aunt?
>
> —LITTLEFINGER

Just as the excessive violence of the show serves to communicate an important truth about reality, much of the sex—though perhaps, not the nudity—similarly serves to communicate a fact about reality. Humans tend to be preoccupied with sex and not just within socially acceptable marriage.

An accurate portrayal of human nature requires depicting this interest in sex—though perhaps, without depicting the unrealistic amount of interest in incest that occurs in Westeros. The human propensity towards violence and excessive sexuality has been noted by several important thinkers. Plato referred this tendency as the appetitive aspect of human nature, Sigmund Freud described it as the Id, and Augustine conceptualized it an expression of original sin. However we describe this tendency, it is often ignored or understated in traditional epic stories.

Game of Thrones is also accurate in that many of its characters' sexual entanglements ultimately have negative consequences. It accurately acknowledges the difficulties faced by those who are born in less than ideal circumstances due to their parents' choices, including bastards like Gendry or Jon Snow. It acknowledges that there can be dramatic social consequences for ill-conceived relationships. For example, Robb's uprising against the Lannisters might have been successful had he not broken his engagement to one of Walder Frey's daughters. Most strikingly, there's an important sense in which the romantic triangle between Rhaegar Targaryen, Lyanna Stark, and Robert Baratheon is responsible for all the deaths and violence in Robert's Rebellion.

The show is also honest in showing that not all romantic relationships are positive and healthy. While some couples have good relationships like Catelyn and Eddard or Robb and Talisa, many others do not. There is physical abusiveness and manipulation in Cersei's relationships as well as Ramsay and Sansa Bolton's; Tyrion Lannister and Shae's relationship ends tragically with betrayal and homicide, Jon and Ygritte's relationship ends violently, and so on.

The only negative aspect of sexual relationships that is understated is the danger of sexually transmitted diseases, since promiscuous people like Tyrion, Bronn, or several other characters, would inevitably be at risk of sexually transmitted infections. Yet, this is a forgivable omission given how many relational dangers it does acknowledge, and the fact that sexually transmitted diseases aren't exactly an exciting, action-packed topic.

Vulnerable Heroes

You wear your honor as a suit of armor because you think it protects you . . . but it weighs you down and makes it difficult to move.

—LITTLEFINGER

Game of Thrones also tells us a neglected truth about heroes: a standard epic storyline since the time of Homer depicts the virtuous hero as virtually invulnerable. So long as morality and virtue shape the hero's character his victory is assured. Inevitably, the hero is able to overcome whatever obstacles come his way more due to his commitment to virtue and right than cunning. The examples of such heroes are legion: Luke Skywalker, Frodo Baggins, Aslan, Ulysses, Aneas, Harry Potter, and so forth.

Yet, the tales of Ned Stark and Robb Stark offer a needed corrective to these romantic stories. To have honor without cleverness or wisdom can result in recklessness and is likely to end badly. While it's important for narratives to hold up virtue as a heroic ideal, a commitment to moral virtue without wisdom is a recipe for failure and personal disaster.

Philosophers from at least as far back as Aristotle have argued that the paradigm of virtue must include both intellectual and moral skill. In this sense, Tyrion Lannister rather than Ned Stark is closer to Aristotle's ideal.

> Those are brave men out there. Let's go kill them!
>
> —TYRION LANNISTER

Game of Thrones tells us the truth about our 'enemies.' It does not give us a simplistic story about larger than life heroes who never make mistakes and inhuman villains who embrace evil for the sheer joy of evil (except, perhaps, for Joffrey Baratheon and Ramsay Snow).

Instead, most of its characters are more like real people, albeit in extreme situations. They have real hopes, real dreams, realistic, and complex motivations. Even the actions of someone like Jaime Lannister 'The Kingslayer' eventually make sense to those who watch long enough to realize that he isn't just the arrogant nemesis of 'the hero' Ned Stark.

Theon Greyjoy commits his atrocities largely out of a desire to reconnect with his own family and culture. Littlefinger wants power. And as in real life, Westeros's villains aren't incompetent fools who reveal their plans and then leave their enemies alive in some unnecessarily complex trap.

Just as the real world isn't truly divided into quickly identifiable heroes in white hats and villains in dark hats, Westeros isn't easily divided into a simplistic dichotomy of 'heroes and villains.' In reality, most people are similar to morally imperfect 'gray' characters. Robert's rebellion may have been justified, but this fact would not justify the assassination of Daenerys, who was merely a child while her father committed his atrocities.

Ned Stark may have been an honorable man, yet even he lied about the nature of his victory over Ser Arthur Dayne. Instead of an honorable victory, Ned only won this fight because one of his allies unexpectedly stabbed Dayne in the back. The Greyjoys may be violent pirates, but no real moral justification of King's Landing's rule over them has been offered other than their centuries-old surrender to the dragon-riding Targaryen conquerors.

In these and many other ways, the moral realism of *Game of Thrones* provides a much-needed counterpoint to the standard simplistic caricatures promoted by other popular epic stories.

Ideals versus Reality

I tell them no one's special. And they think I am special for telling them that.

—THE HIGH SPARROW

Game of Thrones tells us the truth about idealism. It is not unusual for the worst atrocities to be committed in the name of the highest ideals. Even though the egalitarian assumptions of the Free Folk and the Sparrows are closer to the moral assumptions undergirding contemporary politics than the hierarchical monarchies that dominate Westeros, neither of these egalitarian ideals is attractive in its actual applications. The Free Folk's emphasis on absolute freedom and natural equality is actually violent lawless anarchy and the Sparrows' egalitarian religiosity is violent and power-hungry. Of course, the ideals of the hierarchical societies of Westeros aren't any fairer or less conducive to violence and abuse than these egalitarian ideals.

This reflects a truth about the real world in that noble ideals in themselves do not guarantee a just society. In reality, most societies aspire to noble ideals of one kind or another, but fall well short of their own ideals. Yet it's common for societies to misjudge their cultural rivals by focusing upon their worst extremes while turning a blind eye to their own failures.

Much of American society judges Islamic society by its violent extreme. Some secular Americans judge Christians based on their crassest fundamentalist representatives. Some Christians judge secularism by its connections to murderers like Hitler, Stalin, and Robespierre. In each case, they judge the worst representatives of competing worldviews against their own theoretical high ideals.

Now It Ends

Game of Thrones is undoubtedly a violent and sex-filled show. While not everyone watches for the deep plot and engaging characters, it still teaches important truths about reality that are often omitted from epic stories.

It teaches us the truth about the ugliness of violence and war that many stories omit. It teaches us the truth that humans can be a sexually preoccupied bunch, often to their own harm. It teaches us the truth that following noble ideals gives no guarantee of success and that villains can have perfectly understandable motives. It reminds us that lofty political ideals give no guarantee of justice in the real world.

As Littlefinger warns Sansa, "Life is not a song." It's better to see the world as it actually is, rather than in the inaccurate terms of romanticized stories.

27

Was the Red Wedding Massacre a Good Thing?

WILLEM VAN DER DEIJL

For two and a half seasons I loved watching *Game of Thrones*.

Sure, it hadn't been easy to understand why Sansa's wolf Lady had to be killed, or why Daenerys had to become a young widow. And yes, it had been particularly tough to watch the righteous Ned Stark die, executed on orders of the abhorrently vicious boy-king Joffrey, even after Ned had decided to beg for his life for the sake of his children.

Yet, after all the tragedies, I still enjoyed *Game of Thrones* more than anything. But at the end of Season Three the joy ended. The occasion was the Red Wedding.

At this gruesome event Walder Frey turns on his allies at the wedding of his own daughter. The result: Robb Stark, his mother Catelyn, wife Talisa, and wolf Grey Wind are brutally slaughtered along with most of his bannermen and most of his army. The northern rebellion is effectively crushed, and with it, every hope of removing Joffrey from the throne and finding justice for the death of Ned Stark.

Furthermore, the murders took place after Lord Frey had sworn to protect his guests in a traditional sacred vow of hospitality known as Guest Right. For me personally, the shock of this event was so great that I stopped watching *Game of Thrones* for two years.

I should have kept watching. Not only does sweet revenge on King Joffrey finally arrive, but because I stopped watching I did not get to see an important philosophical moment in the series, in which Tywin Lannister defends himself from Tyrion's accusation that he has gone too far in his attempt to keep his grandson Joffrey on the throne. Fascinatingly, Tywin replies:

> Explain to me why it is more noble to kill ten thousand men in battle than a dozen at dinner.

The response leaves Tyrion surprised. Tywin is not the kind of man who seems to act out of moral nobility, and his son does not believe that he is moved by saving innocent lives. But is Tywin right? Could it be at all plausible that Tywin Lannister acted morally in organizing the Red Wedding? Can it ever be morally permissible to organize such an event involving deceit, betrayal of trust, and horrific mass murder?

To Do the Most Good, Get Your Hands Dirty

There is a view in philosophy in which the ends always justify the means. On this view, killing a dozen people to save ten thousand is justified even if the dozen are innocent and the ten thousand are not. This view is called consequentialism.

More precisely, consequentialism is the view that the right moral action is the action that has the best consequences out of all available options. So, if the action with the best consequences involves killing an innocent person, then it is not only morally permitted, but it is even *required*.

But what consequences are to be rated as best? There are a variety of versions of consequentialism, which vary according to what they judge to be good. The most well-known type of consequentialism is utilitarianism. Utilitarians understand "best consequences" as the outcome that maximizes overall happiness, where everyone's happiness counts equally.

Other consequentialists believe that not everyone should count equally in the good, but those who are currently worst off should be prioritized. According to this theory—prioritarianism—it's better to make a miserable person better off than to make someone better off who is already having a very good life. What all consequentialists share is a belief that sometimes lying, cheating, breaking vows, and even stealing may be justified if they are required to bring about the best outcome. They disagree in this matter with their main rivals—deontologists—

who believe that some actions, such as breaking vows, are always morally wrong *regardless of the consequences.*

Consequentialist reasoning, and in particular the associated mantra "the greatest good," has a bad name. Evil fictitious characters like to cite this principle. For example, in the Harry Potter series the dictatorial wizard-lord Grindelwald had it written above the entrance of his prison.

Stalin is said to have defended state terror by citing the principle that "the ends justify the means." However, it may not be fair to discredit a theory by citing the evil characters who have abused it to justify crimes. Clearly, such characters do not actually make the world a better place. In so far as they apply consequentialist reasoning, they are not very good at it.

At this point you might wonder: the Red Wedding was a gruesome slaughter in which many honorable men were killed. How could someone even ask whether such a thing could be morally okay? You might feel compelled to stop reading, because such a suggestion raises questions about the sanity of the person who makes it. But before you do so, please bear with me for three short paragraphs.

While we can all agree that the Red Wedding was a terrible event, there are many political leaders responsible for terrible events that we honor for their bravery. Think about the bombing of German cities in the Second World War. Many innocents died.

Think about the atomic bombs on Japan, ending the war by destroying whole cities. More recently, you can think about the innocents that died in bombings targeted at the Islamic State (ISIS) in Iraq and Syria. Or, consider the targeted drone strikes on high-profile terrorist by the United States, in which often many more people die than the targeted bad guy.

Perhaps, you think that these real cases are actually immoral and should have been prevented, even though some desirable effects came out of them. However, there are also cases where it is more obvious that the killing of innocents is a necessary evil. Consider the situation in which you know that a hijacked airplane is flying straight for a building housing thousands of unwitting innocents. The airplane contains a handful of passengers. A military jet is still able to take the plane down. We may feel that a president who gives the order to take the airplane down is doing something terrible, but at the same time, we might also think it is the best thing he can do.

Killing innocents with bombs is obviously a bad thing, but it also seems that especially in the political arena when the stakes are high, doing the right thing requires doing something terrible. In these situations, the consequentialist perspective has some plausibility. Torturing, bombing, or shooting down innocents is never morally ideal, but when you can save many innocent lives by doing it, then failing to do so may be even worse.

The idea originates from Niccolò Machiavelli: if killing a few innocents can prevent a horrifying war, a rebellion, or an uprising, killing a few innocents may be the best thing to do. In other words, in cases when the stakes are high, a good politician sometimes needs to get her hands dirty.

A Massacre and Its Consequences

Tywin Lannister got his hands dirty by organizing the Red Wedding. But is this a case in which the benefits of the outcome are truly greater than the moral costs? Could the Red Wedding be justified from a consequentialist point of view?

To answer this question, we have to see whether the desirable consequences of the Red Wedding outweigh its evil consequences. Tywin makes exactly such a judgment in his reply to Tyrion: killing a small group of men in a dishonorable way is bad. However, if the Red Wedding had not happened, the military forces of House Lannister would have had to face the Northern Rebellion in battle. Before such a conflict would come to a conclusion each army, and probably both, would suffer major loses.

However, if Tywin had been victorious in battle, then he would not be blamed for the men he had slain, but celebrated. By setting up the slaughter at the Red Wedding he minimized casualties on both sides and avoided a long war, which would have brought unrest, instability, economic downturn, and much unsafety to the people in the country.

In Tywin's Defense

So, what are the consequences resulting from organizing—or choosing not to organize—the Red Wedding? Firstly, the Red

Wedding resulted in many casualties on the side of the Northern Rebellion. According to fan estimates the number of Northern bannermen that died in the slaughter following the Red Wedding was around 3,500. Moreover, being killed in a large manslaughter after a large drinking feast when your guard is down is a particularly bad way to go.

But on the brighter side: the Red Wedding ended the rebellion and brought peace to Westeros or at least brought it a lot closer. The benefits of this should not be underestimated. War has many more casualties than the soldiers that die in battles. In the words of Varys: "Why is it always the innocents who suffers, when you high lords play your game of thrones?"

In subtle details, the series depicts the economic damage that the war and political instability have caused the country: such as the hungry mob begging king Joffrey for food or the popularity of the humble anti-elitist religious order of sparrows. From Tywin's perspective ending the war was an important priority. It not only ensured his own power, but from a more neutral moral perspective there are also clear benefits. A longer war would have been more disruptive and would have resulted in more suffering for everyone. Moreover, the battle deaths from such an extended period of war would most likely far exceed the casualties of the Red Wedding slaughter.

In many ways this parallels some of the modern cases described above, such as the case of the atomic bomb that ended World War II. Surely, the casualties of the Red Wedding were mostly unwitting army men rather than innocent civilians, but that should make little difference (and if anything, makes the Red Wedding less bad). Framed this way, if consequentialist reasoning would have it that the dropping of the atomic bomb on Hiroshima and Nagasaki was justified, then so is the Red Wedding.

It does appear odd to call the Red Wedding morally defensible. The Red Wedding provokes very strong feelings of moral revulsion. But some consequentialist philosophers have argued that on some occasions such moral emotions or instincts may be misleading. We may feel that an act is morally revolting only to realize upon reflection that it was, in fact, the best thing to do. Accordingly, we should not trust our feeling of moral revulsion too much in judging the Red Wedding.

A Closer Look at the Consequences

Our description of the consequences of the Red Wedding has so far been overly simple: 3,500 men died and as a result the war is over. There are problems with this simple characterization. The Red Wedding has more consequences beyond killing 3,500 men and ending the war.

Firstly, not only did the Red Wedding keep the hated tyrant Joffrey in place, but it also replaced the beloved Robb Stark as a ruler of the North with the sadistic Roose Bolton. In defending his act, Tywin does not consider the fact that Robb would have been a much better king for his people than Joffrey or Roose Bolton.

Secondly, the Red Wedding was possible due to a major breach of trust committed by Roose Bolton together with Walder Frey. Surely, most would believe that breaking such a sacred vow of hospitality is bad in itself, but in case of the Red Wedding the tale of betrayal traveled quickly throughout Westeros. As a result, the effect of breaking Guest Right may be worse. Would you still trust someone who offers Guest Right to you after hearing of this recent event?

The fact that even the worst enemies could expect a peaceful visit to a foe under Guest Right encouraged diplomatic negotiations, and with it, more opportunity to prevent or resolve bloody conflicts. The breach of Guest Right at the Red Wedding erodes this important institution of trust. Since, this erosion of trust can have detrimental long run consequences even a consequentialist acknowledges the importance of institutions like Guest Right.

One obvious reason to reject Tywin's defense of the Red Wedding is that Tywin is not really concerned for the greater good. Tywin benefits personally from the Red Wedding. If Tywin truly cared about the good of the people, why did he support his incompetent grandson Joffrey on the throne? You may recall that Joffrey caused the Northern Rebellion by unnecessarily executing Ned Stark.

We can speculate about Tywin's true intentions, about which he is never very open. Perhaps Tywin really believed that he could achieve his personal goals of keeping the political power for his family while promoting the greater good. Maybe he believed that he could keep control over his grandson, and eventually turn him into a more just ruler. Perhaps, he was concerned with the good of the people, but also understood that without a gruesome war, there was no way to get a better king. He may have believed that splitting up the country, as Robb seemed to have wanted, was even worse than having Joffrey as a king. This is all speculation. However, it all seems to be dubious. Tywin Lannister does not appear to be much concerned with the greater good of the people. Even if the consequences of the Red Wedding were ultimately good, which is highly doubtful, this would not be due to Tywin's moral character.

This Massacre Doesn't Cut It

Being in power is difficult, especially if you want to do the right thing. From a consequentialist perspective, in some situations, doing the right thing involves sacrificing your own integrity. President Truman cannot be praised for causing the deaths of the innocents who died in Hiroshima and Nagasaki, but we can appreciate that what he did may have been necessary to achieve the least bad outcome.

Sometimes, in times of war or terror, good politics requires getting your hands dirty. In these situations cold calculation may be required. Just as Tywin said, it may be nobler to kill a dozen men at a dinner table than a thousand on the battlefield.

However, Tywin did not just kill a dozen men, but thousands. It's doubtful that the greater good was ultimately achieved in this particular case. Consequently, the Red Wedding is not a case of justifiable dirty hands, even from a consequentialist perspective.

Rather than a good Machiavellian prince, it seems more appropriate to see Tywin as a power-hungry conspirator driven by evil motives.

28
Severed Heads, Dirty Hands

VIKTOR IVANKOVIĆ AND ZLATA BOŽAC

Westeros is a vile and unforgiving place. We, as readers and viewers, are tuning in at one of its more bloody and brutish episodes.

With half a dozen pretenders to the Iron Throne, the Old Gods, the New Gods, a Drowned God, a Red God, a Many-Faced God, the Iron Bank, many other small-scale tormentors, and a supernatural army of snow zombies, the simple folk seeking a fairly serene life can't seem to catch a break. The cruelty at their expense and the threat of their decimation has become routine. Sometimes it's for a religious cause, or a cause of royal right, or sometimes it's just the Mountain. "It's always the innocents who suffer most when high lords play their game of thrones" (*A Game of Thrones*), for whatever cause they play it.

But not all causes are illegitimate. It's true that a high lord's opportunities for getting his hands dirty in Westeros are as common as gales in Storm's End. However, in some cases, getting our hands dirty is what needs to be done if the innocents are to be helped, or some greater tragedy averted. Sometimes, it means lying about a successor's legitimacy to mitigate public unrest. Or it means avoiding full-on war at the expense of postponing the abolishment of a despicable practice like slavery. Heads will be severed and hands will be dirtied, but the ends are occasionally worthy of the means.

The Paradox of Dirty Hands

... we who presume to rule must sometimes do vile things for the good of the realm.

—Varys to Ned Stark, "The Wolf and the Lion"

Thomas Hobbes, an adviser to kings of another age, held the stern belief that decisions and actions which preserve peace always outweigh the deeds that compromise it. What lies beyond peace is a dismal state of affairs, "a gaping pit waiting to swallow us all," in Varys's words ("The Climb"). Persons are left to fend for themselves, in a war of all against all.

Lives in "the state of nature," says Maester Hobbes, end up being solitary, poor, nasty, brutish, and short. He would counsel us not to lose sight of these facts, for a king's rule might be terrible in its harshness, but would still be better than the horrors of war of all against all. Anything that helps to keep the peace, even if it's peace under Lord Tywin Lannister's iron fist, is moral and praiseworthy.

But this faces us with a paradox. If peace is kept through atrocities, lies, murder, torture, or invasion of privacy—things immoral through and through—how is it that they are moral under a peacekeeping imperative?

Ser Jaime Lannister, Lord Commander of the Kingsguard, is the walking incarnation of this paradox. Following the Battle of the Trident, the mad king Aerys demanded from Ser Jaime, his last Kingsguard champion, to bring him his father's head as proof of loyalty. Aerys then entered into a fit, ordering that King's Landing be burned to the ground. Jaime executed Aerys, earning the title of Kingslayer—a mark of blame for breaking one of the most sacred oaths in Westeros.

But doesn't Jaime deserve some commendation? As Jaime says to Catelyn in *A Clash of Kings*: "I think it passing odd that I am . . . reviled by so many for my finest act." Had his willingness to dirty his hands not saved the masses from a desperate madman? This madman was the King, but one who effectively waged war against his people and withheld the peace he was purposed to provide, as even Maester Hobbes grants. Dirtying one's hands, then, must sometimes be moral, if it's fueled by the greater good.

This paradox escapes Lord Eddard Stark. Ned urged King Robert to send Jaime to the Wall for Aerys's murder, yet, at the same time, he accused Jaime of never lifting a finger when Ned's father and brother were being roasted alive by the Mad King ("Lord Snow"). Ned can't make up his mind between the paramount importance of duty on one side, and the protection of the innocent, in as great a number as possible, on the other. Jaime recognizes he is entrapped in a world of duties and necessities to dirty his hands—a myriad of moral dilemmas:

> So many vows . . . they make you swear and swear. Defend the king. Obey the king. Keep his secrets. Do his bidding. Your life for his. But obey your father. Love your sister. Protect the innocent. Defend the weak. Respect the gods. Obey the laws. It's too much. No matter what you do, you're forsaking one vow or the other. (*A Clash of Kings*)

There is little question that Maester Hobbes is justified in stressing the importance of avoiding the horrors of war. But there might be other legitimate causes for allowing dirty hands. Michael Walzer, the man whose contemplations stirred the very tradition of our thinking about dirty hands, considered them an unavoidable fact in the world of politics. Yet Maester Walzer ended up allowing dirty hands only when the consequences are nothing less than communal death.

But what is communal death? Daenerys Targaryen certainly has an idea. It's when the very moral foundations of community are at stake, for they seem to rest on a terrible and systematic atrocity. In her mind, slavery is one such atrocity. It is indeed true that of all the bleak prospects for happiness beyond the Narrow Sea, those of slaves are utterly barren. Daenerys becomes aware that ruling means dirtying one's hands in other ways than eating a stallion's heart. In "And Now His Watch is Ended," Daenerys swindles the slave sellers of their Unsullied army, while retaining the possession of her prized dragon. She then takes advantage of her new position and brings the slavers to a bitter end. It seems obvious that, for her cause to prevail against a more powerful enemy, she had to resort to ruthless trickery.

The philosophical problem of dirty hands has different readings, all of them taking into account the consequences that our actions will bring. But some will think that any kind of seemingly evil means is justified in achieving the happiness of many. Others will allow for dirty hands, but only when this means preventing tragedy, like an invasion of White Walkers. Our understanding of what it means to be moral tends to be rule-bound, as Lord Stark would see it, and it will undoubtedly limit the reach of dirty-hand methods. The causes for and variations of dirty hands are as numerous as the progeny of Walder Frey, and our exploration will only examine some of these considerations. Our first inquiry might be: How dirty can hands get under circumstances of war?

Doing Necessary Evils

All murderers are punished unless they kill in large numbers and to the sound of trumpets.

—VOLTAIRE

These words uttered by another sage, Maester Voltaire, suggest that even our morality of rules shifts and bends in times of war. The act of killing, which we condemn in other areas of social life, is commonplace in war, and though we regret it, we accept its necessity. Soldiers kill rival soldiers, leaders order assassinations, maesters weigh the relative importance of lives to save.

Staunch rule-followers, like Ned or Stannis, believe in an absolute code of honor according to which wars are fought and dirty hands are minimized. Tyrion, on the other hand, knows that if wars are to be won, they are not to be bound by strict rules. Whilst showing empathy for the plights of the poor and innocent, Tyrion understands that their safety is sometimes promoted only through trickery, manipulation, and cold-hearted acts (such as the annihilation of Stannis's fleet in Blackwater Bay).

Ned rejects his own promotion to the throne and insists on Stannis because the throne is *his by right*. He warns Cersei about his plans because that course of action is *honorable*. He rejects Daenerys's assassination because it is *unjust*. Although Ned is right that certain actions are, in one sense, immoral, his decision not to commit them not only brings his own demise, but plays a decisive role in pushing a country into war. Doing necessary evils is the essence of war.

Until his tragic end, Ned seems to be morally wrong in ignoring the grand architecture of horrific consequences that will befall not only his house, but the innocents of the kingdom. His fixation on moral rules may only be paralleled by that of a certain Maester Kant, who would not even justify lying to save an innocent fugitive facing death.

Stannis comprehends that success in war demands dirty hands. But his response to this awareness is completely out of touch. Not only does he overstep the terrible moral boundary of sacrificing his daughter for his god's favor—which would make even the strongest dirty hands supporters twitch—but he is also blind to the *prudential* reasons for action or inaction. Stannis should have predicted that such an atrocity would be too much for his followers' conventional moralities to take, and that their favor would be lost. Dirtying your hands isn't just about what is *moral* in the grand scheme of consequences. It is also about being *smart*.

Nasty Deeds for the Greater Good

And ofttimes a very small man can cast a very large shadow.

—Varys (*A Clash of Kings*)

The people of Westeros might raise their voices against the moral reasoning of dirty hands. It isn't fair, the commoners might protest, that the Lannisters may cheat and manipulate, that the Cleganes may butcher, that pretenders may sack, pillage, and burn, as long as a righteous cause is proclaimed, while "lesser" men are at the mercy of people above laws and moral rules. Why should the superiors be exempt from rules of morality? Aren't they privileged enough already? How is this peculiar moral division of burdens justified? Is justice merely an advantage of the stronger, as a certain Maester Thrasymachus once said?

The high lords would say that the moral power to do seemingly unscrupulous deeds is not a privilege, but a curse. Great power bears immense responsibility, and with responsibility guilt over actions that those lords too recognize as wretched in some way, if they truly care for the innocent. Lords such as Tywin Lannister may understand that wretched acts need to be done if high goals are to be won, even at the cost of being despised. It requires great fortitude to assume high duties.

People like Varys and Jaime know they are hated, but show resolution and resilience, as they understand that they do what is required. That, they would say, is the mark of a truly moral man.

But as Varys tells us, grand political actions are not only authored by "great" men. If it's true that even "lesser" men can change the course of the future, they might face decisions which demand the dirtying of their hands. Jon Snow, as a mere steward, encounters one such decision when he realizes that in order to pass off as a turncoat he will have to murder the legendary Qhorin Halfhand and suffer the judgment of his brothers whom he seemingly betrays. Both Jon and Qhorin understand that if a greater good is to be pursued—that of standing a chance at fending off the Wildling and White Walker threats—Qhorin will have to sacrifice his life and Jon his honor. Dirtying one's hands seems more a matter of moral decisions with high stakes than that of grand roles.

The Irresponsibility of Being Too Good

There is no creature on earth half so terrifying as a truly just man.

—Varys (*A Game of Thrones*)

It is by now established that Westerosi lords are often not only excused in dirtying their hands for a just cause, but are morally obliged to do so.

But what about the flip side of the Gold Dragon? Are chaste leaders at fault when they refuse to dirty their hands for the greater good? Our oft-mentioned culprit in honorable conduct, Eddard Stark, might be accused of refusing to dirty his hands for preventing tyranny, by not storming the Red Keep at Renly's insistence in "You Win or You Die." But there is a less obvious suspect of this crime—the kind-hearted Maester of the Night's Watch, Aemon Targaryen.

Aemon not only refused the throne, ceding rule to his younger brother Aegon—whom he still considered a boy—but also left for the Wall fully aware of a possible plot against his younger brother. This plot resulted in the succession of his other brother Aerys, whose tyranny requires no illustration. Are Aemon's refusals to take up responsibility a moral crime?

Ned and Aemon would rightly defend themselves by saying that acting justly in the way we describe requires foresight—there's no way of knowing where their deeds would take them. Ned might say that his dirty hands could have still provoked lord Tywin into war. Aemon might say there's no guarantee that his reign would have stopped his brother from ascending the Iron Throne. But one thing is obvious: moral rulers are obliged to make distant predictions about the moral outcomes of their actions and be willing to dirty their hands when they must. Anything else amounts to weakness, which is shown here to be nothing less than a moral fault.

This is why rule-abiding children cannot be good sovereigns—they lack both foresight and mental power to take up grisly responsibility. In order to be good rulers, as Aemon says, younglings need to kill the "boys" and "girls" and let the "men" and "women" be born, as Daenerys does on the ashes of Mirri Maz Duur's pyre. Daenerys grows into moral maturity that includes dirty hands, but keeps, as Jorah says, a gentle heart, indispensable for worthy moral goals.

There is a further wrong in trying to keep your hands clean. It is in the fact that individuals often selfishly try to avoid responsibilities that require the sacrifice of dirtying their hands. This is why we often condemn people for 'washing their hands' of certain duties. Many characters in Westeros are blameworthy of just that under the pretext of honor and virtue.

Finally, is allowing dirty hands opening a pit to ever more horrific deeds? Do dirty hands breed more dirty hands? Perhaps, and perhaps not. It becomes obvious that moral rule-following does not always lead to desirable moral outcomes. And battling evil will sometimes require dirty hands, lest the evil endure. Virtuous leaders will often need to resist the downward spiral of dirty hands—the dulling of their senses to all the violent transgressions they will have to commit. Daenerys and Jon are such characters. They demonstrate the willpower to endure hard and demanding decisions, while keeping an eye on truly moral goals–the best that can be hoped for in the bleak reality of Westeros.

29

The Best of Friends

WESLEY GEYER

Part of what makes *Game of Thrones* a compelling story is its ability to make us question the motives of everyone around us.

Whether it's Theon Greyjoy's betrayal of the Starks, Littlefinger's betrayal of Sansa, or Olly's betrayal of Jon, virtually everyone is driven by hidden motives. With few exceptions, every decision could hide any number of hidden agendas that that will be revealed in the next episode.

There's something truly fascinating about the way George R.R. Martin has written his characters. Their relationships with each other have been defined by their role in the Seven Kingdoms and beyond. Apart from a few stellar cases, we have been led to question the sincerity of almost every relationship formed in the series.

When it comes to friendship Martin's characters are no less devious, and even though there are a number of memorable friendships formed throughout the series, many end too soon for us to make real sense of them. We don't know much about the relationship between Jon and Robb, two boys who grew up as half-brothers with strong family values, or the nature of the relationship between Arya and the butcher boy, whose friendship was ended abruptly when The Hound ran him down on horseback ("The Kingsroad"). But do we have to know anything about the intricate workings of the relationships to decide whether or not they are true friendships?

According to Aristotle, we don't need to know about the inner workings of a friendship to know whether or not it is true. He claims that what makes a friendship perfect is its being based on the highest goal of human life—virtue. Furthermore, the basis of any friendship has a significant effect on whether or not Aristotle would even consider it a true friendship in the first place.

Broadly speaking we can define three types of friendship discussed by Aristotle in his *Ethics*: friendship borne of necessity or mutual benefit, friendship borne of mutual pleasantness, and friendship based on the virtue of both parties. Even though each of these types of friendship benefits those involved, this last one is the only form that Aristotle considers to be true friendship.

Virtue ethics plays a central role in Aristotle's philosophy. He believes that the purpose of human life is to flourish, which is roughly to be happy. He uses the term 'eudaimonia', which translates from Greek to 'happiness' in English, but more broadly means 'flourishing at living a good life'. He claims that happiness is the ongoing activity of being virtuous.

It's this type of thinking that dominates Ned Stark's mentality when he asks Varys, "You think my life is some precious thing to me that I would trade my honor for a few more years . . . of what?" In order to be happy we have to be virtuous, and we can only be virtuous by making use of our rational faculties, which sets us apart from other living beings. To abandon virtue and honor is to lose that which makes life truly worth living.

However, for a virtuous person to flourish and achieve the state of eudaimonia, they must also maintain some essential relationships and have some measure of wealth and power. Aristotle explains that this is necessary because without these goods, a person's virtuous activity might diminish, since they would find fewer opportunities to live out their virtue. After all, rotting alone in the dungeon is hardly a flourishing life.

So now we know that Aristotle values friendship as part of a good, virtuous life. But what kind of friendship would be worth pursuing if we're interested in attaining the deep happiness of eudaimonia? In Aristotle's *Nicomachean Ethics*, the deepest friendship is caring for another person for their own sake based upon their virtuous character.

While there are many examples of friendships in *Game of Thrones*, it's difficult to be sure which of them are based on anything but the prospect of personal gain. However, there are at least three examples of friendships that have been formed in different ways and for Aristotle's three different ends: pleasantness, usefulness, and virtue.

The Usurper and His Hand

I never loved my brothers. Sad thing for a man to admit, but it's true. You were the brother I chose.

—ROBERT BARATHEON, King of the Seven Kingdoms ("A Golden Crown")

The first, a friendship between the King of the Seven Kingdoms, Robert Baratheon, and the Warden of the North, Eddard Stark, both of whom we're introduced to in the first episode ("Winter Is Coming") of the first season of the show and in the first few chapters of *A Game of Thrones*. The friendship has been a lifelong companionship between the two war heroes.

Having both been fostered by Jon Arryn, Baratheon and Stark saw each other as brothers. Their relationship was one that did not start out of choice, but because of the closeness that comes with growing up together. Their relationship prospered into adulthood, at which point they fought together in countless battles. While such a relationship is unarguably legitimate—as legitimate as any relationship between siblings could be—according to Aristotle's standard it does not hold power as a friendship based on virtue for a few reasons. First, Aristotle considers this kind of friendship only 'incidental' because of the ongoing basis of the friendship.

We don't know a whole lot about Robert and Eddard's upbringing in Jon Arryn's care. What we do know is that they formed a brotherly bond that was strengthened by their time in battle together, and we know that Robert was betrothed to Eddard's younger sister Lyanna. His intense love for Lyanna set the events in motion that ultimately led to his rule as the King of the Seven Kingdoms. After she was 'kidnapped' by Prince Rhaegar Targaryen, Robert overthrew the Mad King and killed the man supposedly responsible for the disappearance and death of his betrothed.

It is at this point where we first see Robert and Eddard at odds with each other, with both of them clearly holding different values in the face of the war they had just survived. Robert was happy to see the wife and children of Prince Rhaegar killed as payback for his own loss, and treated them not as innocent people, but as "dragonspawn" cut from the same cloth as the Mad King and his son. Eddard, on the other hand, is enraged at this brutality, and might have held it against Robert if their shared grief over the death of Lyanna had not brought them back together.

Here we see that there is conflict between the two. When Eddard's values and Robert's are brought into such stark contrast their relationship is tested. The core of their friendship, based on closeness brought about by what Aristotle would call pleasantness, is now outweighed by the conflicting values of the two men.

To Aristotle this type of friendship is obviously flawed because, "with increasing age their pleasures become different" (*Nichomachean Ethics*, Chapter 8). Eddard also alludes to the fact that Robert's pleasures differ from his own in the case of Lyanna, stating that Robert never recognized her strength of character, but instead valued her only for her incredible beauty. We could even say that it is because of the death of Lyanna that the imperfection in the friendship came to light, especially since her death caused Robert to be reminded of her every time he saw Eddard.

The Lannister Dwarf and the Knight of the Blackwater

I like you, pampered little shit that you are. I just like myself more.

—SER BRONN of the Blackwater ("Mockingbird")

Another notable friendship from the series is between Tyrion Lannister and Bronn, whom he meets after being captured by Catelyn Stark in Season One ("Cripples, Bastards, and Broken Things"). As one of the most entertaining and important characters in the series, Tyrion is someone who is viewed as an outsider within the most powerful family in the realm. He is taken hostage by an opportunistic Catelyn who believes him to be responsible for the attempted assassination of her son Bran. Her plan to take Tyrion to The Vale to answer for his crimes culminates in his demand for a trial by combat, and after a number of jokes about his physical fighting acumen, he is able to talk himself out of a tricky situation in a way that only a golden-tongued Lannister can by demanding that a champion be allowed to fight on his behalf.

The man who comes to his aide is Bronn, a sellsword who had been travelling with the company to The Vale, who picked up on every subtle hint thrown out by Tyrion as he muttered the famous words, "A Lannister always pays his debts," time and time again. After Bronn's victory Tyrion is freed and the two begin their partnership. It's a friendship that, even though it is heavily reliant on the endless stream of gold that Tyrion has in store for Bronn as payment, every *Game of Thrones* fan knows to hold at least some manner of sincerity.

Even though there are moments where the friendship seems sincere, the standards for genuine friendship according to Aristotle are not met, regardless of how much we want it to be so. To Aristotle, the friendship between the two is doomed to failure at one point or another because, like Robert and Eddard's, it is not based upon virtue.

Tyrion and Bronn saw in each other an opportunity to benefit themselves. For Tyrion it was a way to survive. A bit of gold later and he finds himself free of certain death at the hands of his enemies. For Bronn, the promise of payment from a member of the richest family in the realm is a chance to improve his own situation.

The friendship is doomed to failure though, because in Aristotle's words "the useful is not permanent but is always changing. Thus when the motive of the friendship is done away, the friendship is dissolved." Accordingly, Bronn informs Tyrion that even though he considers him a friend, the prospect of marriage and wealth is a better choice for him than risking his life again in trial by combat ("Mockingbird").

Though disappointed in the fact that his friend has chosen wealth over him, Tyrion understands, and even says that that kind of opportunistic decision-making is what he liked about Bronn. Regardless of whether these friends remain together throughout the series, liking someone for being opportunistic or for having enough money to pay you is not a virtuous reason to like them. So their friendship is considered imperfect according to Aristotle's virtue ethics.

Lord Snow and Sam the Slayer

I need you here, Sam. If you leave, who's left to give me advice I trust?

> —Jon Snow, Lord Commander of the Night's Watch ("Mother's
>   Mercy")

Perhaps the most famous friendship in *Game of Thrones* is one between two of the most likable and honest characters in the series: Jon Snow and Samwell Tarly. The two meet at Castle Black on Sam's first day with the Night's Watch. We learn very quickly that Sam had been sent to the Wall by his father who does not want his legacy passed onto someone who is unworthy (*A Game of Thrones*). Jon Snow, on the other hand, joined the Night's Watch because he feels like an outsider in his family, being the bastard son of Eddard Stark.

He approaches his uncle Benjen—a ranger with the Night's Watch—to join as a result of being treated like an outsider by his stepmother Catelyn. So, Jon and Sam join the Night's Watch to find a place where they belong. Jon quickly takes to life on the wall, having been trained in combat at Winterfell, while Sam struggles due to his timid nature. Yet, Sam eventually learns to stand up for himself as the two become friends in their new life.

What makes the friendship truly interesting in light of Aristotle's characterization of friendship based upon virtue is that they are possibly the only two recruits who actually embody the values of the Night's Watch, since the other recruits are mostly criminals and exiles. The very beginning of their friendship demonstrates the virtuous nature of the two. Though Sam starts out as the most cowardly member of the Watch he learns of his own strength through their friendship and even kills a White Walker when it becomes necessary. Jon joins the watch thinking he is an outcast, and learns by watching Sam that it doesn't matter whether or not you have noble blood—being a good person is what earns a man respect.

Neither of them has any ulterior motive for befriending the other, and as a result their friendship is forged from mutual respect and mutual desire for the good of the other. Aristotle views only this type of friendship, based on character, as truly virtuous. These are friendships that exist between two people who are equally virtuous, and thus are equally concerned with the good of the other.

Since, the relationship between Jon Snow and Sam Tarly is based first and foremost on the shared values of their brotherhood in their new life on the Wall, it becomes an example of a perfectly virtuous Aristotelian friendship. The friendship between Snow and Tarly is based on the stable ongoing virtue of their characters and is the gold standard of virtuous friendship in the face of the approaching Winter.

30
Trying to Do Good with Arya, Tyrion, and the Hound

ROBERT C. THOMAS

It shouldn't take a maester to convince you that the world of *Game of Thrones*—on either side of the Narrow Sea—is full of more bloody conflict and complicated scheming than Machiavelli himself could have imagined.

But amid all the beautifully filmed battlefield chaos and dramatic plot developments, it might be easier to overlook just how hard of a time the most decent people in Westeros have at actually knowing *how* to keep being decent people in the first place. Much like our own world (if with a more consistent dramatic flair), life across Westeros and Essos has a way of throwing curveballs and temptations at its residents that makes being a good person much more complicated than just having good intentions.

This isn't a new problem. Throughout our own history, philosophers have taken a look at how much being moral involves using our heads as much as our hearts. Some of the greatest came up with very different ideas about the relationship between our rationality and our moral life.

Aristotle argued for a close relationship between intellectual and moral virtue. Moral virtues are developed by bringing the non-rational portions of the self into line with rational principles. This sounds easy enough, since it is common sense that a virtue like courage involves fearing only things and situations that are actually dangerous. Yet, just ask someone with an irrational fear of spiders, mice, or snakes whether it is easy to bring fear into line with rational principles.

Similarly, the virtue of temperance requires bringing one's appetite into line with the body's actual needs for nutrition.

Yet, ask anyone on a diet whether desiring only the food that's actually needed for health is easy. Aristotle believed that developing practical wisdom—the kind of knowledge and judgment about real-world conditions that we need to understand *how* to act with courage, prudence, or generosity in a particular situation—was as much a part of leading a good life as those virtues themselves.

In contrast, utilitarians like Jeremy Bentham argued that determining the morality of an action is like solving a complicated math problem, where we add up the total good or harm that an action will do to everyone affected and judge the morality of the action based upon its total results. For Bentham, morality is strictly about the long ranging consequences of actions. Therefore, moral action requires considerable foresight and ability to predict an action's effects.

A third approach to ethics was held by Immanuel Kant, who believed that we could reason our way to firm moral rules that we should follow regardless of their consequences. For example, he believed that lying was an offence against rationality and therefore should be avoided regardless of the expected consequences. He held this view so consistently that he literally claimed that if a homicidal maniac asked you where your innocent neighbor happened to be hiding, it would be morally wrong to lie to him (although you could presumably just keep your mouth shut).

While Aristotle, Bentham, and Kant held very different opinions on morality, they did agree on one thing. Whether it's about the subtle judgment of wisdom, balancing a math problem, or reasoning to the right moral rules, the one thing they all agreed on was that figuring out how to do the right thing takes serious thinking.

Yet, the *kind* of knowledge we'd need to actually do the right thing or be a good person seems difficult to uncover, and neither the Seven, nor the Old Gods, nor the Lord of Light seem very interested in providing answers on that front. If the gods have moral wisdom, they are not very forthcoming with it.

The sixth season of Game of Thrones provides some great examples of the need for moral wisdom. Two of the fans' favorite self-exiled Westerosi—Arya Stark and Tyrion Lannister—face nearly disastrous failures in judgment when trying to do the right thing—and it's not quite clear that any of us would have made a better call in their shoes. Meanwhile, back in Westeros, our favorite cynical swordsman, Sandor 'the Hound' Clegane, provides some sobering reflections on moral certainty after his brush with death.

Unintended Consequences

I can't sleep until I say the names . . . the ones I'm going to kill.

—ARYA STARK

Arya Stark's training with the Faceless Men in Braavos presents her with her own moral dilemma after they restore her sight. In "The Door," she's offered a chance to redeem herself by poisoning the stage actress Lady Crane, but begins to have second thoughts as she gets to know her mark. When she shares her growing doubts with Jaqen H'ghar, he challenges her moral worries with exactly the sort of question we'd expect from a follower of the Many-Faced God: "Does death only come for the wicked and leave the decent behind?" Despite Jaqen's pressure, her own fear, and her obligations to the Faceless Men, our young heroine ultimately abandons her promises and spares Lady Crane in "Blood of My Blood."

Arya's decision seems like a triumph of conscience, but the course of events quickly takes a darker turn. After being wounded by the Waif and being nursed by Lady Crane, Arya's act of mercy ultimately backfires. In "No One," the Waif ultimately kills Lady Crane herself—delivering what she then assures Arya was a more painful death than the poison would have produced if Arya had followed orders. Despite Arya's best intentions, what she intended as an act of mercy turned out to only delay and worsen the sentence on Lady Crane, also resulting in her own injuries, and the need to kill the Waif in self-defense. If good results were the goal, Arya chose a messy path to those results.

The Starks are no strangers to damage caused by unintended consequences. After all, the misplaced mercy that Ned Stark once showed to Cersei Lannister laid the ground for a devastating civil war. Much like her father, Arya thought she was acting out of compassion, only to see the situation blow up in her face. It's fair to ask how she could have known how badly her decision would turn out, but that's always been a challenge to living the moral life.

If what makes an action right or wrong is its consequences, it's not clear how Arya—*or anyone else*—could be expected to *know* in advance whether or not they are doing the right thing. It can involve a dangerous amount of guesswork. The question gets even messier if we stop to wonder how different things might actually have been if Arya had poisoned Lady Crane according to plan. It's impossible for Arya to have predicted longer-ranging consequences as the Waif, Jaqen, and others reacted if she had made different choices. The quest for the moral life marked by actions promoting the good of all starts to seem like nothing more than a wild goose chase.

Good Intentions

We make peace with our enemies, not our friends.

—TYRION LANNISTER

Tyrion Lannister's challenges in Meereen add the extra messiness of politics and war on top of the same moral uncertainties that Arya faced. Season Six opens with Tyrion left to govern the city and put down the ongoing insurgency. As the violence continues and the brave new order in Slaver's Bay slides back into its glorious past of depravity, filth, and oppression, Tyrion and Varys eventually discover that the restored Masters of Astapor and Yunkai are funding the troublesome uprising.

After his experience navigating the political machinations of King's Landing, Tyrion decides to pursue a peaceful resolution to the uprising. In "Book of the Stranger," he invites representatives of the Masters from Astapor and Yunkai to broker a deal, offering them a compromise to phase out slavery more gradually and with compensation, in exchange for an end to the insurgency. Naturally, he throws in some of his signature special of "tits and wine" to sweeten the deal.

Despite objections from Missandei and Grey Worm that the Masters can't be trusted, Tyrion explains "I don't trust the Masters. I trust their self-interest." As his luck would have it, Tyrion misread the Masters' view of their own self-interest with disastrous results. In "No One," the Masters break their deal and launch an unexpected naval attack on Meereen.

Tyrion compromised the dignity and freedom of the enslaved populations of the other cities for the sake of peace and stability. He decided that avoiding the bad consequences of an extended war (or defeat) outweighed accepting the negative consequences of another seven years of slavery in two cities. Instead, he came very close to getting both sets of horrific consequences, if the city hadn't been saved by Daenerys's return.

Just like in Arya's case, it was hard to be certain what the consequences of Tyrion's compromise were when his choices were made. The Masters ultimately broke the deal and left the survival of Meereen teetering on the edge of a knife until Daenerys returned with Drogon and the Dothraki in the nick of time. Then again, it's very possible that the city wouldn't have lasted as long as it did if Tyrion hadn't bought time with the arrangement with the Masters that at least temporarily kept the peace. No one knows what would have happened. The consequences might have been even worse.

One thing that made Tyrion's challenge even more like the one Ned Stark faced was its political aspect. When explicitly dealing with the political goals and strategies of other people, Tyrion and Ned both faced a choice between sticking strictly to a moral principle at all costs and compromising in the hope that getting their hands dirty might turn out better for everyone in the long run.

Ned lost his head and plunged the Seven Kingdoms into chaos by sticking to his principles, while Tyrion may have saved the lives and freedom of thousands by watering down his principles when his political judgment called for it—even though his political judgment very nearly backfired as well. What would Ned, Tyrion, or any of us watching have had to know in advance to be sure we were making the right call in those situations? Making the right calculation and figuring out the right rule both seem frighteningly hard to do when the game is so complicated and the stakes are so high.

Return of the Hound

There's something greater than us. And whatever it is, it's got plans for Sandor Clegane.

—BROTHER RAY

While Arya and Tyrion struggled with the consequences of their own actions, a more reflective take on the moral dilemmas of life in Westeros comes from an interesting source. Despite being left for dead by Arya during the fourth season, Sandor "the Hound" Clegane emerges very much alive in "The Broken Man" after being nursed back to health by Brother Ray. After his rescue and convalescence, the entertainingly cynical Hound is surprisingly mellow and reflective for a man who claims that "hate" is what kept him going when grievously wounded and left for dead. Then again, few characters have been known so well for cutting straight to the point.

After Ray and his flock are visited by rogue members of the Brotherhood Without Banners, Ray explains the pacifistic attitude behind his lack of attention to self-defense by arguing: "Violence is a disease. You don't cure a disease by spreading it to more people." The Hound's bleak response that "you don't cure it by dying, either" proves darkly relevant when the rogues return and massacre Ray and the rest of the group. The Hound sets out for revenge, finding and finishing off one group of the killers before finding the others already slated for execution by the Brotherhood itself in "No One."

After the Hound takes part in a more measured approach to punishment than he admits he would've dealt out when younger, Beric Dondarrion and Thoros of Myr try to recruit him to join their cause. Although he doesn't decisively reject the possibility, he displays his skepticism once again with his warning that "lots of horrible shit in this world gets done for something larger than ourselves." That sentiment is a sobering one when we look back through the series, with events like Stannis Baratheon's sacrifice of his own daughter for a vision of his destiny as a savior of the realm, the death of countless innocents because of Robb Stark's ostensibly just war against the Lannisters, or the schemes and crimes of Tywin for the sake of the family legacy. Principle and purpose, it seems, are no guarantee of a happy ending.

Despite all his skepticism about causes and principles, life didn't leave the Hound with the option to just coast along and dodge the big questions about what to do or how to live. Life forces his hand and he's continued to face unavoidable decisions, as much as anyone else. He and the other characters of Westeros will undoubtedly have still more difficult decisions to make as the story races to a conclusion, whether or not a path to find the right answers to those decisions is clear or obvious.

We all have choices to make and those choices always have consequences, even if what we choose is inaction. Everyone must live by some principles and moral judgments, even if they must choose without certainty.

Forced Choices, Unknowable Results

You know nothing, Jon Snow.

—YGRITTE

Most of our lives are not as exciting as the lives of the characters in *Game of Thrones* (unfortunately) and they aren't as bloody either (fortunately). Even so, we're stuck with the same basic kinds of moral challenges ourselves.

Predicting the good and bad consequences of our own actions can seem impossible and figuring out the right principles to live by—and *how* to act on them—isn't necessarily much easier. Even when we think we have a right answer, the result sometimes turns out uglier than we imagined. Those challenges get even trickier when we throw that peskiest of complications—other people—into the mix.

If obtaining moral wisdom is so difficult are we really any better off than Arya, Tyrion, and the Hound? Well, with any luck, we may make it through life without anyone trying to run a sword through us. Still, we're just as stuck with having to make important decisions about what to do and what kind of people to be, without always having easy ways to answer those questions—and we're just as stuck with the decisions we make.

31
Paying the Iron Price

Tom Hansberger

Theon Greyjoy struggles to be accepted by his family because he does not understand what is expected of him in the Iron Islands. He is not able to develop the virtues valued by the Iron Islanders. Theon's difficulty living up to his father's expectations is also directly related to Theon's identity, as we see when Theon—finally!—admits that Eddard Stark was his true father and that he "chose wrong" in trying to be a Greyjoy ("And Now His Watch Is Ended").

Theon's struggle with virtue begins in "The Night Lands," when Theon meets his sister Yara. Yara does not reveal her identity as she takes him to the castle. Theon thinks she's a peasant girl and attempts to seduce her as they ride together. When Theon finds out—to his dismay—that Yara is his sister, he asks her why she had concealed her identity: Yara responds that she had wanted to find out "what kind of man" Theon had grown up to become.

Yara's response embarrasses Theon because it suggests that his sexual overtures toward her constituted evidence of an overly lustful character. As Aristotle would say, Theon experienced (and showed) *too much* sexual desire—he did not express an appropriate amount of sexual desire by being so forward with a woman he had just met.

Theon's humiliation with Yara is consistent with the tone of his reunion with Balon, his father. Balon Greyjoy immediately criticizes Theon's appearance and asks Theon whether he paid the "iron price" or gold for his jewelry, by which he means to ask whether Theon took the jewelry from the body of an enemy he'd killed or if he had purchased it. When Theon confesses that he'd paid for his jewelry, Balon objects that he will not have his son dress "like a whore" and throws the jewelry into a nearby fireplace.

Balon's disdain for Theon after discovering that Theon had paid good money for his jewelry seems to suggest that, on the Iron Islands, jewelry is used as visible *proof* of courage. According to their customs, a man who wears jewelry is showing off his skill in battle, so anyone who wears jewelry they have bought must be trying to dupe others into thinking they are a better warrior-pirate than they really are.

Theon's Vices

Balon sees Theon as weak and dishonest because of his purchased jewelry. So Theon is not proud enough by the standards of the Iron Islands—not only does Theon experience *too much* lust, he experiences *too little* 'self-respect'. In Aristotle's terms, Theon has a 'small soul;' to achieve greatness of soul requires placing more value on honor and great deeds than on material possessions. For Balon, such honor comes through piracy and martial prowess.

So Theon's return to the Iron Islands reveals his vices to his family (at least, as Balon and Yara see it). This explains why Balon does not trust him with any serious command in his raids on the North; while Yara commands a fleet of ships, Balon only gives Theon command of a single ship. Theon has not shown enough virtue to be trusted with important military tasks. As a result, Theon seems to feel an intense desire to prove his worth to his father, a desire which, ironically, ultimately leads him to be a rash commander.

Theon's doomed command begins poorly in "The Ghost of Harrenhal." When his crew arrives at port and prepares to board the *Sea Bitch*—Theon's ship—Theon greets them and commands them to stop their preparations to leave. For the most part, the crew ignores him—except for one man who suggests that, because of his experience with "reaving and raping," he does not need a commander and sees no reason not to set sail without Theon. In response, Theon threatens to hunt him down and hang him as a traitor if he leaves Theon behind.

The tense situation is only defused when Yara appears, joking that she and the crew "yield" to Theon. Nevertheless, while Theon and Yara talk, the bulk of the crew abandons Theon. Theon is only able to board his own ship when Dagmer, his first mate, appears and offers to take him aboard. Theon's uptight attitude only serves to diminish his crew's respect for him. Theon would be a better leader if he developed a sense of humor, like Yara. Having a sense of humor would probably make him a better commander on the Iron Islands and, therefore, a more virtuous person, even *in the face of* his crew's immoral love of "reaving and raping."

After their meeting, Theon and his first mate, Dagmer, hatch a plot to capture Winterfell, which would be a major victory for the Iron Islands (and for Theon). While he does manage to capture the poorly defended castle by sneaking in at night, he cannot hold it. Not only does he command fewer than twenty men in the castle, Winterfell is also too far from the sea for the Greyjoys to send reinforcements or supplies. Theon's attack on Winterfell turns out to be ridiculously ambitious and impractical, but Theon stubbornly ignores Yara's warning to flee in "The Prince of Winterfell."

Theon's foolish gambit at Winterfell results in his capture and the deaths of all the men he commands. Instead of embodying the virtue of courage, Theon embodied the vice of rashness, failing to recognize the difficulty of holding Winterfell against Northern attacks.

Aristotle's Middle Way

Theon does not know how to wage war 'at the right time and in the right way;' he does not understand what *virtuous violence* looked like. As Aristotle might say, the virtuous soldier neither flees from battle nor seeks it out when they are not sure that they will win. Given that the Iron Islanders are pirates who employ hit-and-run tactics to win, Theon cannot possibly hope to hold Winterfell. Regardless of how distasteful the Iron Islanders' tactics may be, Theon's attempt to hold Winterfell shows that he is not a good leader because he does not understand the men he commands and he is, therefore, a rash commander, not a courageous one.

Aristotle's virtue ethics suggests that individuals ought to behave in such a way that they develop moderate personality traits and meet their social obligations. For example, a courageous soldier will neither flee at the first sign of danger nor will they take unnecessary risks. They fear exactly what they should and to the appropriate degree. By balancing between the extremes of cowardice and foolhardiness, a good soldier is able to fight effectively.

For Aristotle, there's a close connection between the actions which are good for the individual and the actions which are good for society since, in Aristotle's words, "man is a social animal." However, Aristotle holds that not all social obligations are just—society might ask us to do something immoral. Aristotle sees acts like adultery and murder as inherently wrong. These cannot be done 'at the right time and in the right way' and, so, do not fit with the general pattern of virtue ethics.

The society of the Iron Islands values some things that are simply wrong—they encourage theft, murder, and rape as part of their way of life. It's difficult to be a 'virtuous' member of such a society without being complicit in such actions.

Uncertain Identity

Theon's failure to develop virtue also leads to his identity crisis. Theon is unsure, early on, whether he belongs with the Starks or with the Greyjoys. Theon clearly feels more comfortable with the Starks' *customs* (because he spent his childhood with them) but he feels that he *must* find a place with the Greyjoys because he is a member of that family. Across Westeros, loyalty to your family is highly valued. Despite feeling out of place with the Greyjoys, even some Starks might admit that Theon's loyalty to his family should come first. (Catelyn, for instance, might have to agree, given her loyalty to the Tullys and her children.)

So why does Theon fail? The answer seems to be that he lacks self-knowledge. The other Greyjoys know who they are—as Balon says, Yara "knows who she is," which is why Balon gives her a more important command than Theon's. Even the Greyjoys' words express a kind of self-knowledge: "We do not sow." Theon, on the other hand, seems to become more unsure of himself over the course of the story until his identity collapses completely. After months of torture by Ramsay, Theon denies his own name and refers to himself as "Reek," just as

Ramsay wanted. Ramsay's techniques might have similar effects on almost anyone but, because Theon was *already* unsure about who he was, the result is especially dramatic.

At its core, authenticity is to be true to yourself. Personal authenticity often conflicts with the ethical demands that others make of us. The philosopher Charles Taylor claims that, in practice, authenticity is frequently used to justify personal caprice but, nevertheless, it stems from a real ethical insight. An individual's ability to determine their own life and sense of self is ethically important, despite the difficulty we often find in reconciling our wishes with those of others.

Theon's capture by Ramsay brings his quest for belonging to a tragic end. Theon even refuses to co-operate with Yara's rescue attempt, which leads her to acknowledge his failure to know 'who he is.' Afterward, Yara concedes "My brother is dead," acknowledging the loss of Theon's identity ("The Laws of Gods and Men").

The events of Season Six give us hope that Theon may still find his identity, although the contradictions he faces have still not been completely addressed. Although his protectiveness of Sansa caused his revolt against Ramsay at the end of Season Five, Theon heads 'home' to Pyke after Brienne pledges fealty to Sansa ("Home").

In "Book of the Stranger," Theon tells Yara that she should be Queen and that he only wants to serve her. In Season Six, Theon's identity is dominated by guilt for his past crimes and a desire to serve Yara, whom he thinks is the best person to lead House Greyjoy after Balon's death. After "Battle of the Bastards," when Daenerys and Yara agree to an alliance as long as the Iron Islanders stop pillaging Westeros in the future, it seems that Theon's choice to serve Yara may help resolve the tensions in Theon's personality, although this remains to be seen.

Virtue and Authenticity in Balance

While there is hope for Theon, he still does not seem sure of himself, showing that issues concerning his identity and virtue continue to trouble him. This is no accident: The words inscribed over the oracle at Delphi, "Know thyself," suggest that the Greeks were aware of a link between virtue and authenticity. Theon's unsuccessful attempt to 'know who he is' carries obvious implications for his ability to live up to the ideal of authenticity.

If authenticity means 'being true to oneself', then we must obviously *know who we are* in order to do anything that fits the bill. Underlying Theon's failure to develop into a virtuous Greyjoy is his failure to *be* an authentic self. Before Theon even becomes Reek, he is already lacking an identity, preventing him from fulfilling his obligations.

On the Iron Islands, the characters' knowledge of who they are is seen in their sense of *purpose*. For Aristotle, our *telos* is the meaning or purpose of our lives and he derives his account of virtue from the *telos*. Similarly, what the Greyjoys believe they ought to do is derived from their beliefs about themselves. To be a Greyjoy *just is* to be a ruthless and cunning reaver in Balon's mind. Theon's failure to do what a Greyjoy 'ought' to do is ethically wrong in the eyes of Iron Islanders. Furthermore, he is failing *himself*; he is uncomfortable being who he is. According to Balon's twisted version of Aristotelianism, Theon would be happier if he accepted his identity as a Greyjoy by acting in accordance with the Iron Islanders' standards of virtue.

Theon's failure to achieve virtue—in either Aristotle's or Balon's senses—leads to the disintegration of his sense of self. Theon's transformation into Reek dramatizes the insight that who we are is determined by our relationships with others. Thus, Theon's tragic failure to achieve authenticity is a product of his dysfunctional relationships with his family and society.

It turns out that authenticity and virtue are not opposites, despite the fact that one focuses on the individual and the other on society. Rather, authenticity *depends* on virtue—we can only figure out who we are and be true to ourselves through interpersonal interactions.

Although Theon is partly to blame for his failed relationships with others, it is also obvious that the Iron Islanders' conception of virtue is morally bankrupt. Any society that values theft and rape as part of its culture and livelihood is clearly immoral.

But because the Iron Islanders' society and its institutions encourage immoral behavior, there is a paradox for Theon: since Aristotle's virtues are shown by how we meet our social obligations, Theon could not have courage or be a good leader without becoming a murderer and a thief. His murder of two peasant children—whom he passes off as Bran and Rickon Stark—shows how Theon struggled to become as ruthless as Balon wanted him to be ("A Man Without Honor").

If Yara becomes Queen of the Iron Islands and reforms their society, then Theon may be able to attain moral virtue and a sense of belonging there but, failing that, Theon will probably remain a tragic outsider in his own homeland.

No, now it ends.

—EDDARD STARK

References

Adriani, Nicolaus, and Albertus C. Kruyt. 1968. *The Bare'e-speaking Toradja of Central Celebes*. Human Relations Area Files.

Aeschylus. 1956. *The Oresteian Trilogy: Agamemnon; The Choephori; The Eumenides*. Penguin.

Anonymous. 2010. *The Holy Bible: King James Version*. Zondervan.

Aristotle. 1992. *The Politics*. Penguin.

———. 1997. *Poetics*. Hackett.

———. 1999. *Nicomachean Ethics*. Hackett.

———. 1999. *Nicomachean Ethics*. Prentice Hall.

———. 2000. *Nicomachean Ethics*. Cambridge University Press.

———. 2009. *Nicomachean Ethics*. Oxford University Press.

Aston, Trevor Henry, and Charles Philpin. 1987. *The Brenner Debate: Agrarian Class Structure and Economic Development in Pre-industrial Europe*. Volume I. Cambridge University Press.

Augustine. 1998. *Confessions*. Oxford University Press.

Bathurst, Gene. 2015. Who's the Most Evil Character on *Game of Thrones? Blathers of Gene Bathurst* (7th June).

Beck, Lewis White, ed. 1949. *Immanuel Kant: Critique of Practical Reason and Other Writings in Moral Philosophy*. University of Chicago Press.

Bentham, Jeremy. 1907. *An Introduction to the Principles of Morals and Legislation*. Clarendon.

Boyce, Kenneth, and Alvin Plantinga. 2015. Proper Functionalism. In Cullison 2015.

Chaillan, Marianne. 2016. *Game of Thrones: Une Métaphysique des Meurtres*. Le Passeur Éditeur.

Cornet, Roth. 2014. *Game of Thrones*: Joffrey Baratheon's Top 5 Most Evil Acts. *IGN: UK* (12th April).

Cullison, Andrew, ed. 2015. *The Bloomsbury Companion to Epistemology*. Continuum.

Descartes, René. 1993. *Meditations on First Philosophy*. Hackett.

Detmer, David. 2008. *Sartre Explained: From Bad Faith to Authenticity*. Open Court.

Dobb, Maurice. 1946. *Studies in the Development of Capitalism*. London: Routledge.

Eaton, Anne. 2012. Robust Immoralism. *Journal of Aesthetics and Art Criticism*.

Eliade, Mircea. 1959. *The Sacred and the Profane: The Nature of Religion*. Houghton Mifflin Harcourt.

Ellaby, James. 2012. Is *Game of Thrones'* Joffrey TV's Most Vile Character? *Huffington Post* (30th May).

Erickson, Mark T. 2004. Evolutionary Thought and the Current Clinical Understanding of Incest. In Wolf and Durham 2004.

Euripides. 1992. *Iphigenia at Aulis*. Oxford University Press.

Flynn, Thomas. 2006. *Existentialism: A Very Short Introduction*. Oxford University Press.

Freud, Sigmund. 1963. *Sexuality and the Psychology of Love* Macmillan.

———. 1968 [1905]. *Jokes and Their Relation to the Unconscious*. Hogarth Press and the Institute of Psycho-Analysis.

———. *Totem and Taboo*. 2001 [1913]. Vintage.

———. 2012. *A General Introduction to Psychoanalysis*. Wordsworth.

Fromm. Erich. 1981. *On Disobedience and Other Essays*. Seabury.

———. 1994 [1941]. *Escape from Freedom*. Holt.

———. 1992 [1973]. *The Anatomy of Human Destructiveness*. Holt.

Hobbes, Thomas. 1962 [1651]. *Leviathan: On the Matter, Forme, and Power of a Commonwealth Ecclesiasticall and Civil*. Collier.

Hume, David. 1976. *A Treatise of Human Nature*. Oxford University Press.

———. 1988. *An Enquiry concerning Human Understanding*. Open Court.

———. 1992. *Writings on Religion*. Open Court.

———. 1993. *An Enquiry Concerning Human Understanding*. Hackett.

Kant, Immanuel. 1949 [1797]. On a Supposed Right to Lie from Altruistic Motives. In Beck 1949.

———. 1987 [1790]. *Critique of Judgment*. Hackett.

———. 1993 [1785]. *Grounding for the Metaphysics of Morals*. Hackett.

———. 1996 [1798]. *The Conflict of Faculties*. Cambridge University Press.

———. 2002. *Critique of Practical Reason*. Hackett.

Kierkegaard, Søren. 2003. *Fear and Trembling*. Penguin.

———. 2009 [1846]. *Concluding Unscientific Postscript to the Philosophical Crumbs*. Cambridge University Press.

Liew, Tim. 2014. *Game of Thrones*: Why We Love to Hate King Joffrey. *The Metro* 14 (April).

Locke, John. 1988. *Two Treatises of Government*. Cambridge University Press.

MacIntyre, Alasdair. 2007. *After Virtue: A Study in Moral Theory*. University of Notre Dame Press.

Martin, George R.R. 1996. *A Game of Thrones*. Bantam.

———. 1998. *A Clash of Kings*. Bantam.

———. 2000. *A Storm of Swords*. Bantam.

———. 2005. *A Feast for Crows*. Bantam.

———. 2011. *A Dance with Dragons*. Bantam.

———. 2013. *The Wit and Wisdom of Tyrion Lannister*. Bantam.

———. 2014. *The World of Ice and Fire: The Untold History of Westeros and the Game of Thrones*. Bantam.

Marx, Karl H. 1964 [1844]. *Economic and Philosophic Manuscripts of 1844*. International.

———. 1965. *Pre-Capitalist Economic Formations*. International.

Marx, Karl H., and Engels, Friedrich. 1976. *The German Ideology*. Moscow: Progress.

Massie, Pascal L., and Lauryn S. Mayer. 2014. Bringing Elsewhere Home: *A Song of Ice and Fire*'s Ethics of Disability. *Studies in Medievalism* 23.

McNabb T.D. 2015. Warranted Religion: Answering Objections to Alvin Plantinga's Epistemology. *Religious Studies* 51:4.

Mitcham, C. 1994. *Thinking Through Technology: The Path between Engineering and Philosophy*. University of Chicago Press.

Mumford, Lewis. 1967 [1934]. *Technics and Civilization*. Routledge.

Nussbaum, Martha C. 1986. *The Fragility of Goodness: Luck and Ethics in Greek Tragedy and Philosophy*. Cambridge University Press.

———. 1998. Victims and Agents. *The Boston Review* 23.

———. 2006. *Frontiers of Justice: Disability, Nationality, Species Membership*. Belknap.

Plantinga, Alvin. 1993. *Warrant and Proper Function*. Oxford University Press.

Plato. 1992. *Republic*. Hackett.

———. 1992. *Protagoras*. Hackett.

———. 1997. *Complete Works*. Hackett.

———. 2002. *Five Dialogues: Euthyphro, Apology, Crito, Meno, Phaedo*. Hackett.

———. 2003. *The Republic*. Cambridge University Press.

Reid, Thomas. 1983. *Inquiry and Essays*. Hackett.

Sade, Marquis de. 1801 [1797]. *Histoire de Juliette ou les Prospérités du Vice*. Paris.

Sartre, Jean-Paul. 1956. *Being and Nothingness*. Philosophical Library.

———. 1962. *Nausea*. Hamish Hamilton.

———. 1992. *Notebooks for an Ethics*. University of Chicago Press.

———. 2007. *Existentialism Is a Humanism*. Yale University Press.

Sextus Empiricus. 1990. *Outlines of Pyrrhonism*. Prometheus.

Smith, James K.A. 2016. *You Are What You Love: The Spiritual Power of Habit*. Brazos.

Taylor, Charles. 1991. *The Ethics of Authenticity*. Harvard University Press.

Turner, Jonathan H., and Alexandra Marianski. 2005. *Incest: Origins of the Taboo*. Paradigm.

Voltaire. 2012 [1771]. Rights. In Voltaire, *Questions sur l'Encyclopédie*. Ulan.

Walzer, Michael. 1977. *Just and Unjust Wars: A Moral Argument with Historical Illustrations*. Basic Books.

———. 2004 [1988]. Emergency Ethics. In Walzer, *Arguing About War*. Yale University Press.

Wertheimer, Alan. 2003. *Consent to Sexual Relations*. Cambridge University Press.

Westermarck, Edward.1930. *A Short History of Human Marriage*. Macmillan.

———. 1934. Three Essays on Sex and Marriage. Macmillan.

———. 2013. *Marriage Ceremonies in Morocco*. Classics.

Whitehouse, Harvey. 1995. *Inside the Cult: Religious Innovation and Transmission in Papua New Guinea*. Clarendon.

———. 2000. *Arguments and Icons: Divergent Modes of Religiosity*. Oxford University Press.

———. 2004. *Modes of Religiosity: A Cognitive Theory of Religious Transmission*. AltaMira.

Wolf, Arthur P., and William H. Durham, eds. 2004. *Inbreeding, Incest, and the Incest Taboo: The State of Knowledge at the Turn of the Century*. Stanford University Press.

Wood, E. 2002. *The Origin of Capitalism: A Longer View*. Verso.

Yates, Frances. 1964. *Giordano Bruno and the Hermetic Tradition*. University of Chicago Press.

Lineages and Histories of the Great Maesters

MAESTER ARTUR MATOS ALVES is Assistant Professor at Concordia University. His interests are philosophy of technology, cyberculture, and media. He believes that the Iron Bank of Braavos should make the Lannisters pay their debts sooner rather than later.

MAESTER MAX ANDREWS is a philosopher at the University of Edinburgh, Scotland. His research is in philosophy of physics, multiverse scenarios, and modal realism. Max recognizes truth in fiction and would be pleased (and horrified) if the *Game of Thrones* universe turns out to be real somewhere in logical space.

GRAND MAESTER ROBERT ARP works as a researcher for the US Army. He has interests in philosophy and pop culture and the history of Western philosophy. He thinks that Cersei Lannister put forward a false dilemma in claiming, "When you play the game of thrones, you win or you die. There is no middle ground."

MAESTER ERIK BALDWIN teaches in the Philosophy Department at the University of Notre Dame. He has written chapters for several books on pop culture and philosophy, including *Orphan Black and Philosophy: Grand Theft DNA* (2016). His work focuses on philosophy of religion, epistemology, and comparative and cross-cultural philosophy, with an emphasis on Christian, Buddhist, and Islamic philosophy. He thinks that one of the most offensive scenes in the entire series is when Joffrey destroys one of the few remaining copies of *The Lives of Four Kings* written in Grand Maester Kaeth's hand (in "The Lion and the Rose").

MAESTER ADAM BARKMAN has written more than seventy-five books, book chapters, or journal articles, many of which have to do with philosophy in film and philosophy in pop culture. In order to write this much, Barkman has to do a lot of "research" (watch a lot of TV) and each of his five young children have—waking up in the middle of the night—had to endure different shows. Katie, the four-year-old, got *Game of Thrones* and has been known to dance in her sleep to the theme song.

MAESTER ZLATA BOŽAC is currently forging her Maester's chain at the Central European University, Budapest. Before that she spent some years in the Citadel of Zagreb. Her chain is composed of several links in political philosophy, the most precious being in left libertarianism, global justice, the problem of demos constitution and the use of nudging in charitable giving. She hopes to make many contributions to the field in the future, because philosophical thinking is dark and full of errors.

MAESTER MARIANNE CHAILLAN works as a philosophy teacher, across the Narrow Sea, in France. She likes philosophy and pop culture and tries to combine them as often as possible. She thinks Petyr Baelish gives us wise advice when he says, "Don't worry about death. Worry about your life. Take charge of your life for as long as it lasts."

MAESTER KODY COOPER is an Assistant Professor of Political Science at the University of Tennessee, Chattanooga. He has broad interests in law, political thought, American politics, and religion. He believes there is only one thing to do with a bad habit in your own life: chop it off and feed it to the goats.

MAESTER DANIELLE KARIM COX lives in Oklahoma City not far from the plains of the Reach. Having received her Maester's chain at the University of Oklahoma she now teaches Philosophy to the men and women of the Armed Services. She thinks David Hume and Tyrion Lannister would have an interesting conversation about cripples, bastards, and broken things.

MAESTER JONATHAN COX was born North of the Wall in Fairbanks, Alaska. After sneaking his way past the Night's Watch he infiltrated the Citadel and studied under the Maesters at the University of Central Oklahoma. He currently works as the Creative Director of The Escape OKC, using riddles, puzzles, history and logic to entertain and educate. He also wonders if Bernard Suits would either win or die in the Game of Thrones with a proper Lusory Attitude.

MAESTER E.M. DADLEZ is Professor of Philosophy at the University of Central Oklahoma. Her work is mainly on the philosophy of art and literature, and on topics at the intersection (sometimes, more accurately, the collision) of aesthetics, ethics, and epistemology. She is the author of various articles on aesthetics and applied ethics, as well as *What's Hecuba to Him?* (1997) and *Mirrors to One Another* (2009). Like Arya, she has been known to fence, although her wits have of late been more reliable than her rapier when she is on the offensive.

MAESTER AURÉLIA DESVEAUX works in Paris as a lawyer and occasional teacher. She enjoys practicing and explaining law, but advises her clients against declaring that they are guilty of being a dwarf. She has interests in ethics, arts, ancient civilization, and science fiction.

MAESTER WILLIAM J. DEVLIN is Associate Professor at Bridgewater State University. His philosophical interests focus on Existentialism, Ethics, Philosophy of Science, and Philosophy and Popular Culture. He has written chapters on the philosophy of such television series as *The Walking Dead*, *Lost*, and *South Park*, and such films as *No Country for Old Men*, *Gone Baby Gone*, *Terminator*, and *12 Monkeys*. He's also co-editor of the volume, *The Philosophy of David Lynch*. While he admires Stannis's focus on duty and honor, William would rather save his own daughter, Meggie, by accepting a fate from Ser Ilyn Payne (under King Joffrey's decree) than follow Stannis's guide to parenting.

MAESTER KIMBERLY S. ENGELS is a PhD candidate in philosophy at Marquette University. Her main philosophical interests include existentialism and applied ethics. She has published several articles on the application of existentialism to debates in healthcare ethics and environmental ethics. She joins Tyrion Lannister as one who likes to drink and know things.

MAESTER JEFF EWING is a doctoral candidate at the University of Oregon. He has chapters in numerous pop culture and philosophy books, and is currently co-editing *Alien and Philosophy* with Kevin S. Decker. He secretly hopes that one of Daenerys's dragons dies fighting the White Walkers, and gets resurrected as an ice dragon. Then again, why do all dragons have to be so aggressive and dangerous? His new hope is that Tyrion gets a wine dragon who breathes a Pinot Noir of a particularly nice vintage.

MAESTER WESLEY GEYER is currently completing his MA in philosophy at the University of Johannesburg and works as an English teacher. His research interests include various topics in the Philosophy of Science, Biology and Language. He once tried to use a book as an actual whetstone, but ended up with a shredded book and a blunt sword.

MAESTER PAUL GILADI is currently an honorary research fellow at the University of Sheffield, and has published several works on German idealism, pragmatism, and contemporary philosophy. He wonders if Gendry is rowing *ad infinitum*.

MAESTER TOM HANSBERGER is an advanced PhD student and lecturer at Marquette University. Aside from philosophy and pop culture, Tom's research interests include German Idealism and Phenomenology. Whenever the Dothraki say "It is known," Tom can't help but wonder: "By whom?"

MAESTER JARNO HIETALAHTI is a post-doctoral researcher at the University of Jyväskylä, Finland. He's currently conducting his research on Erich Fromm and humor at the Erich Fromm Institute, Tübingen, Germany. There he forges analytical weapons to battle against Tyrion Lannister's prophecy: "Let them see that their words can cut you and you'll never be free of the mockery."

MAESTER JASON IULIANO is a graduate of Harvard Law School and a PhD candidate in Politics at Princeton University. He supposes that makes him something more like a Maester-in-Training. While studying arcane doctrines, however, he often thinks the legal system would be more entertaining if disputes were resolved via trial by combat.

MAESTER VIKTOR IVANKOVĆ is a PhD student in political theory. His research interests are in nudging, democratic theory, and bioethics. He likes structured and orderly philosophy because chaos is a ladder and he's afraid of heights.

MAESTER TIM JONES, PhD, is an elected councillor for Norwich City Council, England, and a sometime teacher of Literature at the University of East Anglia. If the students get bad grades, he's activating the hidden stash of wildfire beneath the classroom.

MAESTER CHRISTOPHER C. KIRBY was once Associate Professor of Philosophy at Eastern Washington University. He was last seen aboard the *Titan's Daughter*, sailing far and away across the Narrow Sea, to Braavos. A man has contributed to other popular culture and philosophy volumes, including *Arrested Development and Philosophy* and *The Ultimate South Park and Philosophy*. If the day comes when you must find him again, say these words: "Valar otapis."

MAESTER TRIP MCCROSSIN teaches in the Philosophy Department at Rutgers University, where he works on, among other things, the nature, history, and legacy of the Enlightenment. He's taken lately, talking to folks after his last class of the day, to saying: "A man is Trip McCrossin of Brooklyn, and I'm going home."

MAESTER MATTHEW MCKEEVER is from Northern Ireland and has just completed his PhD in philosophy at St Andrews, Scotland. He works mainly on philosophy of language and metaphysics. He's confident Tyrion had this book in mind when he said: "The great thing about reading is that it broadens your life."

MAESTER TYLER DALTON MCNABB teaches philosophy and literature courses at Thales Academy. He has authored several articles in the areas of philosophy of religion and epistemology. He disagrees with Ygritte in thinking that Jon Snow knows nothing. At the very least, Jon knows that he knows nothing.

MAESTER LAUREN O'CONNELL holds a PhD in New Testament and Early Christianity and has a long-standing love of Greek philosophy. She currently teaches Theology to undergraduates at Loyola University in Chicago and reminds her students to listen to Jojen Reed when he says, "A reader lives a thousand lives before he dies; the man who never reads lives only once."

MAESTER JEREMY PIERCE is Alchemist of Metaphysics at Le Moyne College. He violated his vows as a maester to marry and sire five children, two of whom have autism, which awakened his interest in thinking more deeply about disability but lost him favor with the Citadel. He lives near Winterfell in Syracuse, New York, where winter is always coming and no one believes his dire warnings about the coming invasion by armies of undead Canadians.

MAESTER STEPH RENNICK is a lecturer in philosophy at Cardiff University, and founder of the Epicurean Cure. Her research interests span metaphysics and epistemology, but she's best known for her work on time travel, foreknowledge, and speculative fiction. She thinks that you, unlike Jon Snow, know lots of things, even about the future.

A man's name was **MAESTER EVAN ROSA**. Before he joined the Faceless Men, he was Director of the Biola University Center for Christian Thought, Editor of *The Table*, and Adjunct Professor of Philosophy at Biola University. *Valar morghulis.*

GRAND MAESTER ERIC J. SILVERMAN is Associate Professor of Philosophy at Christopher Newport University. He has interests in ethics, philosophy of religion, and medieval philosophy. He has authored over a dozen articles and published two other books: *The*

Prudence of Love: How Possessing the Virtue of Love Benefits the Lover and *Paradise Understood: New Philosophical Essays about Heaven*. He likes to believe that Wisdom is Coming!

MAESTER ROBERTO SIRVENT teaches ethics, political theory, and theology at Hope International University. He has interests in philosophy, film, and theories of political resistance. His students are much better than him at following the storylines of *Game of Thrones*, which is quite embarrassing. If he ever has a child with his brilliant and beautiful wife Krista, they will name her Arya.

MAESTER ROBERT C. THOMAS currently works as a government contractor. His research and writing cover topics related to ethics, political theory, economics, and international affairs. He thinks that Aristotle's disappointment over Ned Stark's lack of practical wisdom would probably outweigh his respect for Ned's courage.

MAESTER LORI UNDERWOOD is a professor of philosophy and dean at Christopher Newport University. She is a Kant scholar specializing in ethical and political theory, particularly as it applies to cosmopolitanism and terrorism. She thinks Littlefinger only believes "Chaos isn't a pit. Chaos is a ladder" because he's never been on a college campus when the internet goes down during course registration.

MAESTER WILLEM VAN DER DEIJL is a PhD researcher at the Erasmus University in Rotterdam. He has a background in philosophy and economics, and his work focuses on the philosophical foundations of well-being concepts in economics. While resembling a Lannister in appearance, he believes Daenerys's moral leadership can save Westeros. Also, he is of the belief that dragons are awesome.

MAESTER HANS VAN EYGHEN is a PhD candidate at the VU Amsterdam. His research focuses on cognitive science of religion and general philosophy of religion. He believes bios like these are rather futile because he agrees with Jaqen H'ghar that in the end a boy or girl has no name.

MAESTER JAMES WILLS spent the latter years of his twenties in education, before giving up all that financial security to complete an MA in English Literature. He is about to start a PhD, so although there are plenty of things about the Lannisters he despises, one day he seeks, like a Lannister, to pay off all his debts.

Index

269

POPULAR CULTURE AND PHILOSOPHY®

DOCTOR WHO

AND PHILOSOPHY
BIGGER ON THE INSIDE

EDITED BY COURTLAND LEWIS AND PAULA SMITHKA